THE LUST TO ANNIHILATE

A Psychoanalytic Study of Violence in Ancient Greek Culture

by
Eli Sagan

Psychohistory Press, Publishers
New York, New York, U.S.A.

THE LUST TO ANNIHILATE: A PSYCHOANALYTIC
STUDY OF VIOLENCE IN ANCIENT GREEK CULTURE

Library of Congress Cataloging in Publication Data

Main entry under title:

Sagan, Eli.
    The Lust to Annihilate.

    Includes index.
    1. Civilization, Greek. 2. Violence—Greece—Psychological aspects. 3. National characteristics, Greek. I. Title.
DF78.S18   301.6'33'0938   79-15280

ISBN 0-914434-11-X

This book is for Miriam, Rachel,
Susannah and Daniel

Acknowledgment is made of the generosity of the University of Chicago Press in granting permission to quote from the following works:

Richmond Lattimore, translator: *The Iliad of Homer,* 1962
Richmond Lattimore, translator and editor: *Greek Lyrics,* 1960
David Grene and Richmond Lattimore, editors: *The Complete Greek Tragedies,* four volumes, 1959

Quotations from *Beowulf* translated by Burton Raffel, Copyright © 1963 by Burton Raffel, are reprinted by arrangement with The New American Library, Inc., New York, N.Y.

Table of Contents

v

Thus the Greeks, the most humane men of ancient times, have a trait of cruelty, a tigerish lust to annihilate—a trait that is also very distinct in that grotesquely enlarged mirror image of the Hellenes, in Alexander the Great, but that really must strike fear into our hearts throughout their whole history and mythology....When Alexander has the feet of Batis, the brave defender of Gaza, pierced, and ties him, alive, to his carriage, to drag him about while his soldiers mock, that is a revolting caricature of Achilles, who maltreats Hector's corpse in a similar fashion at night; and even this trait is offensive to us and makes us shudder. Here we look into an abyss of hatred....When the victor in a fight among the cities executes the entire male citizenry in accordance with the laws of war, and sells all the women and children into slavery, we see in the sanction of such a law that the Greeks considered it an earnest necessity to let their hatred flow forth fully; in such moments crowded and swollen feeling relieved itself: the tiger leaped out, voluptuous cruelty in his terrible eyes....Why did the whole Greek world exult over the combat scenes of the *Iliad?* I fear that we do not understand these in a sufficiently "Greek" manner; indeed, that we should shudder if we were ever to understand them "in Greek."

Nietzsche

Introduction

INTRODUCTION: The God of Reverence

The development of culture is impossible without the transformation of ritual modes of thought and action into more liberated forms. During the nineteenth and twentieth centuries, the worship of divinity, for some, has been transformed into reverence for certain abstract ideas, or for particular great men of the past. Like the "G" in the God of old, the initial capital signifies that reverence: Truth, Beauty, Reason, History, Science, Being, Economic Determinism. In Paris, after the French Revolution, altars to Reason were erected before which the faithful worshiped. Only recently has our culture given up the practice of engraving on stone the names of its new gods. Like the tablets of Moses, public buildings, libraries, university edifices proclaim reverence for the new deities: COPERNICUS, GALILEO, NEWTON — SHAKESPEARE, TOLSTOY, HOMER.

An unliberated reverence permeates our relationship to the ancient Greeks. The old gods of the Greeks have not been resacralized; no one today worships Zeus or Athene. In our hearts, however, we have built an altar, not to the gods of the Greeks, but to the Greeks themselves.

To understand, to analyze a people and a culture, one must abandon reverence, no matter how great the human achievement of such a culture may have been. One may love the Greeks—as Ben Jonson loved

Shakespeare—"this side idolatry," but understanding will come only when one can differentiate between love and idolatry. When Nietzsche urges us to understand "in Greek" that "trait of cruelty, a tigerish lust to annihilate,"[1] we should not, like Plato, decide to censor the story, to repress the facts, on the ground that no god should be shown as behaving in such a manner. To understand the Greeks—"in Greek"—it is as important to comprehend what they could not do, and why, as it is to hymn the praises of their great accomplishments.

Some scholars, especially those who have a sympathy with the iconoclastic nature of Marxist thought, have been critical of Greek culture and society. Homosexuality, the degraded position of women, economic inequality, class conflicts, imperialism, and, especially, slavery have been the objects of this attack. George Thomson calls Greek slavery "the irremediable evil which from this time forward was to gnaw at the vitals of ancient society."[2] These criticisms have had great value in demonstrating that the Greeks were not demigods breathing the free air of Athens whose only occupation was creating imperishable works of art, but were people living in the midst of immoral institutions that were also created by these very Greeks.

To criticize a culture from one's own moral view is one thing; to analyze the moral tensions within a society may be something wholly different. It is important to differentiate what is immoral in a society from what is morally problematic for that society. A moral concern is problematic for a culture when *the culture itself* expresses a profound and pervasive ambivalence about an institution within that culture. An attitude within a culture, or an institution within society, may be undeniably immoral; but if there is no profound questioning of that institution or attitude, if there is no pervasive expression of ambivalence towards this immorality, we cannot correctly regard these forms as morally problematic. Greek slavery, like all slavery, was an evil. In order to establish that it was morally problematic it would be necessary to prove that it really did "gnaw at the vitals" of the culture. In my view, neither Thomson nor anyone else has given us such proof.

The importance of identifying what is morally problematic in a culture is that such analysis will underlie the fundamental tensions within society. It is to these areas of moral equivocation that we should look to observe the possibilities of progress—or regress—in society. A culture can only solve the problems it has set itself; one can legitimately talk of "failure" in a culture—as many have in regard to Greek civilization—only in reference to a failure to solve problems that were regarded as such. No society resolves immoralities that are not problematical for it. The failure of a society to resolve the problems created by the morally problematic can threaten the very nature of that society.

Within Western culture today, we can observe the process by which an immoral institution became increasingly problematic. Imperialism—the tyranny of one nation over another—has always been immoral, whenever it was exercised, but it was by no means morally problematic for most people living in the nineteenth century. Few pronounced it an evil. The middle of the twentieth century presents us with a radically different view. The French experience in Algeria, the American catastrophe in Vietnam, the Portugese policy in Africa—all these have demonstrated that imperialism has not only become morally dubious for those practicing it, but also that the argument over its legitimacy can rock the very foundations of the societies involved. Nothing is more important to society than those concerns that are morally problematic.

It is the argument of this book that the characteristic form of immorality and aggression—and primary ambivalence—in Greek culture was a commitment to sadistic violence, a love of killing, "the tigerish lust to annihilate." It is here that we must look to find the moral tension in Greece; here we will find the possibilities of moral advance. In that commitment to violence we may discover the reasons for the ultimate "failure" of Greek culture.

This ambivalent love of killing was present in Greek culture at the beginning, in Homer and the *Iliad*. The *Iliad* is the earliest work of Greek literature that we possess. Previous to it, we have no maxims, no riddles, no songs, no prayers. We do not know, and may never know, who composed the *Iliad,* nor how or when it was first sung. A controversy rages over the questions of whether there ever was a man called "Homer," whether he composed the *Iliad* or merely brought disparate poems together, and whether the same person also composed the *Odyssey*. If not Homer, was it a group of poets or a sequence of poets? And when did this Homer, group, sequence, or anonymous live? For our purposes, it is enough to say that a consensus of scholars holds that the *Iliad* assumed its more or less final form in about 700 B.C., that the *Odyssey* followed a short time later, and that these two poems were the high point of Greek epic poetry.

In the two centuries that followed, approximately 680 B.C. to 480 B.C., lyric poetry, composed by poets whose names and approximate dates we do have, was the most vital form of Greek literature. During this period, the *Iliad* and the *Odyssey* were known and admired—much as the Bible was in Western Europe throughout many centuries—although the greatest poets wrote not epic, but lyric verse.

In the lyric age, the demise of epic poetry did not bring with it a lack of concern with the problems of violence. The love of killing was not merely the product of an heroic age that produced great epic literature, and it did not cease when that age was over. Some lyric poets swallowed whole the world-view of Homer, merely applying it to the new political conditions of the city-state. Others took it as their central interest to reject and transform the Homeric morality of violence. Individuality was the great creation of the lyric poets; that individualism was forged in a struggle against violence.

During the fifth century B.C., lyric poetry was being written by some, and the poems of Homer were still held in reverence, but the men of greatest literary genius wrote history and tragedy. The tragic playwrights almost succeeded in radically transforming Greek culture and its commitment to violence. They went far beyond the limited heroic morality, but they did so only by dealing with it directly—deliberately examining its implications for human existence. For themselves, they succeeded; the culture as a whole rejected their moral message, prolonging its existence with the same old values, as if the tragic poets had never lived.

Thucydides, writing at the end of the fifth century, presents us with evidence that this lust to kill remained a powerful force in Greek life three hundred years after Homer had sung his great poem. We are shown that this passion for killing may have been the very thing that destroyed the Great Age of Athens. Whether or not Thucydides intended us to draw these conclusions from his work is unclear. There is no question, however, that a commitment to violence is one of the most important subjects of his history.

I intend in this book to trace the history of Greek attitudes towards violence from Homer to Thucydides. My primary interest is with values, not with institutions. Behind any system of institutions there lies a system of values. The institution of slavery can exist only when a culture perpetuates a value system that certifies it is legitimate for one human being to own another.

Faith in the efficacy of violence was a central belief in the Greek value system. Violence was not merely one of many important factors, nor was it an incidental expression of the culture. All literature is a reflection of a system of values; great literature has the power to transform received values and thereby change culture. In the literature of the Greeks there was a pervasive interest in the forms of violence, and a continuing debate over the legitimacy of these forms.

My interest is not limited to what some have designated the "contest system"—that Greek capacity to make a competitive game out of almost any human activity. My interest lies at the point where the contest system did not work. This system did not succeed in sublimating the desire to kill into the desire to demolish an opponent in a competitive game. The contest system itself must have contained an element of violence in it that too easily regressed into more primitive forms. As Alvin Gouldner writes: "Yet it is this same contest system that also rends the *polis* and so lacerates its social order that at times it appears that, of all the Greek talents, by far the greatest is mutual destruction."[3] It was not the contest system that led to mutual destruction; it was the failure of this system to transform, to sublimate, the desire to kill into something more civilized. Such a "talent" for destruction the Greeks of the city-states inherited from their great ancestor Homer. In Homer we can see an early configuration of all the moral problems that plagued Greek culture throughout its existence.

Culturally, we are all children of ancient Greece. Biologically, all of us are the offspring of parents who are partially good and partially bad human beings. As we grow up, we incorporate into ourselves the qualities of our parents. The negative qualities—which we unconsciously know to be such—present a problem. About these we feel the necessity to lie, perhaps to pretend they never existed. There is a psychic cost in such a denial of reality—we pay for our denial by having recourse to sentimentality. When we become adult, and parents ourselves, we add a new illusion to our lives—the notion that we are no longer dealing with our parents and our problems with them. We are dealing, we think, with politics or history or with the Greeks, and we do not see that ancient attitudes towards our parents, and the resultant conflicts and sentimentalities, are influencing our intellectual views. We are "shocked" (and delighted) to learn of any new scandal about the great men of history. We are appalled to learn that the humane Greeks could have indulged a love of killing.

The greatest Greek scholars have not been free of this desire to deny certain ugly aspects of Greek life. Gilbert Murray was a firm believer in moral progress: "I must take for granted many fundamental theses. That man has progressed, for one thing, and that the direction in which Western Civilization has moved is on the whole a good one."[4] When Murray writes of Greek society, he comments: "Of course there were bad things, and always have been in all societies."[5] A view if moral progress should have led Murray to address himself to the questions of what was the nature of those "bad things," and how did they differ from the bad things in previous and subsequent societies. However, we do not get such an analysis because Murray's reverence for the Greeks did not permit it.

In *The Greeks and the Irrational,* E. R. Dodds consummately succeeds in destroying the sentimentalized image of the cold, formal, rational Greeks. We wish he had given us a chapter on aggression as an aspect of the irrational, but he does not look directly at the worst in Greek culture.

It takes nothing away from the enormous achievements of Greek culture to say that the people who created that civilization were committed to a barbaric view of violence. No one can legitimately deny his own debt to Greek civilization. Simply stated, the desire to analyze Greek culture critically is an attitude inherited from those very Greeks. However, though we may all be pygmies sitting on the shoulders of giants, we are still not required to forget that in most stories giants eat people.

Teaching the *Iliad* to students presents a particular problem that one does not encounter with other "great monuments of Western Civilization." It is hard work to keep the students' interest. A generation that "turns off" at the slightest provocation has great difficulty in "turning on" to this work. In a way, they are not at fault. For long stretches of the book—in fact, for most of the book—"nothing happens." Nothing, that is, except human beings killing each other. If one lacks a keen interest in this particular brand of homicide, the reading promptly becomes tedious.

At one time, a great deal of effort went into shortening, bowdlerizing, and retelling literary monuments so that people who wished to be familiar with "culture," without understanding it, might have an easy road. By serious people, the practice has fortunately been given up. Except with the *Iliad*. When I. A. Richards, certainly a responsible and sophisticated expositor of literary meaning, abridged the *Iliad* in order to make it readable, he did so not out of some perversity, but because he recognized that this work presents the modern reader with a special problem.

Why did the ancient Greeks find so fascinating what many of us find so dull, or even repulsive? Obviously, for them something very important was happening in all those places where "nothing happens." An oral poem—one that would take a least three eight-hour sessions to recite—could easily have been shortened to eliminate the dull places if those who composed, recited, and listened to it thought of these places as lacking in interest.

Arguments have been advanced to explain why there is so much killing in the *Iliad*—that Bible of Greek culture. One argument claims that the killing is a remnant of the barbaric past—a description of a culture, and cultural values, that no longer existed when Homer sang. Another viewpoint holds that the killing is merely a metaphor for courage and heroism; it is not to be taken literally. The argument has also been made that Homer is horrified by the actions of his heroes; he is really showing us how the use of force destroys the humane potentialities in people's lives. In the course of this book I hope to establish that all these explanations are inadequate. When we come to the discussion of the Anglo-Saxon epic poem *Beowulf,* we shall see that a man can be conceived as a great courageous hero though he does not kill other people. If we are to understand the violence in the *Iliad* we must not generalize about the nature of epic poetry, but try to comprehend the Greek cultural values that left their imprint on this poem.

When primitive peoples were asked why they did a particular thing in a particular way, the common response was, "It is the custom." When we ask why the first great book of the Greeks is dominated by violence, killing, and graphic sadism, we must first understand:

> Custom is lord of everything
> of mortals and immortals king.
> High violence it justifies...
> —Pindar[6]

I
Despair and Redemption

Considering the length of the poem, the essential story of the *Iliad* is remarkable in its simplicity. Previous to the opening of the story, Paris, the son of the Trojan "King" Priam, had visited the mainland of Greece. In the house of Menelaos, the "King" of Sparta, he had seduced Helen, the wife of Menelaos, and brought her back with him to Troy. Subsequently, embassies from the Greeks demanding the return of Helen had been rejected by the Trojans. Agamemnon, the "King" of Mycenae, and brother to Menelaos, had gathered together a great expedition from many states, and sailed to Troy for the purpose of retrieving Helen and destroying the city.

When the poem begins, the Greeks have been besieging the city of Troy for nine years. Achilles—the greatest warrior of the Greek force— quarrels with Agamemnon, the leader of the expedition. As a result of this quarrel, Agamemnon takes from Achilles Briseis, a previously captured concubine. Achilles withdraws from the siege, vowing not to fight again. Not trusting to the natural course of events, Achilles engages the help of his mother, Thetis, a goddess, to convince Zeus to turn the battle against the Greeks in Achilles' absence, so that his revenge may be satisfied.

Zeus consents; the Greeks are beaten back; Agamemnon attempts to assuage Achilles' anger, to no avail; the Greeks are beaten back worse than before. No longer able to watch the defeat, Achilles sends his dearest friend Patroklos into battle, wearing Achilles' armor, but Patroklos is promptly killed by Hektor—bravest of the Trojans and son of the Trojan "King" Priam. To revenge the death of Patroklos, Achilles returns to the battle, takes the life of Hektor, gives Patroklos a barbaric funeral complete with animal and human sacrifice, and refuses to give back to the Trojans the body of Hektor, continuing to work his vengeance on a corpse.

As the twenty-fourth, and last, book of the poem opens, Patroklos is dead; Hektor is dead—his corpse continually degraded by Achilles. Most of the sons of Priam are dead. The city of Troy is doomed to destruction. Nothing avails Achilles in the satisfaction of his grief and anger—neither the death of Hektor nor the mutilation of his body; nor the twelve young, beautiful Trojan warriors and the horses and dogs slain on the pyre; nor even the healing power of the funeral games: nothing. Everything that has happened since the quarrel between Agamemnon and Achilles has been destructive—a waste of life and meaning. There was a time when Achilles believed revenge could bring satisfaction, but with moral collapse comes meaninglessness:

'Do not kill me. I am not from the same womb as Hektor,
he who killed your powerful and kindly companion.'
            So the glorious son of Priam addressed him, speaking
in supplication, but heard in turn the voice without pity:
'Poor fool, no longer speak to me of ransom, nor argue it.
In the time before Patroklos came to the day of his destiny
then it was the way of my heart's choice to be sparing
of the Trojans, and many I took alive and disposed of them.
Now there is not one who can escape death, if the gods send
him against my hands in front of Ilion, not one
of all the Trojans and beyond others the children of Priam.
So, friend, you die also. Why all this clamour about it?
Patroklos also is dead, who was better by far than you are.
Do you not see what a man I am, how huge, how splendid
and born of a great father, and the mother who bore me immortal?
Yet even I have also my death and my strong destiny,
and there shall be a dawn or an afternoon or a noontime
when some man in the fighting will take the life from me also
either with with a spearcast or an arrow flown from the bowstring.'
                                                    [XXI 95-113][1]

Achilles, killing him, hurls his dead body into the river:

'Lie there now among the fish, who will lick the blood away
from your wound, and care nothing for you, nor will your mother

lay you on the death-bed and mourn over you, but Skamandros
will carry you spinning down to the wide bend of the salt water.
And a fish will break a ripple shuddering dark on the water
as he rises to feed upon the shining fat of Lykaon.
Die on, all; till we come to the city of sacred Ilion,
you in flight and I killing you from behind; and there will not
be any rescue for you from your silvery-whirled strong-running
river, for all the numbers of bulls you dedicate to it
and drown single-foot horses alive in its eddies. And yet
even so, die all an evil death, till all of you
pay for the death of Patroklos and the slaughter of the Achaians
whom you killed beside the running ships, when I was not
    with them.'

[XXI 122-135]

For the tragic hero, redemption comes from insight and the willingness
to accept responsibility for actions and mistakes. Achilles, giving no
thought to the fact that his own rage has brought them all to this point,
throws off any check to primitive wrath. Many times in the poem men
have been compared with lions feasting on the blood and inward parts.
Facing Hektor, who is pleading for an agreement with Achilles that
whoever is the victor in their death-duel should return the corpse of the
vanquished to family or friends for proper burial—a reasonable request
within the value system of these aristocratic warriors—Achilles refuses
the plea and accepts the simile; he will be such a lion.

'Hektor, argue me no agreements. I cannot forgive you.
As there are no trustworthy oaths between men and lions,
nor wolves and lambs have spirit that can be brought to agreement
but forever these hold feelings of hate for each other...'

[XXII 261-264]

Lower than this, we feel, the human spirit cannot go. We are
mistaken:

'No more entreating of me, you dog, by knees or parents.
I wish only that my spirit and fury would drive me
to hack your meat away and eat it raw for the things that
you have done to me...'

[XXII 345-348]

Homer makes us feel that from this nadir of dehumanization only one
thing can restore order to the world: an act so grand in its morality and

humanity that it would triumph over the debasement of human values to which the reader has been witness. For the poet, two great concerns dominate the story: one is the use of ransom to compensate someone who gives up an aggressive satisfaction—killing or maltreating another; the other involves the reverential burial of a hero whose life has been destroyed by an aggressive act. These two themes come together in the last book of the poem, when Priam ransoms the body of his slain son Hektor from Achilles in order to give him a hero's burial. Only then are meaning and order restored to the world.

In each of the three dramatic climaxes of the poem, the central question is whether or not ransom or gifts to compensate loss will be accepted. In the first book Agamemnon, out of arrogance, refuses to accept a ransom for the girl Chryseis, whom he had captured and made his concubine, despite the fact that the ransom was offered by the girl's father, who was a priest of Apollo, and despite the fact that "all the rest of the Achaians cried out in favour that the priest be respected and the shining ransom be taken." This refusal of Agamemnon leads directly to the quarrel with Achilles and Achilles' withdrawal from the fighting.

Later, when Agamemnon attempts to end his quarrel with Achilles, he sends ambassadors with promises of great treasure if Achilles will give over his anger and return to the fighting. Achilles' refusal of these gifts, and the subsequent defeat of the Greeks, lead to the death of Patroklos.

In sharp contrast to the dire consequences that followed the refusals of Agamemnon and Achilles, in the last book Achilles accepts the ransom offered by Priam and returns to him the body of Hektor. Achilles has been commanded by Zeus himself to accept this ransom. Should Achilles refuse Priam, it would signify that even the gods are incapable of morally ordering the world.

Homer's interest in the question of whether or not ransom is accepted is not restricted to these three high climaxes. The question of whether ransom should be taken is frequently raised. Within the body of the poem there is not one instance when anyone spares the life of another warrior and takes him captive for ransom—in spite of the fact that there are numerous references to the practice in the past. Several previously ransomed heroes appear in the poem, only to greet death this second time.

Homer heightens the tension by making his heroes act during the course of the poem in ways that are even more violent than their previous modes of behavior. Menelaos, the brother of Agamemnon, had Adrestos at his mercy; the latter pleaded to be taken alive: "my father would make you glad with abundant repayment" and he "moved the spirit inside Menelaos." Agamemnon came running to argue that such compassion is no longer appropriate; Menelaos shoved Adrestos away as Agamemnon killed him.

Similarly, Odysseus and Diomedes have been out on a spying expedition to the Trojan camp; they have captured a Trojan spy Dolon, promised him that his life will be spared, for ransom, learned what they could from him, and cut off his head, and "Dolon's head still speaking dropped in the dust."

After Achilles has rejected the gifts of Agamemnon and continued his refusal to fight, the Trojans bitterly beat back the Greeks. Many of the great heroes of the Greeks were wounded and retired from the battle. Under these desperate circumstances, Achilles, though deciding not to return to the fighting himself, sends Patroklos into battle wearing the armor of Achilles. When Hektor then takes the life of Patroklos, he also takes from him Achilles' armor, and puts it on his own person. Achilles returns to battle with a new set of armor made for him by the god Hephaistos, of which the most remarkable piece is a great shield on which Hephaistos had embossed a multitude of scenes from daily life. The first scene of human life described on this shield is one of marriage and festival, followed by a scene in which two men are arguing over the blood price of a man killed. When they cannot agree they resort to the justice of the court, which will determine how much compensation is to be paid.

Civilization, Homer tells us, depends upon the capacity of men to give up personal blood-revenge, and to rely instead on the justice of the whole community. Of the three ambassadors sent by Agamemnon to Achilles, only Ajax succeeds ever so slightly in moving Achilles, with these words:

'Pitiless. And yet a man takes from his brother's slayer
the blood price, or the price of a child who was killed, and the guilty
one, when he has largely repaid, stays still in the country,
and the injured man's heart is curbed, and his pride, and his anger
when he has taken the price; but the gods put in your breast a spirit
not be placated, bad, for the sake of one single
girl...'

[IX 632-638]

The concern over whether Achilles will allow Hektor's body to be ransomed is not merely a personal, psychological question. We are aware that such a refusal will prevent Achilles' return to a meaningful life; we are affected by the desire of Priam for some consolation before his world closes around him. But our deepest involvement is with the crucial question—the great moral concern of whether civilization is possible, whether or not barbarian rage can be controlled and transformed either by human affection or by the power of the gods.

Equally significant for Homer is a second concern—the proper burial of a hero. We are told in the very first lines of the poem that the wrath of

Achilles not only brought destruction to multitudes, but, even more, "gave their bodies to the ... feasting of dogs." Homer suggests no horror in the fact that they died fighting; he feels pity for a brave death, but no terror. That their dead flesh should be rended by dogs is a moral and psychological horror. That the bodies of the brave should be denied a loving burial and be left to the birds and the dogs, or that a great hero should maltreat the body of another great hero, is a barbarian outrage unworthy of the civilized warrior who wants to kill, who wants to sack cities, who wants slaves and treasure, but who also needs the sense that there are some things he will not do. It is, and is not, an hypocrisy. It is nothing less than one of the means by which people have climbed out of the barbarian past.

Sarpedon, a mortal son of Zeus, is killed in the fighting. Zeus decides not to save the life of his son, not to interfere with the process of fate. Hera, his wife, comforts him in his loss:

'No, but if he is dear to you, and your heart mourns for him,
then let him be, and let him go down in the strong encounter
underneath the hands of Patroklos, the son of Menoitios;
but after the soul and the years of his life have left him, then send
Death to carry him away, and Sleep, who is painless,
until they come with him to the countryside of broad Lykia
where his brothers and countrymen shall give him due burial
with tomb and gravestone. Such is the privilege of those who have
perished.'

[XVI 450-457]

This incident is one example of an asymmetrical symmetry between heaven and earth that pervades the *Iliad*. In this case, the king of the gods, having lost a son, assuages his grief by a proper burial—with the aid of magic. When the "king" of the Trojans loses his son, the gods arrange that his son also receive a funeral worthy of his life. This time, Zeus decrees, there shall be no magic; the device of the god Hermes' stealing Hektor's body away from Achilles is rejected. Homer will not resolve this great human problem by magical means; Zeus decrees that Priam must bring ransom and ask for the corpse, and Achilles must comply.

At the time of the siege of Troy, Priam is an old man, incapable of fighting. He had been a great killer in his youth—like all the others. When the delegation from the Greeks appeared in Troy before the war, and demanded the return of Helen, Priam had joined the others in "heroically" refusing to send her back. After Hektor's death, despite the commands of the gods, Priam's wife urges him not to go to Achilles, fearing for his life. He rejects her advice, determined to perform one last great act of courage before he dies. With only a mule, a cart, and a driver, he crosses the great plain in front of the city and makes his way to the ships of the Achaians. Fearful that someone may take his life; fearful, as well, that his hatred for this man who has killed so many of his sons may overwhelm him and cause him to spit out his anger at Achilles, thereby destroying his mission and his life, Priam enters the hut of Achilles. Our response to this old killer begging for the return of the body of his dead son, slain in a war for which the father is also responsible, is the only time in the entire poem that we feel pity and terror in the same person.

Faced with his son's killer, Priam shows that courage includes more than a willingness to kill one's enemy; through his love for his dead son he redeems the moral order of the world. He moves the cold, barbaric heart of Achilles:

> 'Honour then the gods, Achilleus, and take pity upon me
> remembering your father, yet I am still more pitiful;
> I have gone through what no other mortal on earth has gone through;
> I put my lips to the hands of the man who has killed my children.'
>   [XXIV 503-506]

For the first time since Patroklos had been killed, Achilles does not refuse an appeal to his humanity:

> So he spoke, and stirred in the other a passion of grieving
> for his own father. He took the old man's hand and pushed him
> gently away, and the two remembered, as Priam sat huddled
> at the feet of Achilleus and wept close for manslaughtering Hektor
> and Achilleus wept now for his own father, now again
> for Patroklos. The sound of their mourning moved in the house.
>   [XXIV 507-512]

Achilles, reminded by Priam's presence of his neglect of his own father, unburdens himself to Priam: " 'I give him no cure as he grows old, since far from the land of my fathers I sit here in Troy, and bring nothing but sorrow to you and your children.' "

[XXIV 540-542]

For this brief moment, we may imagine that Achilles has clearly read the message of life's possibilities that Hephaistos had wrought on the great shield. It would be incorrect to make this connection, however, because the shield has no dramatic value for the poem; it adds nothing to the essential story. It is, nevertheless, one culmination of the Homeric view of the world. Achilles' shield is a vision of how beautiful the world might be if there were no Troy, no Paris, no Helen, no Achilles, no Hektor; it is a garden of earthly delights. It is a vision because its dream of peace does not proceed from any action in the poem. The shield relates to the rest of the poem as do the background and foreground of a painting—some imagined painting by Bosch or Brenghel, full of the siege of a great city, the warriors engaged in spilling the entrails and the lives of each other onto the ground, the smoke of battle almost obscuring the doomed city, the colors shades of grey and black night. And in the background, in soft colors of Spring, we see the tilled fields and the grapevines, dancing and music—the whole filling us with longing and sadness for we do not know how to get from the reality of the destruction to that vision of peace.

Hephaistos renders peaceful and joyful scenes as if oblivious of the use to which the shield will be put. Achilles waits with animal impatience for his new armor so that he can begin his killing. When Achilles takes up the shield with his "manslaughtering" hand, we are forced to leave that beautiful vision—and we never return to it.

Unlike the return of Helen, unlike the destruction of Troy, and all the plunder and all the slaves, and all the glory—which are themselves dreams of a different kind—here at last we are given a vision worth risking one's life for:

> And the renowned smith of the strong arms made elaborate on it
> a dancing floor, like that which once in the wide spaces of Knosos
> Daidalos built for Ariadne of the lovely tresses.
> And there were young men on it and young girls, sought for their
>   beauty
> with gifts of oxen, dancing, and holding hands at the wrist. These
> wore, the maidens long light robes, but the men wore tunics
> of finespun work and shining softly, touched with olive oil.
> And the girls wore fair garlands on their heads, while the young men
> carried golden knives that hung from sword-belts of silver.
> At whiles on their understanding feet they would run very lightly,
> as when a potter crouching makes trial of his wheel, holding
> it close in his hands, to see if it will run smooth. At another
> time they would form rows, and run, rows crossing each other.
> And around the lovely chorus of dancers stood a great multitude
> happily watching, while among the dancers two acrobats
> led the measures of song and dance revolving among them.
>
> [XVIII 590-605]

This description appears in the eighteenth book of the poem, the scene between Priam and Achilles at the very the overwhelming preoccupation of the poem, that which takes more words, more energy than any other subject is another kind of dance: The killing dance.

> This man Peneleos caught underneath the brow, at the bases
> of the eye, and pushed the eyeball out, and the spear went clean through
> the eye-socket and tendon of the neck, so that he went down
> backward, reaching out both hands, but Peneleos drawing
> his sharp sword hewed at the neck in the middle, and so dash downward
> the head, with helm upon it, while still on the point of the big spear
> the eyeball stuck. He, lifting it high like the head of a poppy,
> displayed it to the Trojans and spoke vaunting over it...
>
> [XIV 493-500]

Many scholars have noted that there is much deliberate expurgation in this poem. The primitive magical aspects of religion and ritual, though they seem to have existed since the beginning of human culture and were still matters of intense interest in the fifth and fourth centuries B.C., have practically no place in the poem. We may assume that people in Homer's time maintained a concern with such practices and that Homer was making a deliberate decision in excluding them from his work. The grosser forms of excretory and sexual humor—attributes of all literature from primitive times and still used with great success by Aristophanes in the fourth century B.C.—are nonexistent in the *Iliad*. The language is never vulgar or gross, but always maintains a lofty, aristocratic tone, when we are told:

> ...the two Aiantes in the fury of their fierce war strength,
> as two lions catch up a goat from the guard of rip-fanged
> hounds, and carry it into the density of the underbrush,
> holding it high from the ground in the crook of their jaws,
> so the lonely
> two Aiantes lifted Imbrios high and stripped him
> of his armour, and the son of Oileus, in anger
> for Amphimachos, hewed away his head from the soft neck
> and threw it spinning like a ball through the throng of fighters
> until it came to rest in the dust at the feet of Hektor.
>
> [XIII 197-205]

If a deliberate decision was made by the poet and the poetic tradition to exclude matters of a primitive and gross nature, we can only conclude that the same deliberation went into the decision to *include* these human activities, and this paean to the strength of Agamemnon:

> Hippolochos sprang away, but Atreides killed him dismounted,
> cutting away his arms with a sword-stroke, free of the shoulder,
> and sent him spinning like a log down the battle.
>
> [XI 145-147]

These are among the most graphic examples that can be found within the poem, but they are at one with literally hundreds of descriptions of men being killed in the fighting. In these passages there is no ambivalence, no ambiguity, no irony, no indication that these killings are anything but the brave, heroic actions of manly, courageous heroes. The heroes' work is killing; they do it with passion and efficiency; they are heroes because they accept the fact that they themselves may die in such labor. The glory, the high opinion of their peers, makes all this risk of life worth it. One wonders why the same poet, or the same culture, has given us the scene of Priam and Achilles, the descriptions of the high possibilities of life on Achilles' shield, and the spinning, log-like body, the rolling ball head, and the poppy-eye stuck on the point of a spear.

In the history of the development of society and culture, there was a time when violence and the morality of the warrior-hero played a progressive role. Society did not develop from "primitive" to "civilized" in one great revolutionary step forward. Between the "primitive" and the "civilized" another significant stage of cultural development existed. Some call it "The Heroic Age"; others name it "Barbarism," to differentiate it from "savage" primitive society. I prefer less perjorative terms for our ancestors, to whom we owe so much. The sequence Primitive Civilization, Barbaric Civilization, and Archaic Civilization has the advantage of not implying that Primitive culture was simple, nor that "civilization" was that civilized.

There is general agreement among scholars as to which cultures would fall under the heading "Archaic Civilizations." Such cultures were literate; their peoples lived in cities and used metals; they developed complex religious lives, which included moral anthropomorphic gods; they lived under systems of law, not custom; and they instituted a strong kingship. The earliest Archaic Civilizations existed in Egypt, Mesopotamia, China, the Indus valley, and the Aegean.

Primitive Civilizations were illiterate; their peoples lived in villages and did not use metals; magical practices dominated their spiritual lives; the morality of their gods was extremely vague; custom, and not law, was the means of social control; at most, they developed weak chieftainships as the highest social office. Kinship structures dominated political life.

Very few writers have concerned themselves with Barbaric Civilization. Many have incorrectly included Aztec or Polynesian society under the primitive rubric. The Aztecs, the Incas, the pre-literate kingdoms of Africa, the ancient Polynesians, the Germanic, Norse, and Celtic tribes of Europe before their conversions to Christianity—none of these lived in a Primitive Civilization. All these peoples were representative of Barbaric Civilization. The institutions and values that differentiated Barbaric from Primitive society were: aristocracy, a professional priesthood, complex myth, fully developed anthropomorphic gods, the beginnings of law and kingship, and the destruction of the stranglehold of kinship forms that primitive society had maintained against individual expression. The physical and psychological courage of the warrior-hero, and his willingness to risk his life in battle, were crucial factors in the establishment of Barbaric Civilization. That courage, that energy, was of enormous importance in the transformation of primitive culture; when speaking of that time, it can truly be called "progressive."

It is important to place the *Iliad* in this evolutionary scheme. The culture of the eighth century B.C. in Greece was not a Barbaric Civilization emerging out of the Primitive; neither was it a fully developed Barbarian Civilization developing towards the Archaic. Eighth-century Greece was a fully developed Archaic Civilization that was about to burst forth in a frenzy of creation that would, in a mere two or three hundred years, produce a culture that went far beyond anything early Archaic Civilization had known. In these circumstances, the preservation of the Barbaric morality of the warrior-hero was a moral anachronism. That warrior mentality was no longer progressive as it had been when it helped shatter the confines of Primitive society. It no longer served the interests of cultural development; it had become a conservative, if not regressive, force within society.

It is also true that there are occasions when Homer tires of the killing and begins to question the validity of the heroic morality. He never does more than raise the question about its value; outright condemnation, the proposal of a radically new morality, is impossible for him. Out of deep feelings of ambivalence, out of an unconscious notion that something is wrong, comes not an alternative mode of human action, but irony—an irony that reflects the inability to give up values that no longer serve moral interests.

An instance of this ironic view occurs in the scene where Hektor, having returned to the city from battle, meets his wife, Andromache, and their small child Astyanax, on the ramparts. Andromache pleads with Hektor to take a defensive stance in the battle—not an aggressive one—to save the city and keep her from being widowed and the boy from becoming fatherless. He does not hear what she says and cannot respond to her pleas; he gives her very small comfort: "But may I be dead and the piled earth hide me under before I hear you crying and know by this that they drag you captive."

Since Hektor is incapable of discourse when his wife questions heroic values, he turns to their child, lifts him up, and utters a prayer to Zeus the child shall grow up to be as he is—a killer:

'Zeus, and you other immortals, grant that this boy, who is my son,
may be as I am, pre-eminent among the Trojans,
great in strength, as am I, and rule strongly over Ilion:
and some day let them say of him: "He is better by far than his
    father,"
as he comes in from the fighting; and let him kill his enemy
and bring home the blooded spoils, and delight the heart of his
    mother.'

[VI 476-481]

By stating that the "blooded spoils" will "delight the heart of his mother," when the mother has just finished pleading with the boy's father to abandon the madness of this killing-morality, Homer makes us witness to irony. Whether this irony is conscious or not we cannot tell. What we do know is that Homer shows us Hektor ensnared in an absurd morality, and the poet himself shows no alternative way—he knows no way to escape from this entrapment.

How can we reconcile these contradictions? How can one poem hold within it the profoundly moving encounter of Priam and Achilles, the deep irony of the noble heroes trapped in a morality of (self-) destruc- and the verse after verse after verse of human slaughter, a poem that many times makes us feel that it has taken as its task to act out Lear's Lear's great cry of desperation: "Kill, kill, kill, kill, kill, kill!"?

I have previously set down two hypotheses concerning human aggression and cultural form[2]: one, that all cultures distinguish specific acts of aggression as either legitimate or illegitimate; two, that the fundamental attitude expressed by culture towards acts of aggression is one of ambivalence. Any work of literature will accurately reflect the value system within the culture that produces it. As Dodds said of the Bacchae, we must regard it "not only as a piece of Greek but as a work of art and at the same time (like all works of art) a social document."[3]

The Iliad can be analyzed to determine: Which acts of aggression are considered legitimate, which illegitimate? How does ambivalence about aggression manifest itself? Is there more ambivalence about some acts of aggression than about others? And, most importantly, what are the relationships in the poem of legitimate acts, illegitimate acts, and ambivalence—of all of these—to morality? Such analysis will underline contradictions, not reconcile them. The disparate and ambivalent attitudes towards aggression in all cultures, and in the Iliad, may be understood, but they cannot be reconciled one with another.

When attempting to distinguish between legitimate and illegitimate acts of aggression, it is important clearly to indicate from what source the judgment comes. Homer presents four distinct sources of morality and aggression in the poem: Zeus, the gods other than Zeus, the men and women of the story, and the poet himself. The same act may be illegitimate to Zeus, illegitimate to Hera, not subject to any judgment by the heroes, ambivalent to Homer, and a morally chaotic act to us. One cannot ask, simply, what the attitude of the *Iliad* is to an act which challenges authority, or what stance is taken in the poem toward sadistic killing. There is no single attitude or stance, only a plurality of stances and attitudes. When we read the *Iliad* we often get a sense of things morally off center; this does not happen when we read the Bible or the tragic poets. This confusion emanates from the fact that there is no single source of normative judgment in the poem.

For Homer, the gods as a whole are sharply distinguished from Zeus. With respect to aggression and morality, they are indistinguishable from the men and women in the poem. No god or goddess other than Zeus expresses any moral concern more elevated than the human characters in the poem express. In the great debate on Olympos concerning what is to be done about Achilles' "shameful" treatment of Hektor's body, Apollo passionately speaks out that "Achilles has destroyed pity" and "does dishonor to the dumb earth in his fury." But all the gods except Zeus have taken sides in the war. Apollo, for example, has been on the side of Hektor and the Trojans from the first. The gods who have been the succor of the Achaians—Hera, Athene, Poseidon—are not moved by Hektor's plight, nor by the speech of Apollo. They are willing that Achilles should have his way, no matter how barbaric it may be.

Zeus stands alone, distinguished from both his fellow gods and the mortals who struggle below. Like the poet, he takes no side in the fighting; his heart goes out to Trojans and Achaians alike. Somehow he is helpless when he receives no confirmation from any of the other gods in his unsuccessful attempts to bring order:

'Let us consider then how these things shall be accomplished,
whether again to stir up grim warfare and the terrible
fighting, or cast down love and make them friends with each other.
If somehow this way could be sweet and pleasing to all of us,
the city of lord Priam might still be a place men dwell in,
and Menelaos could take away with him Helen of Argos.'

[IV 14-19]

The violence of Hera's negative reaction to this peace proposal prompts Zeus to cast accusation at her:

'If you could walk through the gates and through the towering
     ramparts
and eat Priam and the children of Priam raw, and the other
Trojans, then, then only might you glut at last your anger.'

[IV 34-36]

As powerful as Zeus is, he can do nothing more than taunt Hera. He
cannot transform the world and "cast down love." When Hektor is dying, Achilles echoes Zeus' words, ascribing to himself the desires of the
cannibal.

Homer, unlike the lesser gods and the mortals, is capable of complexi-
ty of feeling, of irony and ambivalence. He is able to express doubt about
the heroic ideal, going so far as to put into the mouth of Achilles these
words:

'Why, I wish that strife would vanish away from among gods and
     mortals,
and gall, which makes a man grow angry for all his great mind,
that gall of anger that swarms like smoke inside of a man's heart
and becomes a thing sweeter to him by far than the dripping of
     honey.'

[XVIII 107-110]

Achilles is referring only to the anger that produced the quarrel between himself and Agamemnon. After these pious words, he sets out to
destroy as many Trojans as he can and to take the life of Hektor in
revenge for the death of Patroklos. At another time, Homer has
Menelaos cry out that there should be satiety in all things, even in killing.
These humane sentiments proceed from no logic of story or character;
one may question whether they are merely lip-service to a higher notion
of the good.

Homer's stance in regard to violence is ambiguous, ambivalent and
contradictory. To insist that he has one consistent attitude is to misread
the poem. When Simone Weil says: "In this poem there is not a single
man who does not at one time or another have to bow his neck to
force,"[4] she is not speaking for Homer, even though what she says is
truly in the poem, because *she* speaks with a single moral voice. That evil
in the world comes from peoples' reliance on the use of force in their
relationships to each other is true, and we can see it in Homer's poem,
but Homer has shown us this without truly meaning to say it.

Weil wished that Homer were as moral as she. In the interest of
preserving that sentimentality, she misread the poem. "Patroklos," she
wrote, "throughout the *Iliad* commits no cruel or brutal act."[5] Weil's
logic was correct—if Homer is moral, as she understands the term, he

must have presented us with at least *one* hero who was unambivalently loving. Patroklos, Weil said, was such a hero. Let the poet speak for the hero Patroklos. We shall learn what heroism means:

> The sharp stone hit him in the forehead
> and smashed both brows in on each other, nor could the bone hold
> the rock, but his eyes fell out into the dust before him
> there at his feet, so that he vaulted to earth like a diver
> from the carefully wrought chariot, and the life left his bones. Now
> you spoke in bitter mockery over him, rider Patroklos:
> 'See now, what a light man this is, how agile an acrobat.
> If only he were somewhere on the sea, where the fish swarm,
> he could fill the hunger of many men, by diving for oysters;
> he could go overboard from a boat even in rough weather
> the way he somersaults so light to the ground from his chariot
> now. So, to be sure, in Troy also they have their acrobats.'
>
> [XVI 739-750]

No one in the poem is exempt from the commitment to Barbaric-heroic morality, and certainly not Homer. This does not mean that we are not clearly shown that everyone is destroyed by it. It is this double-vision that makes the poem so powerful and so terrifying.

I use the words "ambiguous" and "ambiguity" in a special sense. The dictionary definition of "ambiguous" reads "doubtful or uncertain ... equivocal." I do not use it in this way. For me "ambiguous" and especially "morally ambiguous" means "complicated, complex, not easily understood, containing elements which seem to contradict logic and each other." Others have used the word in this way; I know of no other word which has these meanings, and have, therefore, appropriated it for this special use.

When Hegel tells us that the way of the mind is "roundabout"; when Aeschylus announces that "Zeus, who guided men to think,...has laid" it down that wisdom comes alone through suffering ... From the gods who sit in grandeur grace comes somehow violent" *(Agamemnon,* 176-182)[6]; when Nietzsche proclaims: "Man's highest good must be bought with a crime"[7]; when Thomas Mann recollects that "Degas once made the remark that the artist must approach his work in the same frame of mind in which the criminal commits his deed,"[8] or says that Dostoevski is one "in whom saint and criminal are one";[9] when Apollo, the god of light and healing, commands Orestes to murder his mother; when Hamlet laments that "conscience doth make cowards of us all"—these observations about human behavior are not unclear or equivocal; they are ambiguous; they are representative of the highest wisdom of which human beings are capable.

Cultural development contains its own ambiguities. Primitive society was egalitarian and democratic; leadership existed, but any man was free to obtain the position of a leader. When Barbaric Civilization destroyed the Primitive world-view, it put an end to this equality. In many Polynesian societies, a special heaven was created for those who died in battle, whereas in Primitive cultures all who died suffered the same fate. The Maori of New Zealand evolved a tradition of esoteric learning available only to those who were privileged; in Primitive society there was a common store of knowledge and tales available to all. All Barbaric societies created the institution of aristocracy, where status, privilege, and honors were established by birth; Primitive culture knew nothing, or very little, of such an institution.

Was it "moral" or "progressive" for human beings to take that great step out of Primitive Civilization, putting an end to equality between people, when equality is undeniably good? In my terms, it is profoundly ambiguous—ambiguous because there is no clear-cut, simple "good" or "evil" in the situation. That advance came, like wisdom for Aeschylus, only with suffering.

To live with ambiguity, to recognize that our lives and the history of our culture are not simple or one-dimensional, is an experience of freedom. Keats wrote, in praise of Shakespeare, of his *"negative capability; that is, when a man is capable of being in uncertainties, mysteries, doubts, without any irritable reaching after fact and reason."*[10] Dogmatism knows nothing of ambiguity. Conservative, frightened members of any society have always been incapable of ambiguity, rejecting it in others, and insisting that moral truth is logical and one-dimensional. Homer was not capable of ambiguity; his way was the way of ambivalence. This was not true of the whole of Greek culture; some lyric poets and all the tragic poets took the morally ambiguous as a central theme of their work. Tragic form, an invention of Greek culture, is in essence a form built out of the ambiguity of the human condition.

I turn now to the most ambiguous place of all, in order to see how Homer dealt with that human experience that Freud names for a Greek hero—that psychic state which pushes us to act (imaginatively) towards the parents who brought us up in the most barbaric manner, insisting that if we are not capable of imagining the consummation of these foul deeds, we will never grow up and become adult. Oedipus complex—the womb of ambiguity.

II
The Quarrel of Achilles and Agamemnon: Oedipal Aggression Brings Disaster

The most common recollection of the first book of the *Iliad* is that Agamemnon was the instigator of the dispute with Achilles, that his arrogant behavior was the cause of the quarrel. Those holding this view recall that Agamemnon, having been forced to give back his prize female captive, Chryseis, seized Achilles' captive girl, Briseis, and thus began a chain of events that brought disaster to them all. Even experts have shared the confusion. W. P. Ker, a pioneer in the study of epic poetry, summarizing the *Iliad* in 1896, placed all the blame for the initial aggression on Agamemnon: "A certain man [Achilles] taking part in a siege is slighted by the general [Agamemnon], and in his resentment withdraws from the war..."[1] More recently, Alvin Gouldner, ordinarily a perceptive reader of texts, wrote: "The conflict between Achilles and Agamemnon was *precipitated* by a quarrel over the booty taken by Agamemnon from Achilles..."[2]

Homer's description of these events clearly indicates that Agamemnon was not the initial aggressor in the quarrel. Agamemnon had captured and made a concubine of a girl named Chryseis. Her father, a priest of Apollo, appeared with gifts to ransom his daughter, but Agamemnon refused the ransom. The priest then appealed to Apollo, who, sympathetic, sent a plague on the Greek army. In an attempt to end this misfortune, Achilles called an assembly of the army, where a seer revealed the cause of the plague.

Agamemnon reluctantly agreed to return Chryseis in order to persuade Apollo to lift the plague. Like a child, however, Agamemnon demanded something to comfort him, something to replace what he had lost. He did not specify his consolation prize, not even that it must be another girl, and certainly not Achilles' concubine:

'Find me then some prize that shall be my own, lest I only
among the Argives go without, since that were unfitting;
you are all witness to this thing, that my prize goes elsewhere.'
[I 118 - 120]

It was not necessary that Achilles respond to this request, since it was not directed at him. Everyone knew that Agamemnon was susceptible to flattery and that it would be sufficient to answer him by praising his greatness and assuring him that a suitable prize would be found. Achilles, however, wanted a quarrel: Agamemnon was vulnerable because his arrogant rejection of the priest's ransom had imperiled the army. Even though Agamemnon was fully prepared to correct the situation, Achilles refused to lessen the tension. Achilles had Agamemnon on the defensive and pursued the attack:

'Son of Atreus, most lordly, greediest for gain of all men,
how shall the great-hearted Achaians give you a prize now?
There is no great store of things lying about I know of.'
[I 122 - 124]

Liberality in the giving of gifts was an important virtue of all warrior chieftains, and calling a chieftain "greediest for gain of all men" was rank provocation. Agamemnon's pride and his position as leader of the expedition required him to respond to this provocation. In his answer, Agamemnon came close to saying that the would take away Achilles' girl, but he stopped just short of it:

...Are you ordering me to give this girl back?
Either the great-hearted Achaians shall give me a new prize
chosen according to my desire to atone for the girl lost,
or else if they will not give me one I myself shall take her,
your own [Achilles'] prize, or that of Aias, or that of Odysseus...
[I 134 - 138]

Even at this point, Agamemnon had no wish to push the quarrel to an ultimate break with Achilles: "Still, these are things we shall deliberate again hereafter." In the meanwhile, plans had to be made to send back

Chryseis. One responsible man, said Agamemnon, would be in charge of
taking her back—Aias or Idomeneus or Odysseus. He even offered the
honor to Achilles, along with an epithet of praise: "most terrifying of all
men..."

Achilles' insult and provocation were answered by Agamemnon's
praise. Agamemnon had offered peace to Achilles; Achilles refused the
offer. The central issue of the quarrel was not the taking away of
Achilles' concubine; the primary question was whether Agamemnon or
Achilles held the greater authority.

After Agamemnon's offer of peace, Achilles was determined to
challenge Agamemnon further, to dare him to prove his authority. Firstly, Achilles hurled insult at the King: "O great shamelessness,"—"you
with the dog's eyes." Then Achilles defiantly dared Agamemnon to take
away his girl: "and now *my* prize you threaten in person to strip from me
[my italics]." Agamemnon had said he might take Achilles' girl; he had
never said he would definitely do so. Finally, Achilles gave voice to the
reasons behind the quarrel; he spit out what had been gnawing him for
some time:

'Never, when the Achaians sack some well-founded citadel
of the Trojans, do I have a prize that is equal to your prize.
Always the greater part of the painful fighting is the work of
my hands; but when the time comes to distribute the booty
yours is far the greater reward...'

[I 163 - 167]

Everyone knew that it was customary for the leader of an expedition to
retain a greater share of the booty than any other individual warrior. In
challenging Agamemnon's right to the largest share, Achilles was
therefore challenging nothing less than Agamemnon's position as the
head of the expedition. It was this challenge to legitimate authority that
brought sorrow to Achilles and so many of the Achaians. Agamemnon
was not being overly imperious; if he had let Achilles' challenge pass, he
would have abdicated his kingship.

Agamemnon finally responded to Achilles' revolt. If you cannot respect
my authority, "Go home then with your own ships and your own companions, be king over the Myrmidons. I care nothing about you."
Agamemnon takes Briseis, no longer merely to compensate himself in his
loss, but:

'...that you may learn well
how much greater I am than you, and another man may shrink back
from likening himself to me and contending against me.'

[I 185 - 187]

No longer able to contain his anger at having been defeated, Achilles began to draw his sword from its scabbard in order to kill Agamemnon. The goddess Athene caught him by the hair, checked his rash action, and persuaded Achilles to give up the notion of killing the King. Achilles then hurled vile insults at Agamemnon. Achilles did not go home, as Agamemnon had suggested; instead, he withdrew to his ships, refused to fight, and waited until the Achaians should suffer defeat because of his absence from war.

Achilles' wishes were fulfilled; the Greeks were beaten back by the Trojans; Agamemnon was persuaded to beseech Achilles to return to the fighting. He sent three ambassadors to Achilles—Odysseus, Aias, and Phoinix—with the promise of great gifts if Achilles would resume the war. Agamemnon also offered to return Briseis, along with his oath that he had never slept with the girl. Achilles refused all this. The quarrel was never really about Briseis; she was the occasion, not the cause, of Achilles' rebellion. What Achilles wanted was the one thing that Agamemnon could never give: the chieftainship itself.

Agamemnon had given detailed instructions to the ambassadors, listing each gift he was offering Achilles, concluding:

'All this will I bring to pass for him, if he changes from his anger.
Let him give way. For Hades gives not way, and is pitiless,
and therefore he among all the gods is most hateful to mortals.
And let him yield place to me, inasmuch as I am kinglier
and inasmuch as I can call myself born the elder.'

[IX 157 - 161]

For thirty-six lines, Odysseus, in typically Homeric manner, repeats to Achilles word-for-word the instructions of Agamemnon, but he does not repeat the last four lines of Agamemnon's speech. Odysseus knows what the quarrel is really about; he knows that Achilles will not yield to Agamemnon's authority.

Odysseus vainly attempted to persuade Achilles to accept Agamemnon's gifts and return to the fighting. Phoinix then tried to bring about the same result in a long speech full of Homeric digressions. One of these "digressions" concerned Phoinix's own life story—the most blatantly Oedipal story in the poem. Phoinix's father had taken a concubine, angering his wife. In order to take revenge, Phoinix's mother asked Phoinix to seduce his father's concubine. When his father learned of it, he symbolically castrated Phoinix through a curse that Phoinix should never have a son of his own. Phoinix was angry enough to dare to kill his father, "but one of the immortals checked my anger...that I might not be called a parricide among the Achaians."

It is an exact duplication of Athene's checking the threatened killing of

Agamemnon by Achilles. The digression turns out to be no digression at all—its function is to underline what Achilles' quarrel is really about. Aggression against authority brings disaster, Homer tells us; the ultimate aggression—killing a father or a king—is the most disastrous course of all. Divine power is required to check such an excess of anger.

Homer's concern with revolt against legitimate authority does not end with the story of Achilles and Agamemnon. No moral problem is of greater interest for Homer than the question of how subordinates should act towards those who hold authority. In contrast to the disastrous actions of Achilles, Homer gives us many instances where those who have less power know how to respect a greater authority. Giving such respect, Homer tells us, is always the wiser way. Diomedes, for instance, was one of the youngest of the heroes. Still, he argued against one of Agamemnon's periodic half-hearted pronouncements that they should all abandon the war and go home. "I will be the first to fight with your folly...," Diomedes said; yet he was most careful to acknowledge that he feared Agamemnon's power: "then do not be angered." Diomedes acted like a good son, showing his father where he had gone astray, but being very careful not to challenge the father's right to make the decision.

Nestor was the oldest of the Achaian warriors, a king in his own country, a man of great authority and wisdom. Homer shows us that even he maintained the highest respect for Agamemnon's kingship. When Nestor appealed to Agamemnon to appease Achilles with gifts as inducement to return, he was most circumspect to heap praise on Agamemnon's head before he dared to speak words that the king might not wish to hear:

'Son of Atreus, most lordly and king of men, Agamemnon,
with you I will end, with you I will make my beginning, since you
are lord over many people, and Zeus has given into your hand
the sceptre and rights of judgement, to be king over the people.
It is yours therefore to speak a word, yours also to listen,
and grant the right to another also, when his spirit stirs him
to speak for our good. All shall be yours when you lead the way.
　　Still
I will speak in the way it seems best to my mind...'

[IX 96 - 103]

Homer is not presenting us with hypocritical flattery; Nestor does not debase himself with such an introduction; it is proper respect owed a legitimate king and chief of a warring expedition.

Homer maintains a keen interest in two themes that are closely related to the idea of legitimate authority: young men are impetuous and not to be trusted; old men are worthy of the highest respect.

'Bring, that he may seal the pledges, the strength of Priam:
Priam himself, for his sons are outrageous, not to be trusted;
lest some man overstep Zeus' oaths, and make them to be nothing.
Always it is, that the hearts in the younger men are frivolous,
but when an elder man is among them, he looks behind him
and in front, so that all comes out far better for both sides.'

[III 105 - 110]

The same tension between old and young marred the funeral games
that followed the cremation of Patroklos. Like all rituals after death,
these games served the function of healing and reconciliation. Even here
Homer introduces the theme of the rash young man who challenges the
authority of age, only to retreat from such rebellion, as a good son
should. In those games, Antilochos, a young hero, defeated Menelaos in
the chariot race by cutting off Menelaos in a narrow passage—a strategy
that was not exactly legitimate. The older protested after the race was
over, claiming that he should be declared the victor over Antilochos.
Repenting his rashness, Antilochos, the proper son of the good Nestor,
responded:

'Enough now. For I, my lord Menelaos, am younger
by far than you, and you are the greater and go before me.
You know how greedy transgressions flower in a young man, seeing
that his mind is the more active but his judgement is lightweight.
       Therefore
I would have your heart be patient with me. I myself will give you
the mare I won, and if there were something still greater you asked for
out of my house, I should still be willing at once to give it
to you, beloved of Zeus, rather than all my days
fall from your favour and be in the wrong before the divinities.'

[XXIII 587 - 595]

Homer believes that old men who can no longer fight live in a different
world from that of the young hero. The death of a young warrior brings
glory; when the aged are killed, there is only pity. Young men are expected to be impetuous, heedless of death, whereas the old become
cautious and protective of life. After Achilles returned to the fighting in
order to revenge the death of Patroklos by killing Hektor, Priam pleaded
with Hektor to retreat into Troy so that he might save the city and save
his father from dolorous death:

'for a young man all is decorous
when he is cut down in battle and torn with the sharp bronze, and lies
       there

dead, and though dead still all that shows about him is beautiful;
but when an old man is dead and down, the dogs mutilate
the grey head and the grey beard and the parts that are secret,
this, for all sad mortality, is the sight most pitiful.'

[XXII 71 - 76]

Old men who were still able to fight maintained the values of the
warrior-hero. Kindly old Nestor, an aged warrior, encouraged the
Achaians to battle, by crying out that they shall not go home until each
warrior has taken a Trojan woman to his bed.

We have observed that Homer makes a connection between killing a
king and killing a father: a god checked Phoinix when he was about to
strike his father, just as Athene kept Achilles from killing Agamemnon.
In both instances, only the external force of the gods had prevented the
catastrophe. Killing a father and killing a king are brought together in
the last book of the poem when Priam confronts Achilles. Priam is a
father and a king, and Achilles responds to him with affection and
hatred. On entering Achilles' hut, Priam immediately calls upon Achilles
to remember his father, "one who is of years like mine, and on the door-
sill of sorrowful old age." Achilles weeps "now for his own father, now
again for Patroklos." He even takes the old man by the hand "in pity for
the grey head and the grey beard." Such feelings, however, do not last
long. Achilles' aggressive feelings for both fathers and kings are soon
manifest and only the orders of the gods prevent new violence. Achilles
cautions Priam not to make too much of mourning:

'Therefore
you must not further make my spirit move in my sorrows,
for fear, old sir, I might not let you alone in my shelter,
suppliant as you are; and be guilty before the god's orders.'

[XXIV 567 - 570]

The poem began with Achilles' attempted revolt against Agamemnon.
Agamemnon refused to yield and Achilles withdrew into sulking anger.
The poem ends when Achilles has another king at his feet, kissing his
hands in supplication, begging for mercy. For the moment, Achilles'
feelings of revenge over Agamemnon were satiated by the power of
humiliation he held over Priam. Only after he had satisfied his desire for
revenge was he able to equate "father" and "affection," was he capable
of human love. The moment of reconciliation quickly passed; the power
of Zeus, rather than Achilles' own inclination, prevented the killing of
Priam and assured the ransom and burial of Hektor's body. Divine
power could not transform Achilles' hatred against those who held
authority.

Homer's concern with legitimate authority—and the revolt against it—includes the gods on Olympos. The gods also have a king, who is actually the father of many of them. Like Achilles, they are continually angry that they have to take commands:

> '...and all the gods rose up
> from their chairs to greet the coming of their father, not one had courage
> to keep his place as the father advanced, but stood up to greet him.'
> [I 533-535]

> 'He [Zeus] spoke, and the goddess the ox-eyed lady Hera was frightened
> and went and sat down in silence wrenching her heart to obedience...'
> [I 568-569]

> Still Athene stayed silent and said nothing, but only
> sulked at Zeus her father, and savage anger took hold of her.
> [VIII 459 - 460]

Unlike Achilles, the gods had learned from the past that revolt cannot succeed. They had defied Zeus, but his power was too much for them, and they reluctantly learned to submit. When Achilles asked his mother Thetis to go to Zeus and ask a favor, he reminded her that Zeus owed her assistance because she had aided him "that time when all the Olympians sought to bind him, Hera and Poseidon and Pallas Athene." Similarly, the god Hephaistos refers to old rebellions when he counsels his mother Hera not to go against the wishes of Zeus:

> 'It is too hard to fight against the Olympian.
> There was a time once before now I was minded to help you,
> and he caught me by the foot and threw me from the magic threshold,
> and all day long I dropped helpless...'
> [I 589 - 592]

No savagery is illegitimate for a tyrant faced with revolt. Zeus threatens his rebellious wife:

> 'I do not know, perhaps for this contrivance of evil
> and pain you will win first reward when I lash you with whip strokes.
> Do you not remember that time you hung from high and on your feet

I slung two anvils, and about your hands drove a golden
chain, unbreakable. You among the clouds and the bright sky
hung, nor could the **gods** about tall Olympos endure it
and stood about, but could not set you free...'

[XV 16 - 22]

Homer shows the gods oscillating between two modes of action, both
unfulfilling: revolt and be punished, or repress anger and submit. For
them, there is no possibility of either successful revolt against a tyrannical power or willing submission to a moral authority. We hear this sad
wisdom from the lady Hera:

'Fools, we who try to work against Zeus, thoughtlessly.
Still we are thinking in our anger to go near, and stop him
by argument or force. He sits apart and cares nothing
nor thinks of us, and says that among the other immortals
he is pre-eminently the greatest in power and strength. Therefore
each of you must take whatever evil he sends you.'

[XV 104 - 109]

As Achilles vented his frustrated revenge against Agamemnon upon
the helpless Priam, just so the gods turn their thwarted anger at Zeus
towards helpless mortals, when these dare to be disobedient. In the *Iliad,*
many stories are cited that teach the lesson that those who attempt to
rival the gods are cruelly punished. The poem itself contains a scene
where Aphrodite has rescued Paris from a duel with Menelaos, when
Paris was about to be defeated. Aphrodite brought Paris to his bedroom
and commanded Helen to go to his bed. Helen had no desire to solace her
second husband after he had not been man enough to defeat her first
husband in the duel. She refused to obey Aphrodite's command:

'Go yourself and sit beside him, abandon the god's way,
turn your feet back never again to the path Olympos
but stay with him forever, and suffer for him, and look after him
until he makes you his wedded wife, or makes you his slave girl.'

[III 406 -409]

Aphrodite, far from the most intelligent of the gods, had learned from
her father how one treats such rebellion. It was not a difficult lesson to
learn; Aphrodite quickly instructed Helen as to the consequences of
disobeying a goddess:

'Wretched girl, do not tease me lest in anger I forsake you
and grow to hate you as much as now I terribly love you,

lest I encompass you in hard hate, caught between both sides,
Danaans and Trojans alike, and you wretchedly perish.'

[III 414 - 417]

Having talked defiance and been challenged, Helen does as they all do:
becomes frightened, represses her anger, and becomes obedient.

In summary, Homer's interest in revolt against legitimate authority
permeates the entire poem. The central story of the *Iliad* begins with
Achilles' revolt against Agamemnon. For Homer, all revolt is an illegitimate expression of aggression; it brings disaster, it should be suppressed, no matter what the cost. Homer cannot repress, however, his
own fascination with the subject. He is like the righteous suppressors of
pornography who insist on obtaining—first-hand—evidence of the evil
that must be extirpated. This fascination with, and revulsion from,
rebellion had enormous implications for Greek culture. If we are to
understand this ambivalence it is helpful to comprehend the nature of the
Oedipus complex.

Freud's discussion of the Oedipus complex and its fundamental importance in the development of the psyche is one of the cornerstones of his
theoretical structure. The clarity of his thought becomes clouded,
however, when he discusses the termination, or dissolution, of the complex—the period when the child turns away from intense sexual feelings
towards one parent and aggressive feelings for the other, and enters a
period of sexual latency. In the course of this discussion, Freud fails to
distinguish between the cause of this dissolution and the form it takes.

There is a significant difference between asking *why* the Oedipus complex dissolves and asking *what form* it takes when it does dissolve. One
may ask why an elephant has a trunk, but to answer: in order to wash its
back, is to confuse biological development with the use to which that
development may be put. The confusion implies some deliberate purpose
in the cosmos, a Grand Engineer of the Universe who not only watches
the sparrow's fall, but makes sure it has the proper feet on which to land.

Freud does admit into consideration the general view of biological-
psychical development: that the Oedipus complex dissolves because it is
in the nature of the psyche that it should do so. He writes: "[T]he
Oedipus complex must collapse because the time has come for its
disintegration, just as the milk-teeth fall out when the permanent ones
begin to grow."[3] However, on the very next page he writes: "Now it is
my view that *what brings about* the destruction of the child's phallic
genital organization is [the] threat of castration."[4] It is of the utmost importance to note that Freud is not saying that the form which the dissolution of the Oedipus complex takes includes a fear of castration, but that
such a fear brings it about—causes it.

Freud does not imply that this may be a neurotic manner in which to terminate the complex. The view applies to all males, potentially neurotic or not. "In boys...the complex is not simply repressed, it is literally smashed to pieces by the shock of threatened castration."[5]

I believe that there is a more accurate way to view the demise of the Oedipus complex, a way which also sheds light on problems in Greek society. In all that follows, I will be talking of the Oedipus problem in the male child; firstly, because I believe I comprehend it much better than the equivalent situation in the female child; secondly, because Greek society was a male-dominant society—its problems and its inadequacies are traceable to a male view of the world.

The Oedipus complex has its uses for the developing psyche. The child begins to entertain ideas of concentrating its genital sexual energy on an object; the child conceives of replacing the father. Aside from the notion of killing, these emotions also mean growing up, becoming powerful, being a man, having a woman, being in love, begetting a child, ordering the world, taking responsibility—it is a preview of adult life. After a period of sexual latency, in adolescence the original Oedipus situation is revisited; the child has a second chance to deal with the intensity of these feelings. Now, however, these drives are no longer biologically premature; the child is now biologically and psychologically prepared to be an adult.

If the original experience of Oedipal desires terminated because of the fear of castration, is it not reasonable to assume that the second round might also end on the same note? This is not to put aside the idea that for some, or many, the original dissolution takes the form of a fear of castration, and that for such people the adolescent revisiting ends in the same way. But is this not a situation of neurosis, a situation that inhibits or makes impossible the attainment of adult satisfactions? If, for everyone, the Oedipus complex is "smashed to pieces by the threat of castration," who could ever risk becoming an adult in later years? The traumatic effect of that first experiment with genital sexuality would haunt all later attempts to become adult, and ultimately make it impossible.

It may also be true that the threat of punishment, if not of castration, hangs over the imaginative fulfillment of Oedipal desires in all people—that even for a healthy, non-neurotic child there is a fear connected with the carrying out of these "foul deeds." It may be a problem with which everyone has to deal, but clearly the healthy solution to the problem and the neurotic non-solution are not identical.

I would like to propose a description, exactly opposite to Freud's, of what happens at the end of the Oedipus complex. In the healthy child, the Oedipus complex is resolved because the child has had the courage to imagine it could do what that complex seeks to accomplish: replace the father and obtain the mother. Far from dissolving on a note of incapacity, the Oedipus complex resolves with a conception of efficacy. Having had the courage to imagine carrying out those desires as a child, the adolescent is then free to direct his sexual and aggressive energies outside his family, and eventually establish his own family. The person who had not the imaginative courage to accomplish Oedipal desires as a child will keep returning to these desires; the thing which inhibited their imaginative accomplishment in the first instance will continue its power of inhibition; such a person will have grave problems in becoming adult. If the threat of castration has originally prevented the imaginative accomplishments of that task, that threat will never go away—all subsequent attempts will more than likely be equally threatened.

In his imagination, the child does not kill the father; what he does is incorporate the father in himself. He takes into himself the attributes of the father, just as the cannibal warrior takes into himself the courage of his enemy by eating him and taking his name. The child becomes the father; the old father is now, somehow, inside the child. Inside the child, the father's voice is still heard: giving orders, demanding moral action, calling for punishment when correct actions are not forthcoming. The father inside the child is conscience. The concept of conscience signifies that moral authority has been internalized.

Freud said that the super-ego, conscience, is the heir to the Oedipus complex, that the pre-Oedipus child has no conscience as we know the term. My notion of incorporation of the father is different from the idea of identification with the father used by Freud to explain the origin of the super-ego. Most importantly, this conception of the origin of conscience implies that, to the degree to which the goals of the Oedipus complex are carried out imaginatively, conscience will lodge *inside* the child; to the degree that these goals are not carried out, the dictates of conscience will appear to come from *outside* the child. The degree to which conscience is internalized is the degree to which the psyche is mature. If the imagination is fearful of accomplishing the goals of the Oedipus complex, because of some imagined fear of castration or anything else, one result will be an insufficiently internalized conscience.

In order to have a strong conscience, boys must have the courage to imagine possessing their mothers by sexual means and incorporating their fathers; it is no wonder that morality is ambiguous, that wisdom comes only with suffering, or that man's highest good is bought with a crime.

It is not surprising that the child is ambivalent about carrying out Oedipal desires, that the psyches of many, faced with such a task, find safety in flight. One important form that this flight may take, in the male child, Freud states, is a renunciation of the sexual feelings towards the mother and the assumption of a passive sexual role towards the father. "The Oedipus complex offered the child two possibilities of satisfaction, an active and a passive one. He could put himself in his father's place in a masculine fashion and have intercourse with his mother as his father did...or he might want to take the place of his mother and be loved by his father, in which case his mother would become superfluous."[6] "[I]n boys the Oedipus complex has a double orientation...a boy also wants to take his *mother's* place as the love-object of his *father*—a fact which we describe as the feminine attitude."[7] For Freud, a fear of castration lies in back of this sexual reversal: "*in boys the Oedipus complex is destroyed by the castration complex,*...the castration complex always operates in the sense implied in its subject-matter: it inhibits and limits masculinity and encourages femininity."[8]

Note that Freud does *not* say that assuming a passive sexual role towards the father and making the mother superfluous is a *reaction to* the Oedipus complex; he says that this development is an inherent factor in the complex itself: "the Oedipus complex has a double orientation." In other words, the Oedipus phase is a period when the male child has intense genital sexual feelings for his mother, a strong desire to eliminate the father, *and* intense drives to become the sexual object of the father. Would it not be simpler to say, and nearer the truth, that this assumption of a passive role towards the father is one possible, or even inevitable, reaction formation to the problems of the Oedipus complex? Freud treats this assumption of passivity, just as he treats the fear of castration, as an intrinsic element of the complex itself. He fails to differentiate between the conditions of the Oedipus complex and the inevitable *reactions* of the psyche to the contradictions and ambivalences that result from the complex.

In my view, the degree to which the young male child will assume a passive sexual role towards his father as a result of the Oedipal situation is in inverse relationship to the degree to which he is willing to imagine carrying out Oedipal wishes. The greater his capacity to imagine those things, the greater will be his own masculine stance, the less will be his passive sexuality towards his father and towards all males in authority.

A young male's retreat from the goals of the Oedipal situation because he feels he cannot achieve them may remind one of the case among some animals where the males fight for dominance over the females. In some situations, the defeated male is not killed, but he does withdraw and turns his rump to the victorious male, in mock sexual submission.

Freud's discussion of the male child's turning sexually passive towards the father in connection with the Oedipus complex can give us insight into the pervasive male homosexuality of Greek culture, and into the subject position of women in that society. Homer carefully and deliberately taught that Oedipal aggression brings disaster—a notion that persisted in Greek culture through the fear of *hybris,* of striving for too much. The characteristic form of Greek homosexuality was the relationship of an adolescent boy and an older man—where the adolescent assumed precisely the passive sexual role that Freud describes. I cannot avoid the hypothesis that there was a close connection between Greek homosex-uality and the fear of Oedipal aggression.

This is not to argue that Greek homosexuality was "caused" by the fear of Oedipal aggression, nor the reverse. In the complex situation presented by cultural form, no one important configuration is the cause of another important configuration. All such configurations are the "causes" of each other. A fear of Oedipal aggression may well lead to a homosexual response, but once that response has been institutionalized it, in turn, will reinforce the dread of Oedipal *hybris*. It is not a question of cause, but a situation of interlocking, mutually compatible views of the world.

The totality of such important configurations of world-views makes up the value system of a culture. Within any complex system of values, some particular values are compatible with each other; they reinforce each other and help perpetuate the existence of one another. Some particular values may be incompatible with each other; they contend against each other; that contention produces strain and ambivalence within the culture. The dread of Oedipal aggression and the dread of male homosexuality in Greek culture were compatible values, each reinforcing the existence of the other.

Freud's discussion of the fear of castration in connection with Oedipal drives can be made less controversial, and possibly closer to the truth, by substituting the idea of fear of punishment in general for the specific fear of losing the penis. When Oedipus finally learned that he had killed his father and married his mother, he put his eyes out. No matter whether or not we regard that self-blinding as a symbolic castration, one thing is cer-tain: he punished himself. When Achilles rebelled against the father-king Agamemnon, and the rebellion failed, he punished himself when he deliberately refrained from fighting; he gave up the most important thing in his life: the activity of the warrior. Why does Achilles send Patroklos into the fighting instead of going himself? A sense of doom hangs over the decision, as if Achilles knew that Patroklos would be killed. It could be that Achilles expected to suffer a great loss, or punishment, as a result of his *hybris* in contending against Agamemnon. He acted like a man who felt the necessity of sacrificing something before he could be assured of forgiveness, and he did send to sacrifice the most valuable thing he possessed—his dearest friend Patroklos. Achilles gave Patroklos his own armor to wear, making Patroklos a mock Achilles—a real sacrifice.

This discussion of the healthy resolution of the Oedipus complex has placed great stress on the imaginative fulfillment of Oedipal drives. Myth and art can aid the imagination in this work. To become adult, it is not necessary to kill one's father and have intercourse with one's mother; it is helpful, however, to have available to the imagination myths and works of art that deal with such behavior. Greek culture created not only the story of Oedipus, but also a mythology wherein the king of the gods, Zeus, had attained his power by overthrowing his father, Kronos. Kronos had become the king of the gods by supplanting—and castrating—his own father, Uranos. Homer's art rejects this imaginative working through of Oedipal desires. Don't—he tells us—it will only lead to disaster.

Homer's belief that aggression against authority brings chaos illuminates the dread of *hybris* in classical times. The fear of going too far, of striving for too much, is symbolically set, in Herodotus and Pindar in the fifth century, as a conflict between mortals and the gods, where the gods punish any mortal who rivals their power. With reiteration that borders on tedium, Pindar exhorts us to follow the way of Diomedes and not that of Achilles. "Some men are great in one thing; others in another: but the crowning summit is for kings. Refrain from peering too far!"[9] "Strive not to become Zeus; you have everything if destiny of such splendours befall you. Mortals must be content with mortality."[10]

Dodds has observed that the origin of the fear of *hybris* lies not in Heaven but in the bosom of the family: "The peculiar horror with which the Greeks viewed offences against a father, and the peculiar religious sanctions to which the offender was thought to be exposed, are in themselves suggestive of strong repression. So are the many stories in which a father's curse produced terrible consequences...and when Plato wants to illustrate what happens when rational controls are not functioning, his typical example is the Oedipus dream."[11]

Family life and the religious life are two areas where fundamental questions concerning authority are raised. Politics is a third such area. The *Iliad* hardly concerns itself with any conflict between higher and lower social classes. The one place where it does deal with these ideas is, in the second book, when Thersites berates Agamemnon and is beaten by Odysseus for his insubordination. It is not clear to what actual social class Thersites belongs. There is no evidence that he is a commoner, although he is obviously not of the same social class as Diomedes or Aias or Achilles—otherwise he could never have been humiliated as he was by Odysseus. Homer's fascination with Oedipal revolt extends even to this lowly, ugly creature. Thersites' challenge to Agamemnon is a caricature of Achilles' rebellion. He even parrots Achilles' words: " 'Your shelters are filled with bronze, there are plenty of the choicest women for you within your shelter, whom we Achaians give to you first of all whenever we capture some stronghold.' " But he has no power; he can only threaten with Achilles' spear: " 'But there is no gall in Achilleus' heart, and he is forgiving. Otherwise, son of Atreus, this were your last outrage.' "

It is appropriate that Odysseus should beat Thersites into submission, since Odysseus has already stated the canon before Thersites expresses his outrage:

> 'Surely not all of us Achaians can be as kings here.
> Lordship for many is no good thing. Let there be one ruler,
> one king, to whom the son of devious-devising Kronos
> gives the Sceptre and right of judgement, to watch over his people.'
> [II 203 -206]

One king in Heaven, one king on earth, one authoritarian father in the home, and woe to him who will not let it be. Odysseus beats Thersites; all the men praise his action; they even laugh at the now submissive rebel. The social consequences of the world-view that certifies all authority as good are the preservation of aristocracy and kingship—the inhibition of democracy.

Homeric ambivalence about legitimate authority was transformed, two centuries later, by the tragic poets into an attitude of ambiguity. The tragic conception of the hero differs from the Homeric. Achilles is a great hero because he is huge, beautiful, born of a divine mother, and the greatest fighter of them all; and the order in his life is destroyed by Oedipal *hybris*. Achilles, however, would have been a great hero without his *hybris,* as the example of Hektor so clearly demonstrates. Hektor rebels against no one; he is a good son and a great fighter—a true hero.

The tragic hero achieves his heroism only with the very act of defiance that destroys either him or his happiness. Prometheus, Orestes, Oedipus, and Antigone are heroic because they are willing to assume the glories and the consequences of *hybris* and revolt. All suffer, but unlike Achilles, who should not have done what he did. Their suffering comes because they have done noble and glorious things. This ambiguity was the gift of the tragic poets. They had the courage to imagine what it feels like to confront, and not retreat from, Oedipal drives. Antigone revolts against a legitimate authority; Prometheus rebels against the king of the gods; Orestes kills his own mother; Oedipus is told by his mother-wife Jocasta, before they learn the truth, that "in dreams too...many a man has lain with his mother." [*Oedipus the King,* 981-982][12]

The concern of the tragic poets with the ambiguity of revolt against legitimate authority was closely connected with political democracy. It is no coincidence that Athens was the first city in history to establish a viable democracy and was also the place where the tragic form was invented. Both tragedy and democracy are impossible when all authority is seen as good and blind obedience to authority is considered a high virtue.

Homer's ambivalence about Oedipal revolt was never resolved within Greek culture. Ultimately, Homer's final judgment prevailed: tragedies ceased to be written; democracy was destroyed. Plato understood well the connections among tragedy, democracy, Oedipal revolt, and ambiguity. Plato's political solution was to propose a system wherein we might be assured of having virtuous, not tyrannical, fathers of the city so that we could all be good children again and there would never be any need for rebellion or even a peaceful challenge to authority. The first order of business in Plato's new state was the institution of censorship. Before doing anything else, he told us in the second book of the *Republic* what stories could not be told in his state. The very first story to be suppressed was the castration of Uranos by Kronos.[13] In great detail, Plato then went on to repress any tale of the gods or mortals that had in it even the slightest ambiguity.

The wheel had come full circle. The openings to freedom represented by tragedy, democracy, and the ambiguity of revolt were closed. Plato joined hands with Homer, declaring that such freedoms would only bring disaster.

III
The Illegitimacy of Barbaric Regression

In his telling of the story of the Oedipal revolt of Achilles against Agamemnon, Homer reveals in himself a deep-seated ambivalence about the legitimacy of such behavior. Towards the barbaric regression of Achilles that follows the death of Patroklos, Homer has no ambivalence; for him, it is unquestionably illegitimate—an unmitigated disaster.

The story of Achilles' wrath is presented in two distinct stages: that which precedes, and that which follows the death of Patroklos. In each stage there is a difference in the nature of Achilles' anger and in the reaction of the poet to that anger.

When Achilles failed in his rebellion against Agamemnon, he did what many little boys do when their efforts to become the captain of the team are thwarted: he had a tantrum, vowed not to play the game anymore, and went crying to his mother for comfort. Achilles was determined that the Greeks would someday regret that they had slighted him; he prayed for their defeat when he was not fighting with them, so that they would come to him, begging him to return.

But Achilles was not a little boy; he was an adult with great power. His mother was a goddess and the two of them were capable of enlisting the most powerful force in the universe, the great god Zeus, to aid Achilles in his revenge-tantrum. When adults with great power behave like little boys, they bring destruction. Many died to comfort Achilles.

Despite the dire consequences of Achilles' plan, in this first stage of

Achilles' anger Homer's judgment of his behavior is lenient, almost indulgent. Homer pities Achilles in his sulking, passive tantrum. Even Zeus, a god of some moral sensibility, agreed to aid Achilles in bringing the scheme to fulfillment. It is a story of one man and his troubles; civilization is not on trial; Achilles' regression in this first phase is personal and psychological; it would be inappropriate to call it "Barbaric."

With the death of Patroklos, everything changed. Achilles' sulking anger was transformed into rage of god-like proportions. No longer trapped in the masochistic tantrum of the little boy comforted by his mother, he became destructive of the hard-won values of Archaic Civilization. It was a descent into Barbarism. "[A] last flicker of the superhuman rage so furiously against his foes must show itself....It is as though a primitive and long suppressed savagery had broken out for a last effort."[1]

The rage that followed the death of Patroklos destroyed not only the life of Hektor but all those forms of cultivated life that had become the pride of the Archaic hero. Achilles' wrath makes us witness to human sacrifice, mass killing, the degradation of the corpse of a hero, and the flesh-eating desires of the cannibal. Society itself comes under attack: "as proof that without envy, jealousy, and ambition in the contest, the Hellenic city, like the Hellenic man, degenerates. He becomes evil and cruel; he becomes vengeful and godless; in short, he becomes 'pre-Homeric.' "[2]

Homer has no sympathy with this "pre-Homeric" man. He tells us the story of Achilles' Barbaric regression as an example of how the true hero should not act. He shows the reader what real Barbarism looks like, so that it may be rejected. Ultimately, Homer's main interest is in defending the values of his warrior-heroes. We should not, Homer is saying, condemn the everyday killing done by Hektor or Menelaos. It could be much worse, he tells us; look at the barbarized Achilles.

Achilles' descent begins with an orgy of killing. In a mere thirty-five lines at the end of Book XX he takes the life of no fewer than ten Trojan warriors. It is a frenzy of destruction unequaled elsewhere in the poem. The poet cannot hold back his horror: "The son of Peleus was straining to win glory, his invincible hands spattered with bloody filth."

Human sacrifice—the characteristic form of aggression in Barbarian society—is the means Achilles chooses to honor his dead companion, Patroklos. Nowhere else in the poem is such a practice even hinted at.

> Then he set beside him two-handled jars of oil and honey
> leaning them against the bier, and drove four horses with strong necks
> swiftly aloft the pyre with loud lamentation. And there were
> nine dogs of the table that had belonged to the lord Patroklos.
> Of these he cut the throat of two, and set them on the pyre;

and so also killed twelve noble sons of the great-hearted Trojans
with the stroke of bronze, and evil were the thoughts in his heart
    against them,
and let loose the iron fury of the fire to feed on them.
                                            [XXIII 170-177]

Achilles was tempted to eat the body of Hektor raw. Such regression is
infectious; Hektor's mother wanted to deal with Achilles in the same
manner: "I wish I could set teeth in the middle of his liver and eat it.
That would be vengeance for what he did to my son." As we know from
cannibal societies, there is no end to that chain of vengeance for
vengeance.

In Homer's view, however, the primary offense in Achilles' barbaric
behavior is not the orgy of killing or human sacrifice, or the talk of
eating human flesh. Homer's main interest is the degradation and
mutilation of Hektor's body. When he describes this mutilation, he
demonstrates no ambivalence; he takes no hidden pride in Achilles'
power to do such a terrible thing. For Homer there is absolutely nothing
to admire in such behavior:

He spoke, and now thought of shameful treatment for glorious
        Hektor.
In both his feet in the back he made holes by the tendons
in the space between ankle and heel, and drew thongs of ox-hide
        through them,
and fastened them to the chariot so as to let the head drag,
and mounted the chariot, and lifted the glorious armour inside it,
then whipped the horses to a run, and they winged their way unreluc-
        tant.
                                            [XXII 395-400]

Homer expresses no sympathy for the twelve anonymous Trojan
sacrifices. All his concern is for the corpse of Hektor:

'Good-bye, Patroklos, I hail you even in the house of the death
        god.
All that I promised you in time past I am accomplishing,
that I would drag Hektor here and give him to the dogs to feed on
raw, and before your burning pyre to behead twelve glorious
children of the Trojans for my anger over your slaying.'
        He spoke and thought of shameful treatment for glorious
        Hektor.
He laid him on his face in the dust by the bier of Menoitios'
son.
                                            [XXIII 19-26]

Why is the treatment of Hektor's body so shameful and the sacrifice of warriors mentioned only incidentally? For us there is more horror in the fresh killing of twelve human beings than in the mutilation of the body of a man who is already dead. Why does Homer not see it in this way? The answer may lie in the fact that for Homeric society cannibalism and human sacrifice were not real possibilities; they had become metaphors for ultimate anger; no actual warrior would do such things. They had become matters of art, not matters of life.

It may be that the mutilation of a dead corpse—especially the taking of the head, which I will talk of later—was a real possibility among the Greeks, and therefore problematic in their culture. Even in historical times the threat of engulfment by the barbarian past lay heavy over Greek culture. Gilbert Murray writes: "What strikes one most in Greek society is not so much any bad things that were actually done. Of course there were bad things and always have been in all societies. It is rather the frightful proximity of worse things still. Practices that to us seem like the scarcely credible stories of a remote past were to the fifth-century Athenian possibilities and even dangers. The jungle grew thick and close all around them, and the barrier between seemed very weak, impalpable."[3]

Despite the fact that the myths—and the tragedies—were full of stories of cannibalism and human sacrifice, there was no eating of human flesh in Greek society and the existence of human sacrifice is still not proved— if it did exist, the number of incidents is extremely small. The treatment afforded the dead bodies of warriors, however, was a major concern. Over and over, Thucydides pointedly mentions that during the Peloponnesian war, after battle, a truce was concluded and the dead bodies exchanged.

Herodotus tells us a story of the war with the Persians. Lampon is urging the victorious Spartan general Pausanias to increase his glory and renown: "When Leonidas was slain at Thermopylae, Xerxes and Mardonius commanded that he should be beheaded and crucified. Do thou the like at this time by Mardonius, and thou will have glory in Sparta, and likewise through the whole of Greece. For, by hanging him upon a cross, thou wilt revenge Leonidas, who was thy father's brother."[4]

Pausanias replies: "...thou has cast me down to the ground, by bidding me maltreat the dead, and, saying that thus I shall raise myself in men's esteem. Such doings befit barbarians rather than Greeks; and even in barbarians we detest them."[5]

The story may or may not be true. Three hundred years after Homer composed the *Iliad*, Herodotus still felt the necessity of teaching this lesson.

The magical obliteration of the gulf that separates life from death is the barbaric essence of the mutilation of a dead body. To continue to hurt the dead body of Hektor may only be done on the assumption that Hektor is still in the corpse of Hektor; Achilles insists that it is Hektor, transformed into a dead body which can still feel pain and humiliation. "Apollo had pity on him [Hektor]," Homer tells us, "though he was only a dead man." Achilles refuses to believe that dead is dead; he will not see that it is only a dead man.

Seen from another point of view, Achilles has no real interest in Hektor's corpse; his interest lies in Hektor, and killing. If he could magically bring him back from the dead, he would do so, so that he might kill him again. Lacking this magical power, he resorts to killing Hektor, symbolically, over and over again.

The refusal to give back the corpse for proper burial is a denial of a fundamental value of the heroic morality. The concept of the hero had heightened the value of human life and its possibilities. The reverential burial of a hero signified that the life that had been lived by such a person had a meaning beyond mere existence. It was incumbent upon the friends—and the enemies—of a hero slain in battle to indicate the value of the life he had lived. To give the body back is a recognition that Hektor was a hero, with a mother and a father, with a wife and a child, who lived a life that had meaning for a whole city. To continue to degrade the corpse is to insist that Hektor was the killer of Patroklos and the object of revenge—nothing more. To kill another human being, one must first make him or her into an object. To continue to kill that person, even after he is dead, is to continue to deny his reality, to prolong his status as object.

Achilles' regression into Barbarism threatened to destroy fundamental values of Archaic life. For Homer, it is an evil which could destroy the world—a totally illegitimate form of aggression. So deep was this regression that the restoration of the heroic world could only be accomplished with divine power. After several half-hearted failures to bring morality into the chaos produced by the gods and the people on earth, Zeus finally overrules the objections of Hera, Athene, and Poseidon and insists that "Achilleus is given gifts by Priam and gives back the body of Hektor."

The "moral order" that is restored by the command of Zeus includes the day-by-day killing of noble heroes by one another. Homer has no interest in transforming that cultural order into something more humane. His only criticism is for regressive behavior. "It could be worse," he tells us. "We could all, like Achilles, regress into barbarism."

When Achilles resorts to a cataclysmic funeral, to human sacrifice, talk of cannibalism, and head-hunting, he is indulging in the customs of the Barbarian peoples who surrounded the Greek world. He is regressing not only to a more primitive psychological state; he is actually going back in cultural time.

In the Dark Age of Greece, about 1050 B.C. to 750 B.C., a time when the *Iliad* was in the process of development, the kind of lavish funeral that Achilles provided for Patroklos did not exist, but: "A society of this kind almost certainly did exist at the very period, but not in Greece: if we look at the material traces from Urnfield Europe, and particularly at the rich graves from the Hungarian plain, we shall find all these heroic attributes which are missing from the Greek world—lavish single burials in large tombs, with paraphernalia of war, feasting and sheer acquisitive wealth generously provided."[6]

Human sacrifice, especially on the occasion of the death of a great warrior, was the custom of many Barbaric peoples. "The funeral of the pagan Norse chieftain may often have been as splendid as that of Patroklos: ornaments and armour were piled up around him, hell-shoes for his distant journey were provided, his wife and some of his slaves were induced to accompany him..."[7]

Herodotus gives us a description of the kind of funeral Achilles provides. Of the Scythians: "In the open space around the body of the king they bury one of his concubines, first killing her by strangling, and also his cup-bearer, his cook, his groom, his lacquey, his messenger, some of his horses, firstlings of all his other possessions, and some golden cups..."[8]

Cannibalism was not unknown among the surrounding Barbarians. Herodotus describes the funeral rites among the Issedonians in which the flesh of the corpse was eaten by the mourners.[9] The Scythians drank the blood of the first man killed in battle.[10] These same Scythians made good use of the dead bodies of slain foes. "The Scyth is proud of these scalps, and hangs them from his bridle-rein; the greater the number of such napkins that a man can show, the more highly he is esteemed among them. Many make themselves cloaks, like the capotes of our peasants, by sewing a quantity of these scalps together. Others flay the right arms of their dead enemies, and make of the skin, which is stripped off with the nails hanging on it, a covering for their quivers."[11] We know, from modern observations of Primitive and Barbaric tribes, that these descriptions of Herodotus are not fanciful horrors, but remarkably accurate. No Homeric hero, except Achilles in the depths of his despair, was capable of this kind of behavior. Achilles destroyed the barrier which separated Archaic society from its Barbaric alternative.

Archaic civilization is the great hero of the *Iliad*. A hero is defined primarily by the nature of his or her antagonist: what he or she struggles against. The Homeric heroes strive not only against one another, but also against the ever present temptation to regress into Barbarism. Just as the non-cannibal head-hunter may be praised because he does not eat the flesh of the enemy whose body he has degraded, just so the heroes of the *Iliad* can be judged by what they do not do. They do not eat the flesh of their enemies; they do not engage in human sacrifice; they do not take the heads of slain warriors and decorate the walls of their huts with them; they do not mutilate the bodies of those they have killed. Achilles, of course, does some of these things. The response of the poet and of Zeus to these actions is the moral climax of the poem.

One great strength of the *Iliad* is its willingness to accept power, force, and courage as civilizing virtues. The heroes of the *Iliad* were as courageous, as willing to lose their lives, as completely committed to killing as were the Barbarian warrior-heroes. Just as the non-cannibal head-hunter gave no quarter to the cannibal in the extent and strength of his violence, so the heroes of the *Iliad* gave no quarter to the Barbarian in the strength of their violence. For cultural development it was the quality of the violence that mattered most. It was worse to eat the body of one slain enemy than to kill a thousand and give them proper burial. To be civilized, however, one was required to have the courage of the Barbarian—and more, one had to have the courage not to be a Barbarian. Only the denial of the temptations to eat human flesh or sacrifice other people or mutilate their bodies could transform the force of Barbarism. Out of such courage comes the real heroism of the *Iliad*.

Homer's concern for the mutilation of Hektor's corpse is closely connected with the vague memories of head-hunting that haunt the latter part of the poem:

> But Hektor, when he had stripped from Patroklos the glorious armour,
> dragged at him, meaning to cut his head from his shoulders with the sharp bronze,
> to haul off the body and give it to the dogs of Troy...
> [XVII 125-127]

And when Iris, the messenger of the gods, describes the scene to Achilles:

> '...and beyond all glorious Hektor
> rages to haul it away, since the anger within him is urgent
> to cut the head from the soft neck and set it on sharp stakes.'
> [XVIII 175-178]

In the heroic poetry of other nations, there is a frank concern with the taking of heads. The barbarism of these events contrasts sharply with the manner of fighting in the Homeric poems. "In Irish heroic sagas we meet with this practice everywhere. In the *Story of Mac Datho's Pig*, cap. 16, Conall Cernach boasts that he has not often slept without the head of a Connaught man under his head and produces on the spot that of their greatest champion, whom he has just slain. In the *Slaughter of Mag Murtheimne*, Lugaid cuts off CuChulainn's head. He is subsequently over-

taken by Conall Cernach, who cuts off his head and carries it off with
him. In another version of the same story Conall cuts off the heads of
many more of CuChulainn's enemies and affixes them to a rod. In the
Tain Bo Cuailnge, when Conchobar arrives to take part in the war, he
and Celtchair cut off eight score heads of the enemy at their first
attack."[12]

In the *Iliad* the practice is only hinted at, but the clues are strong
enough to indicate what the original mutilation of Hektor's body may
have entailed:

> I will not bury you till I bring to this place the armour
> and the head of Hektor, since he was your great-hearted murderer.
> [XVIII 334-335]

After Achilles cries that he wishes he had the fury to eat Hektor's flesh
raw, he declares: "So there is no one who can hold the dogs off from
your head."

The head has a very special meaning in the Homeric poems. It
represents the life of a person who is now dead: "A man is referred to as
a 'head': 'Teukros, dear head'...is Agamemnon's greeting. But with the
exception of this one instance it is the dead that are thus referred to in
Homer. 'Why, trusty head..., hast thou come hither?' says Achilles to
the [*psyche*] of Patroklos...'But now I go to reach the slayer of the dear
head,' says Achilles...So too it is a 'ransom for Hector's head' that
Priam takes and Achilles accepts, though quite clearly the whole body is
in question. It is as if the head were all that mattered after death. Striking
is the action of Hecuba and Andromache when Priam approaches with
Hector's body. They 'first plucked out their hair for him, darting upon
the fair-wheeled wagon and laid hold of his head.' "[13]

One has to struggle to comprehend the logic in this symbolism. The
head-hunter, however, believes that after a person dies, his spirit, his life,
his strength, his capacity to give blessings and benefits survive in the
preserved head. He believes that death does not destroy all that a person
was; certain things live on. For the head-hunter such ideas are faith, not
metaphor.

This discussion of head-hunting leads us to an understanding of the
crucial role that the taking of armor plays in the poem. No great cultural
development takes place without the sublimation of aggression. No
sublimation of aggression take place without the creation of new forms
which incorporate and transform older forms of aggressive satisfaction.
The Homeric hero regards the armor of his foe as the head-hunter
regards the head. The armor is a great trophy of victory; at much risk to
life, great struggles occur, determining whether or not the armor shall be

stripped from a fallen warrior; after the armor has been taken, it is hung around the walls of the huts, exactly in the manner of the head-hunter; the prowess of any soldier is determined by the amount of captured armor (number of heads) that he can display. The Homeric heroes do not take heads, but they live very close to the desire to do so. Head-hunting is the room they have just left.

When Hektor killed Patroklos, he did not—as some Barbarian chieftain might have—cut off the head and wear it as a trophy on his girdle or saddle, in order to incorporate the power of his dead foe. He stripped the armor and put it on himself, exactly as some cannibal warriors take the name of those whose lives they have destroyed. He incorporated the identity of the slain Patroklos into himself. That armor, however, was the armor of Achilles. When Achilles went out to kill Hektor, he knew that he was shortening his own life, that his fate was to die young if he persisted in fighting; it was a suicide as well as a murder. What symbol of that strange interchange of identities between killer and victim could be better than Hektor, in the armor of Achilles, killed by Achilles? "I tell you, he is alive, and killing the dead." [*The Libation Bearers*, 886.][14]

The concept of the sublimation of aggression sheds light on transformations of rites for the dead. One crucial purpose of all funeral rites is the expression and containment of the violent force of aggression that accompanies the death of any person, and especially one who is of importance in society. The brutality of Barbaric culture showed itself in its response to death. Human sacrifice, the killing of horses and dogs, the destruction of all kinds of valuable property—these are the characteristic ways that Barbarian society responded to the death of one of its great warriors. The invention of funeral games as a means of sublimating aggression—the substitution of competition for destruction—was an extraordinary achievement of the Greek mind, and the minds of other cultures, crucially important in the task of sublimating Barbaric aggression and making civil life possible. "The contest was to play a tremendous part in Greek public life in later centuries. Nothing defines the quality of Greek culture more neatly than the way in which the idea of competition was extended from physical prowess to the realm of the intellect, to feats of poetry and dramatic composition."[15]

In Greek society, these sublimated forms served the development of culture. For Achilles, nothing works. During the games that follow the funeral of Patroklos, he behaves in a manner appropriate to his power and leadership, bestowing the prizes with grace and organizing the contest with quiet determination. After they are over, he remains inconsolable, neither his grief nor his anger assuaged.

When sublimation will not work for some, only force will prevent barbaric emotion from destroying culture. Only the fear of the power of the gods makes Achilles give up the body of Hektor, not his realization that he cannot act in that manner. The horse is a wild barbarian by nature. By force he can be trained to perform acts of great service for society. First he must be broken—forcibly made to depart from barbaric life. Such a horse lives inside every Homeric hero. Sublimation alone does not work; affection, by itself, does not have enough strength to prohibit regression; little is achieved without the forcible repression of barbaric feelings. The poem ends with the funeral of Hektor, "breaker of horses."

Homer makes no connection between the unique, extraordinary excursion of Achilles into Barbaric regression and the ordinary, everyday aggressive activities of his warrior-heroes. He draws no moral lesson from the savage excesses of Achilles' behavior that would shed light on the motives that drive all his admirable killers. What Homer does is exactly opposite to making such inferences. He morally isolates and insulates the excesses of Achilles from the common violence of the rest, in order to pronounce one evil and the other admirable. Nowhere does he say or imply that what Achilles is doing is an extreme case of what all the heroes do all the time. What we learn from Achilles is merely that we should not regress into earlier modes of violence.

Other writers have dealt with regressive violence without presenting it as Homer did—insulated from "normal" aggression. The treatment of aggression—human hatred—is far different in the plays of Aeschylus. In *Agamemnon* the central act of violence is the murder of Agamemnon by his wife Clytaemestra. Many other acts of aggression—some of greater, others of lesser, evil—are either presented in the play or reference is made to them. As an act of revenge, Atreus, Agamemnon's father, had served his brothers' children to that very brother in a cannibal feast. When the Greek fleet, under the leadership of Agamemnon, had set out for Troy, contrary winds had caused it to stay in Aulis for many weeks. Agamemnon had sacrificed his daughter, Iphigenia, so that the fleet might sail. Agamemnon had led the forces that destroyed the city of Troy; that destruction is ambiguously "heroic" for Aeschylus. After sacking the city, Agamemnon had enslaved Cassandra, the daughter of Priam, had made her his concubine, and had had the arrogance to bring her home and ask his wife to treat her kindly. Previous to this, Cassandra had been loved by Apollo, and had refused him; in revenge for her resistance, Apollo had decreed that no one would ever believe the prophecies that Cassandra was to make.

In the climax of the play, Clytaemestra, having stabbed Agamemnon to death, appears on the stage, and vaunts over the killing:

> Thus he went down, and the life struggled out of him;
> and as he died he spattered me with the dark red
> and violent driven rain of bitter savored blood
> to make me glad, as gardens stand among the showers

of God in glory at the birthtime of the buds.

[1388-1392]

An image of horror—as evil, as regressive as anything Achilles could imagine or do—it is like nothing so much as human sacrifice in Barbaric
Civilizations, where the blood of the sacrifice is used to fertilize the soil.

But Aeschylus does not isolate this act of Clytaemestra's, setting it
apart from the enslavement of Cassandra, the destruction of Troy, the
child sacrifice, or the cannibal feast. For Aeschylus they are all of a
piece; they are all connected; they are all violence; they are all manifesta-
tions of human hatred; they are all evil. None of these acts of human
violence is excused as more civilized than its savage counterpart.

Joseph Conrad's *Heart of Darkness*, like the *Iliad*, is a work about the
regression of a man of great power. It, also, defines this regression in
cultural as well as psychological terms. Unlike Homer, Conrad does not
tell us that as long as there is no regression everything will be all right in
the world. Kurtz, an agent of "civilized" Europe, has gone into the
depths of the Congo, and has become the lord of the savages, but not
without having that which is savage within himself become lord over
him. Before he dies he redeems himself, and preserves for us the
possibility of redemption, with insight into his own condition: "The horror! The horror!" he says before he dies.

Outside of a few heads stuck on poles near Kurtz's hut, and the sight
of Kurtz crawling on his hands and knees to the fires of the Primitive
people, we are shown no other horrors in connection with Kurtz and his
regression. The book, however, is full of horrors—not horrors
perpetuated by Primitives or those who have regressed into savagery, but
horrors committed by European high civilization, the emissaries of
"pity, and science, and progress, and devil knows what else."[16] Imperialism is the name of the system that brings these horrors.

Marlow, the narrator of the story, arrives at the Congo to be treated to
a vision of hell and hatred. The natives who can no longer work are left
to die: "They were dying slowly—it was very clear. They were not
enemies, they were not criminals, they were nothing earthly now, nothing
but black shadows of disease and starvation, lying confusedly in the
greenish gloom. Brought from all the recesses of the coast in all the
legality of time contracts, lost in uncongenial surroundings, fed on unfamiliar food, they sickened, became inefficient, and were allowed to
crawl away...."[17] To die: "Near the same tree two more bundles of acute
angles sat with their legs drawn up. One, with his chin propped on his
knees, stared at nothing, in an intolerable and appalling manner: his
brother phantom rested its forehead, as if overcome with a great
weariness; and all about others were scattered in every pose of contorted
collapse, as in some picture of massacre or a pestilence. While I stood

horror-struck, one of these creatures rose to his hands and knees, and went off on all fours towards the river to drink. He lapped out of his hand, then sat up in the sunlight, crossing his shins in front of him, and after a time let his woolly head fall on his breastbone."[18]

Conrad does not say that civilization is irrelevant; he is not a simplistic cultural relativist; he regards Kurtz's regression as an unmitigated catastrophe; but he insists on the connection, on the continuity of human violence. Civilized violence differs from Primitive aggression, but they are of a piece. They are both violence; they are both horrible and evil. Imperialism is not excused because it is the common, ordinary experience of civilized men, whereas Kurtz's regression is extraordinary. For Conrad, Kurtz's experience is an extreme case of what all "civilized" people do all the time. "And this also...has been one of the dark places of the earth,"[19] says Marlow of England at the very beginning of the story. There is a profound continuity of savagery and aggression. Imperialism, Conrad tells us, is the savagery of the twentieth century.

What Marlow cannot stand is the hypocrisy that surrounds the whole experience: "You know I hate, detest, and can't bear a lie....There is a taint of death, a flavor of mortality in lies—which is exactly what I hate and detest in the world—what I want to forget."[20] Before leaving for the Congo, Marlow's aunt had preached to him of the white man's burden. He responded, "I ventured to hint that the company was run for profit."[21]

This same kind of hypocritical lie exists in Homer. Homer's lie announces that, if we all avoid the Barbaric regression of Achilles, the world will make sense. Homer's lie says that what Achilles does in the midst of his Barbaric madness is unconnected to what Hektor, Odysseus, and Diomedes do all day long. Homer's lie proclaims that our primary fear should be the fear of regression, that the morality of the warrior-hero contains no evil and should be reverenced and perpetuated. Homer's lie begins in his declaration that we have, indeed, progressed; we are not Barbarians; however, we have come as far as we shall ever go —there will be no more progress.

IV
Legitimate Aggression: Violence and Irony

"Through cruelty force confesses its powerlessness to achieve omnipotence."[1]

[Bespaloff, p. 57]

I have discussed Homer's failure to work through the problems of Oedipal aggression. When a person—or a culture—is fascinated, frightened, and ultimately paralyzed by Oedipal assertion, he or she will approach it, try it, and retreat into more primitive forms of violence. There will be no escape from this ambivalence and no resolution through the birth of conscience—only violence and ambivalence about that violence. The perpetuation of violent aggression results from the failure to work through Oedipal aggression and come out on the other side.

It is not accurate to say that a person, or a culture, trapped in these circumstances will have no conscience. Conscience will still exist, but it will be external; it will seem to come from outside the person. The power of conscience will be diminished; it will be heard as some dim voice demanding moral action, not as a loud and clear moral imperative.

Homer's conscience was strong enough to establish in him the unconscious notion that there was something immoral in the commitment to sadistic violence. However, it lacked the power of transformation which would have enabled him to abandon that commitment. The result was ambivalence about violence and an unconscious irony in the face of that am-

bivalence. Irony is one of the possible results of those occasions when we
recognize that we are powerless to change the circumstances under which we
live. Homer's irony in the face of the demand of conscience that violence be
abandoned was not conscious. Nevertheless, it permeates the poem. He
knew that violence was immoral, but he was powerless to give it up.

One of the first impulses of anyone trapped in a state of ambivalent
aggression is to justify the legitimacy of aggression. Homer justifies aggression with four distinct positions: 1. Violence and courage are identical. 2. The killing is accomplished without the aid of magic. 3. The gods
love violence. 4. Animals and human animals are violent by nature.

1. *Violence and courage are identical.* The ambiguity within the notion
of courage is that force creates, as well as destroys, the warrior-hero. The
limited Homeric world-view had only one definition of courage: willingness to do battle. It would not have been valiant to return Helen, after
she was abducted by Priam's son Paris, even to avoid the destruction of
war; it would not have been brave of Hektor to return to the city, saving
it and himself and avoiding the duel with Achilles. These heroes—admirable in their courage—knew only one, limited definition of power. In
the midst of battle, Idomeneus encouraged and praised his companion
Meriones in a set speech that accurately presents the Homeric view of
courage:

'I know your valour and what you are. Why need you speak of it?
If now beside the ships all the best of us were to assemble
for a hidden position, and there man's courage is best decided,
where the man who is a coward and the brave man show
     themselves clearly:
the skin of the coward changes colour one way and another,
and the heart inside him has no control to make him sit steady,
but he shifts his weight from one foot to another, then settles
     firmly
on both feet, and the heart inside his chest pounds violent
as he thinks of the death spirits, and his teeth chatter together:
but the brave man's skin will not change colour, nor is he too much
frightened, once he has taken his place in the hidden position,
but his prayer is to close as soon as may be in bitter division:
and there no man could make light of your battle strength or your
     hand's work.
Even were you to be wounded in your work with spearcast or
     spearstroke,
the weapon would not strike behind your neck, nor in your back,
but would be driven straight against the chest or the belly
as you made your way onward through the meeting of champions.'
                                                          [XIII 275-291]

This restricted view of courage—defining it as a willingness to die in battle, regardless of the moral implications of the particular battle—unfortunately did not die with the decline of epic poetry. No culture that we know of has been immune from this disease.

There is something admirable in all the varieties of courage—moral, intellectual, artistic, even in that of the warrior. One should not condemn the human capacity to risk one's life. In war, however, the crucial question, the one standard of judgment, is not courage in itself, but what interest of society and culture does that courage serve? It was one thing to be an Athenian in the first part of the fifth century and risk one's life in battle for freedom against a Persian oppressor. It was quite another thing, fifty or sixty years later, to be an Athenian and bravely die in a battle the purpose of which was to take from other Greeks their liberty and establish over them an imperial tyranny. Like the late fifth century Athenians, Homer had no interest in the moral consequences of the war being fought. For him, physical courage was all.

The courage of the Archaic warrior was a necessary condition for the preservation of Archaic Civilization against Barbarism and Barbarians. It was essential that becoming "civilized" did not mean becoming effete and physically cowardly; otherwise, no Archaic culture could have survived in what was overwhelmingly a Barbarian world.

It is wrong, however, to read Homer and the *Iliad* in a way that implies that the crucial problem of Archaic Civilization, in the time of Homer, was one of survival against Barbarian attack. When Homer sang, Archaic culture was already a thousand years old in Greece, and much older than that if we include the experience of Crete. Greece was not a Barbarian society struggling to become Archaic, or a newly established Archaic Civilization fighting to preserve its existence. Less than 150 years after the *Iliad* assumed its more or less permanent form, Hesiod was crying for justice in the courts and Solon (c. 594 B.C.) was attempting to solve problems in the life of Athens that resulted from a conflict of economic classes. Eighth-century Greece was a fully developed Archaic culture, but Homer wrote as if that culture did not exist. Homer was not singing of the beginnings of great things; he was praising the preservation of what had become the rearguard, not the forward edge, of the process of moral development. His own ambivalence about heroic violence allows us to see that even he did not fully believe in the values of the warrior-hero.

Courage in the face of death in battle, worthy of praise as it is, was not invented by Archaic warriors. They differed little from their Barbarian forebears. Homer's heroes, like the Barbarian warriors who preceded them, learned nothing from their experiences of warfare and death. Hektor met his death bravely, but from his mouth issued words he, or anyone, could have spoken in the very first book of the poem, words expressing the heroic morality unchanged and unenlightened:

> '...But now my death is upon me.
> Let me at least not die without a struggle, inglorious,
> but do some big things first, that men to come shall know of it.'
>
> [XXII 303-305]

What he wishes to do is what he had been doing from the first, what they all did: meet battle and the possibility of death bravely. His death gave no deeper meaning to his life. The Homeric view of courage remains what it was before all the events of the poem took place; there is no transformation.

2. *The killing is accomplished without the aid of magic.* Compared to other heroic poetry, the *Iliad* is remarkably free of magical devices that aid the warrior. No warrior possesses a magical cap to make him invisible, or the capacity to fly at will, or a horse with magical power to aid him in his killing. With the exception of the ability to prophesy the future, which is not a warrior's function, all the magical powers belong to the gods: men who disappear from the fighting, spears which return to the hand of the thrower, horses that talk. Whatever the hero does—as destructive as it may be—he does with his own physical strength. Hear Achilles in the midst of his madness:

> 'Not Ares, who is a god immortal, not even Athene
> could take the edge of such masses of men and fight a way
>   through them.
> But what I can do with hands and feet and strength I tell you
> I will do, and I shall not hang back even a little
> but go straight on through their formation, and I think that no
>   man
> of the Trojans will be glad when he comes within my spear's
>   range.'
>
> [XX 358-363]

What Max Weber calls "that great historic process in the development of religions, the elimination of magic from the world which began with the old Hebrew phophets,"[2] did not begin with those venerable prophets alone. The air in the *Iliad* is sharp and clear; things and people are painfully real. One of the most powerful elements of the poem is its psychological realism. The manner in which people behave, in their relationships with each other, is always believable. In these relationships there is nothing fantastical or magical. Agamemnon in his arrogance, Achilles in his tantrum, Helen in her petulant despair—all are true images of the way people really behave. In the *Iliad*, we always feel that we are being shown real people, in real personal situations. Homer's insight into what is most important in peoples' behavior towards each other is remarkably clear, unclouded by magical distortion. The extirpation of magic extends to the methods of killing. The heroes kill, but they kill with "hands and feet and strength."

3. *The gods love violence.* Nowhere is the fact that the lesser gods exhibit morality no higher than the people on earth more patent than in the almost ludicrous scenes of the gods and goddesses in battle. For them, such fighting can be nothing but a game, like the games of war that little boys play. Neither the gods nor the little boys can die in their war-play. The scene of head-hunter Ares carrying off the armor of a slain hero approaches burlesque; it is absurd that he should feel the necessity of proving his "manliness" by taking possession of a battle trophy. For Homer, however, it is natural that the gods and the heroes should share the same ideals.

The conception of gods who behave like people is full of possibilities of ambiguity. The creation of three-dimensional anthropomorphic gods is one great achievement of Archaic Civilization; another is the conception of heroes who are willing to engage those gods in human struggle. Abraham bargains with Jahweh; Jacob wrestles with his angel; Gilgamish derisively rejects the advances of the destructive Ishtar; Odysseus, in the *Odyssey*, scornfully inquires of Athene where she has been during his worst troubles. In the *Iliad* men contend with the gods in the one limited thing they care most about: fighting and killing, and in no other way. Homer tells us that the gods love battle; it would be unreasonable, he implies, to ask mere mortals to be morally superior to the divinities.

4. *Animals and human animals are violent by nature.* There is an intellectual theory abroad in the world today that seeks to "prove" the instinctive aggressiveness of human beings by demonstrating an inherent aggressiveness in animals. The fact that birds will fight to the death to defend their territory is one "proof" called upon to demonstrate that aggression is the order of nature. Such an argument was first made by Homer in poetry, not through intellectual discourse. The most powerful images in the *Iliad* concern themselves with the inevitable violence—and oral aggression—of the natural world, a world of which men are only a part:

> And they, as wolves
> who tear flesh raw, in whose hearts the battle fury is tireless,
> who have brought down a great horned stag in the mountains,
>   and then feed
> on him, till the jowls of every wolf run blood, and then go
> all in a pack to drink from a spring of dark-running water,

lapping with their lean tongues along the black edge of the surface
and belching up the clotted blood; in the heart of each one
is a spirit untremulous, but their bellies are full and groaning...
[XVI 156-163]

For Homer, these bloody comparisons are praise, not criticism, of the
heroes. Menelaos is commended for being as brave as a lion; the blood
seems to be inseparable from the bravery:

As when in the confidence of his strength some lion
hill-reared snatches the finest cow in a herd as it pastures;
first the lion breaks her neck caught fast in the strong teeth,
then gulps down the blood and all the guts that are inward
savagely, as the dogs and the herdsmen raise a commotion
loudly about him, but from a distance, and are not willing
to go in and face him, since the hard green fear has hold of them;
so no heart in the breast of any Trojan had courage
to go in and face glorious Menelaos.
[XVII 61-69]

A lion may, indeed, be glorious. But what of eels and other fish? As
the barbarism of Achilles uncoils itself, the imagery in the poem grows
increasingly repulsive. Achilles does not eat raw the flesh of the slain
Asteropaios; he leaves that to "nature." We are no longer dealing with
simile but with what actually occurs:

And about
Asteropaios the eels and the other fish were busy
tearing him and nibbling the fat that lay by his kidneys.
[XXI 202-204]

Even the sweet dream on Achilles' great shield is interrupted, as
dreams can be by nightmare visions:

But the two lions, breaking open the hide of the great ox,
gulped the black blood and the inward guts, as meanwhile the
herdsmen
were in the act of setting and urging the quick dogs on them.
[XVIII 582-584]

In the poem these images do not serve only literary purposes; for
Homer, they are also moral justification. The violence and sadism of the
heroes—as savage as anything expressed by the wolves and the lions—is
excused and legitimized because men, alas, cannot escape from their

origins in the natural world. Nature is brutal; the cruelty of man is explained and excused.

****

We have yet to understand the prevalence of graphic sadism in the poem. Violence—fighting, killing, sacking cities, taking slaves and booty —was necessary to the heroic morality. To give these up would mean abandoning the whole conception of the warrior-hero. But detailing sadistic action was *not* a poetic necessity. These heroes would still have been heroes, within their own and Homer's terms, without the guts of men spilling on the ground or the eyeball on the spear's point. Much heroic poetry does not indulge in the kind of graphic sadism that we are presented with in the *Iliad*. Why, then, does Homer deliberately treat us to these delicacies?

We may ask the same question about a similar situation in our own society. Why do well-dressed middle-class couples go to movie houses to witness graphic scenes of machine-gun bullets perforating the body of some unfortunate victim, or a group of small boys pouring gasoline on the body of a derelict before setting him afire? Why has our culture returned to the detached eyeball and the inward guts? It is reasonable to make the assumption that the escalation of graphic sadism in the popular arts of our society indicates that we are going through a cultural situation similar to that faced by Homeric society. The cause may lie, in both cases, in a conflict within the value system of the culture.

A society which has set for itself a moral advance which it refuses to implement is under great internal strain. All moral advances involve, among other things, the giving up of previously legitimate modes of institutionalized aggression. The promptings of the super-ego demand a new order of sublimation of aggression; the response of the ego is negative; the ego becomes more violent in order to protect itself against the demands of conscience. The level of social violence in the United States rose precipitously during the "debate" over the war in Vietnam; the same thing occurred in France in regard to Algeria. The demands of black people in America that society abandon the institutionalized aggression that has been directed at blacks has provoked a white "backlash"—white violence demanded at that demand of conscience.

When those in a culture will not do what conscience demands, the tension rises. One response to this tension is the attempt to escape from the conflict. Like Oedipus, who fled from his "parents" directly to his parents, the culture flees from the problem into the heart of the problem. The conflict originated with problems about legitimate aggression; the escape from the conflict consists of movies of graphic violence. A movie is, after all, "only a movie." The vicarious, fanciful brutality of the movies serves the purpose of making all violence unreal. The real violence in our society, directed against real people, goes unnoticed. Blinded by all this fairy-tale blood, who can see human beings dying for lack of adequate medical care in "the richest country in the world"? I do not know what the specific forms of social aggression in eighth and seventh century Greece were or what the forms of moral ambivalence were that were held by those who wielded power in that society. The detailed, recurrent sadism of the *Iliad* would lead one to believe that that culture did not live at ease with its own conscience.

****

Certain aspects of human aggression are so legitimate in the Homeric world-view that there is hardly any ambivalence concerning them. The subordinate position of women to men is so completely assumed as just and proper that it raises no questions; not even from the unconscious super-ego does there arise any perceptible ambivalence. One searches the *Iliad* for any evidence that would indicate that the secondary position of women is understood as unjust, but one finds none.

In similar fashion, sympathy for slaves occurs only once in the *Iliad*. When the body of Patroklos is brought back from the battlefield, Briseis, the captured concubine of Achilles, laments his death:

> So she spoke, lamenting, and the women sorrowed around
> her
> grieving openly for Patroklos, but for her own sorrows
> each.
>
> [XIX 301-303]

This small handful of words of sympathy hardly constitutes an important ambivalence.

The sacking of cities is also unambivalently legitimate for Homer. It is never described in detail and is always referred to in the past tense. It is described in a matter-of-fact way, without emotional charge, without any conflict in feelings, as we might describe a visit to a supermarket. The *Odyssey* provides an illustration:

> 'From Ilion the wind took me and drove me ashore at Ismaros
> by the Kikonians. I sacked their city and killed their people,
> and out of their city taking their wives and many possessions
> we shared them out, so none might go cheated of his proper
> portion.'
>
> [IX 39-43][3]

There is an important relationship here between unambivalent aggression and morality. Forms of aggression about which there is no, or insignificant, ambivalence obviously do not lie on the frontier of moral progress. Moral advance—the increasing humanization of human beings—will occur in those areas of aggression in which ambivalence and ambiguity are intense.

In regard to the position of women and slaves, Greek culture made no progress from the time of Homer until the period when Pagan culture was replaced by Christianity. Not only was there no progress, there was hardly any discussion. Fighting and killing—their connection with the Barbarian past, and the possibility of their sublimation through working out the problems of Oedipal aggression—here was the real stage on which the struggle of morality with aggression was played in Greek culture.

It remains to catalogue the many ways that Homer expressed his ambivalence about violence through irony. Tell us now, you Muses who have your homes on Olympos, how Homer of old sings this great double vision, how he, like some magnificent wild boar trapped by the hunter in a thick grove of trees, when the hunters approach from two or three sides at once, not knowing which way to charge, or which way to flee, charges first in one direction and then in another, to avoid or break the death-dealing spears, and at times, in his confusion, seems to rush in two directions at one and the same time, fleeing and charging, and never escaping his entrapment.

Homer uses images of peace and plenty to intensify feelings of violence:

> Like the multitudinous nations of swarming insects
> who drive hither and thither about the stalls of the sheepfold
> in the season of spring when the milk splashes in the milk pails:
> in such numbers the flowing-haired Achaians stood up
> through the plains against the Trojans, hearts burning to break
> them.
>
> [II 469-473]

Metaphors of flowers have been used by all poets; only Homer could conceive of using a simile of a flower to describe a man whose throat has just been slit:

> He bent drooping his head to one side, as a garden poppy
> bends beneath the weight of its yield and the rains of springtime;
> so his head bent slack to one side beneath the helm's weight.
>
> [VIII 306-308]

In a similar circumstance, making due allowance for the use of formula and repetition in oral poetry, one wonders if what follows was the only formula available to the poet at this moment:

> No longer
> could a man, even a knowing one, have made out the godlike
> Sarpedon, since he was piled from head to ends of feet under
> a mass of weapons, the blood and the dust, while others about
>   him
> kept forever swarming over his dead body, as flies
> through a sheepfold thunder about the pails of overspilling
> milk, in the season of spring when the milk splashes in the buckets.
>   [XVI 637-643]

Homer tells us that courage—the highest of virtues—ironically brings destruction to him who exercises it:

> As when among a pack of hounds and huntsmen assembled
> a wild boar or lion turns at bay in the strength of his fury,
> and the men, closing themselves into a wall about him,
> stand up to face him, and cast at him with the volleying spears
>   thrown
> from their hands, and in spite of this the proud heart feels not
> terror, nor turns to run, and it is his own courage that kills him...
>   [XII 41-46]

Before Patroklos is sent into battle at Achilles' behest, he gives the strongest reprimand to Achilles of anyone in the poem: " 'But you, Achilleus; who can do anything with you? May no such anger take me as this that you cherish! Cursed courage.' " [XVI 29-31] And bitter is the irony with which Hektor rejects sane counsel when Polydamas urges him to retreat into the city and not go down under the spear of Achilles: " 'The war god is impartial. Before now he has killed the killer.' " [XVIII 309] Not only the killer, but those he has loved may also be killed by the war god, whose instrument is the vengeance of those who have been deprived of their companions. Andromache, Hektor's wife, says to her son:

> ...or else some Achaian
> will take you by hand and hurl you from the tower into horrible
> death, in anger because Hektor once killed his brother,
> or his father, or his son; there were so many Achaians
> whose teeth bit the vast earth, beaten down by the hands of
>   Hektor.

> Your father was no merciful man in the horror of battle.
>
> [XXIV 734-739]

The very greatness of Hektor as a warrior will eventually destroy his off-spring. We have already noticed what the killer Hektor wished for his son.

In the contrast of their violence and their innocence, these grand heroes are, ironically, like small children:

> They streamed over
> in massed formation, with Apollo in front of them holding
> the tremendous aegis, and wrecked the bastions of the Achaians
> easily, as when a little boy piles sand by the sea-shore
> when in his innocent play he makes sand towers to amuse him
> and then, still playing, with hands and feet ruins them and wrecks
> them.
>
> [XV 359-364]

Unlike children, they play for real stakes. In their game of forfeit, real lives are given up—Achilles chases Hektor over the great plain: "...since he was no festal beast, no ox-hide they strive for, for these are prizes that are given men for their running. No, they ran for the life of Hektor, breaker of horses." [XXII 159-161]

The most significant indication of Homer's inability to abandon heroic morality is his incapacity to create a character in the poem who either embodies a radically different world-view or one who, through his experiences, transforms that heroic morality into something else. When Homer finally expresses the cry of conscience that this insane killing should stop, he can only put the words into the mouth of a killer. The effect is incongruous and ironic—that Menelaos or Achilles should call for an end to killing. Menelaos has just killed Peisandros, smashing the bones in his head, "so that both eyes dropped, bloody, and lay in the dust at his feet before him," and after performing this bloody deed he cries out:

> '...these Trojans
> whose fighting strength is a thing of blind fury, nor can they ever
> be glutted full of the close encounters of deadly warfare.
> Since there is satiety in all things, in sleep, and love-making,
> in the loveliness of singing and the innocent dance. In all these
> things a man will strive sooner to win satisfaction
> than in war; but in this the Trojans cannot be glutted.'
>
> [XIII 633-639]

Where else in all literature can one find a character who has just dashed
the eyeballs of his opponent in the dust, calmly talking of "the loveliness
of singing and the innocent dance?" If one were to come upon this
passage with no indication as to who had spoken it, one would not be
able to say which hero might have given it utterance—not because it
sounds like all of them, but because it speaks with the voice of none of
them. It speaks with the ambivalent voice of Homer and produces merely
irony.

Freud states in *Civilization and its Discontents* that people are able to
love each other insofar as they direct their collective aggression outward
against a foreign object; and it is true that Achilles can give up his anger
toward Agamemnon only when a more powerful aggression is directed
outward toward an enemy—when he seeks revenge for Patroklos'
murder. Before going out to kill Hektor, he gives voice to a pious statement that rings hollow in the mouth of this new convert to Barbarism:

> 'why, I wish that strife would vanish away from among gods and
>   mortals,
> and gall, which makes a man grow angry for all his great mind,
> that gall of anger that swarms like smoke inside of a man's heart
> and becomes a thing sweeter to him by far than the dripping of
>   honey.
> So it was here that the lord of men Agamemnon angered me.
> Still, we will let all this be a thing of the past, and for all our
> sorrow beat down by force the anger deeply within us.
> Now I shall go, to overtake that killer of a dear life,
> Hektor; then I will accept my own death...'
>
> [XVIII 107-115]

When Heraclitus quotes these words about strife disappearing—in order
to argue against them—he does not attribute them to Achilles, but to
Homer. It is clear that they are the voice and the words of the poet; no
character in the poem could really say them.

The fighting will not stop; references to peace turn out to be merely
lip-service. After the reconciliation between Priam and Achilles, Achilles
asked how long it would take to perform the burial rites for Hektor.
Priam responded with the saddest words in the whole poem:

> '...Nine days we would keep him in our palace and mourn him,
> and bury him on the tenth day, and the people feast by him,
> and on the eleventh day we would make the grave-barrow for him,
> and on the twelfth day fight again; if so we must do.'
>
> [XXIV 664-667]

The moral ambivalence of one generation has repercussions in the generations that follow. In the eighth book of *The Republic,* Plato discusses the causes of transition of one form of government to another, and finds the reason for these changes—sometimes—in the reaction of a son to his father's view of, and his father's position in, the world. Whether or not governments fall because of the ambivalence of fathers, the response of children to the moral ambivalence of their parents is an important element in cultural change. Ambivalence about moral ideals in parents creates three possible characteristic responses in children: One response is that they may despair of ever resolving these contradictions, declare that all morality is of no importance, and live an amoral or immoral existence.

A second response is to swallow the parents and their equivocations whole, become the identical person the parent was, and preserve inherited truth, with all its contradictions, as the only truth possible.

A third reaction is to emphasize whatever teachings of the parents are truly moral, reject the contradictions and ambivalences, and spend one's life struggling against the lies, hypocrisies, and equivocations of ancestral truth.

The first response is anarchic, and produces no art. The second reaction is conservative and produces art in which form is more important than moral ideas. In the third response, the violence in despair may be used by artists of progressive stance; they may even, like Dostoevski, Kafka, or the maligned Euripides, create works of art that superficially resemble the cry of despair and pessimism—and may be misread by some as asserting just such a cynical view—when their real purpose is to shatter the complacency of inherited morality.

Some of the *epigone* of Homer recreated his ambivalences about violence and morality, and merely changed the setting from a heroic war to the battles of the city-states. Others struggled against inherited contradictions— attempting to create a radically new morality. Ultimately, these last failed to convert Greek culture. However, the importance of ambivalence is that it leaves the door open to those who follow, to enter places where none have been before.

V
The Revolt Against Heroic Values: The Lyric Poets

Less than a hundred years after the *Iliad* assumed a permanent form, Archilochus (fl. 650 B.C.)— arrogant and shameless—heralded a moral revolution:

> The shield I left because I must, poor blameless armament! beside a
> bush, gives joy now to some Saian, but myself I have saved. What
> care I for that shield? It shall go with a curse. I'll get me another
> e'en as good.[1]

Throughout the whole of Greek history, Sparta was the political power most committed to the Homeric view of the world. Plutarch relates that, when Archilochus visited Sparta, he was driven from the city immediately after it was discovered that he had written such a poem.[2]

The revolutionary implication of this fragment of poetry lies in the fact that it criticizes a basic tenet of the heroic morality, and, even more radically, the attack includes as its target the *source* of that morality. The basic assumption of the heroic world-view is that the true identity of a person is external; what matters most in a person's life is what happens to something which is *outside* of him: his head, his armor, his shield, his glory, and, finally, his dead corpse. The origin of this mode of thought is easily traced back to that primitive view Frazer called "the external soul."

What Archilochus says—so easy for us to comprehend, so revolutionary in the seventh century B.C.—is that his identity lies not in the abandoned shield, nor in the opinion of others who would cry "Shame!" at such behavior; his identity is internal; it exists only in his sense of himself. He has no desire to become a glorious corpse because all the glory in the world cannot resurrect his sense of himself when he is dead.

Archilochus was a professional soldier; war was his occupation. His business was to fight well, but he had no desire to go bankrupt; his job, as he conceived of it, could only be done if he stayed alive—a far different view from that of the Homeric hero.

Very little remains of the poetry of Archilochus. In that little, however, Archilochus managed to attack every basic tenet of the heroic value system. One such value was external beauty. The Homeric hero, even if not beautiful, was still grand to look upon; his outward appearance gave pleasure to the eye. Homer, believing that identity was external, could not conceive of an ugly, admirable person. Thersites, created by Homer for our disdain, was all things that a hero was not; the poet of the *Iliad* says he was "the ugliest man who came beneath Ilion....bandy-legged and went lame of one foot, with shoulders stooped and drawn together over his chest...." [II, 216-218.] In Homer's view, the ugliness of his appearance is one with the ugliness of his actions. Archilochus insists that the value of a person is internal; what shows is of no account:

> I love not a tall general nor a straddling, nor one proud of his hair
> nor one part-shaven; for me a man should be short and bowlegged
> to behold, set firm on his feet, full of heart.[3]

The Homeric hero gambled all in the course of battle. If victorious, he boasted loudly of his glory; if defeated but not killed, his identity was demolished by that defeat. Archilochus has no truck with this extremist view of the world:

> Give no ground; and if you beat them, do not brag in open show,
> nor, if they beat you, run home and lie down on your bed and cry.
> Keep some measure in the joy you take in luck, and the degree
> you give way to sorrow. All our life is up-and-down like this.[4]

If Archilochus had given such advice to those assembled before Troy, if he had dared to suggest that victory in battle might result from luck as much as from glorious courage, he would have been fortunate to escape with a mere beating of the kind that Odysseus administered to Thersites.

In the seventh century B.C., the characteristic mode of aggression was not conquest and destructive raiding. Money and political tyranny were the new ways in which power dominated over humane values. Archilochus expressed no admiration for any form of tyranny, heroic or otherwise:

> Nothing to me the life of Gyges and his glut
> of gold. I neither envy nor admire him, as
> I watch his life and what he does. I want no pride
> of tyranny; it lies far off from where I look.[5]

This negative response—I have not saved my shield, but myself; "I love not a tall general"; "I want no pride of tyranny"—demonstrates that Archilochus was consciously and deliberately attacking a view of the world that he found inadequate, and not merely giving voice to some vague personal feelings of his own. The opinions of others are always in his mind; those opinions are nothing but the Homeric view of the world. Archilochus creates his own identity only by an attack on, and dissent from, those views. In one line, he can destroy—for those who will listen—the whole value system on which the *Iliad* is erected:

> Erxias, where is all this useless army gathering to go?[6]

This revolution, led by the attack of Archilochus, gained many adherents. These radical views became an accepted part of the Greek value system, but they did not replace the older heroic values. Instead, two contradictory systems of values existed and fought with each other throughout the subsequent history of Greek culture. The reputation of Archilochus himself grew with time; eventually, many would mention Homer and Archilochus in the same breath as the two great poets of Greece, ignoring the fact that they had praised opposite value systems. The great age of Greek lyric poetry, which lasted until the beginning of the fifth century B.C., expanded and developed this anti-heroic view of the world and prepared the way for the full development of tragedy in the fifth century.

One effective method of attacking the heroic world-view was to rewrite the moral history of the Trojan war. Instead of regarding that war as a glorious page in Greek legendary history, some writers portrayed it as a catastrophe destructive of human values. This attack on Homer's conception culminated in the views of the tragic poets, especially in the *Agamemnon* of Aeschylus and in the anti-war plays of Euripides. As early as the late seventh century B.C., Alcman (fl. 630 B.C.) ambiguously relates the idea of heroism to the catastrophic results of the war: "Paris-of-ill, Paris-of-dread, an evil unto Greece, the nurse of heroes."[7]

Like the magical view of the external self, the assumed legitimacy of anger and aggression against one's enemies is a basic source of heroic values. We have observed the semi-hypocritical manner in which Homer talks of how strife should disappear from the world. The lyric poet speaks in his own voice, does not put his sentiments into the mouth of Achilles or Menelaus, and does not obscure what he really believes. The new moral view comes down strongly against the evil of anger and aggression. Alcman calls strife "internal monster."[8] Anacreon (560-490 B.C.) laments of someone that he "fell in love with the tearful strife of war."[9] Ibycus (fl. 525 B.C.) recollects the oral origin of anger when he writes: "There may well be one with a mouth greedy of strife who shall rouse battle against men."[10] And for Evenus (fl. 460 B.C.) aggression is not heroic, but insane: "Often the anger of men unveils a hidden mind much worse than madness."[11]

Aggression will not go away simply because one deems it an evil. Means of sublimation must be found if anger is to be adequately dealt with. The Homeric hero led an impoverished life because he could find no imaginative satisfaction for his aggressive impulses. If he had a desire to kill and destroy, he was forced to act out such impulses. The imaginative satisfaction of aggressive desires can lead to sublimation. The development of this and other imaginative capacities is an essential achievement of lyric poetry. Theognis (550-500 B.C.), in a powerful poem with a clear echo of the imagery of the *Iliad,* instructs us that we may be courageous and adult without having to kill anyone:

> Like a lion sure of his strength, I have drunk not the blood of the
> fawn my claws seized away from his dam; I have climbed the high
> walls and yet not sacked the city; I have yoked the horses and not
> mounted the chariot; I have done and yet not done, and achieved
> and yet not achieved, accomplished yet not accomplished, finished
> yet not finished.[12]

The lyric assault on heroic values included criticism of the sacred concepts of death and ritual burial. Attention has been called to Homer's pervasive concern with the proper burial of the hero, how intimately that ritual was involved with the concept of glory, how both death and glory were touched with the magical notion that the hero continues to feel things and touch the living after his death. None of this made any sense to Archilochus. Plutarch related that Archilochus was criticized, after his sister's husband was drowned at sea, for fighting his grief with jest and wine. Impervious to shame, the poet responded: "for I shall no more heal a wound by weeping than make it worse by pursuing joys and feasts."[13]

The brilliance of Archilochus' response results from his attack on the *magical* notion that the way we act has influence with the dead. It was a common primitive belief that one could heal a wound by applying soothing medicines to the arrow or spear that produced the wound, or aggravate the injury by applying irritants and foul substances to the weapon. The connection between the wound and the weapon, after the fact, was purely magical. Archilochus attacked this concept in order to demonstrate that his dead brother-in-law could care not at all about how the poet spent his time after the funeral, since the deceased was beyond knowing or caring.

In the heroic view, to attack honor and glory was the gravest sacrilege. Such heresy was not beyond Archilochus' vision:

> No man getteth honour or glory of his countrymen once he be dead; rather do we pursue the favour of the living while we live; the dead getteth ever the worst part. [14]

Stesichorus (?610-550 B.C.) pronounced the same view on the value of being gloriously dead:

> 'Tis a vain and impotent thing to bewail the dead. [15]

> When a man dies, all his glory among men dies also. [16]

Having broken the magical touch of death, the poet's perception of death's inevitability is internalized, and it is seen as an integral part of our lives and our selves. With a Shakespearean sense of reconciliation, Simonides (556-468 B.C.) writes: "Some one rejoices that I, Theodorus, am dead; another will rejoice over him; we are all debts due to death." [17]

When a nation is attacked, and its freedom threatened by external force, transformed heroic values are necessary to the preservation of that freedom. The capacity to distinguish between just and unjust wars, between the morally legitimate and the morally illegitimate use of heroic power and glory, was impossible for Homer, as it became impossible for Pericles and Athens in the fifth century. The lyric poets were capable of making that crucial distinction. Simonides, who had written so wisely of an internalized notion of death, faced with the defense of Greece against the Persian invasion, returned to the praise of immortal glory, but did not fail to indicate that the ideal for which men die in battle is the true cause of their glory:

> If the greatest part of virtue is to die well, that hath Fortune given, of all men unto us; we lie here in glory unaging because we strove to crown Greece with freedom. [18]

The existence of spirits of the dead—an actuality for the primitive mind—became metaphor for the poet:

> These crowned their dear country with fame inextinguishable by
> wrapping round them the mist and gloom of death; though they
> died, they are not dead, for their valour brings them back in glory
> from the world below.[19]

Strength in battle was then no longer an end in itself, as it had been for
Homer. The moral ideal pre-empted violence.

The incessant criticism of heroic values on the part of the lyric poets is
demonstrated by the particular antithetical way in which certain
emotions are expressed. These poets do not simply declare that the fairest
or sweetest thing in all the world is to be with one's love, or to celebrate a
feast, or to make and sing poetry; they are compelled by the cultural
situation in which they find themselves to set these values in opposition
to war and fighting in battle. The early poetry of many peoples contains
this kind of antithetical poem that debates the question of which is the
better life: town life is set opposite rural life; the work of the farmer is set
against the work of the craftsman; the life of the soldier is opposed to the
life of the tiller of the soil. In Greek lyric poetry, most antitheses set a
particular personal value against the destructive values of warfare. The
Greek lyric poet creates his sense of identity in large part by declaring
what he is not—that which Homer had taught one should be.

Anacreon (560-490 B.C.) will sing of love, but not before he has
rejected the alternative mode:

> I like not him who at his drinking beside the full mixing-bowl tells
> of strife and lamentable war, but rather one that taketh thought for
> delightsome mirth by mingling the Muses and the splendid gifts of
> Aphrodite.[20]

Stesichorus, also, cannot sing of the joys of the feast without first
rejecting inherited values.

> Come, Muse, thrust wars away, and with me in honour of a
> wedding of Gods and a feast of men and eke a merrymaking of the
> Blest...[21]

At great length, Ibycus explains what he is *not* going to sing of. "With
a cheerful and playful mockery"[22] he parodies the heroic style and
declares it is not for him:

> They sacked the great, famous, wealthy city of Dardanian Priam,

stirring from Argos by the plans of mighty Zeus, maintaining for
fair-haired Helen's beauty in tearful war that is sung in many
songs; and doom came upon patient Troy because of the golden-
haired Cyprian. But now it is not my desire to sing of Paris, who
tricked his host, or of slender-ankled Cassandra, and Priam's other
children, nor of the nameless day when Troy of the tall gates was
taken...[23]

In like fashion, Sappho (620-550 B.C.), the great poet of love, makes the
antithesis of heroic values and amorous feelings the very subject of one
of her finest poems:

> Some there are who say the fairest thing seen
> on the black earth is an array of horsemen;
> Some, men marching; some would say ships; but I say
>   she whom one loves best
>
> is the lovliest. Light were the work to make this
> plain to all...

*   *   *

> Since young brides have hearts that can be persuaded
> easily, light things, palpitant to passion
> as I am, remembering Anaktoria
>   who has gone from me
>
> and whose lovely walk and the shining pallor
> of her face I would rather see before my
> eyes than Lydia's chariots in all their glory
>   armored for battle.[24]

Sappho does not condemn the love of "Lydia's chariots in all their
glory." If this image had no appeal for her, she would have given it in the
first verse, and rejected it. The fact that she closes the poem with this
strong image is indicative that she finds something attractive in it. The
tension in the poem develops from the fact that Sappho considers
valuable that human impulse which makes people love anything. Her interest lies not in suppressing the love of chariots and glory but in
transforming that love into something nobler. The impulse to admire
something, the capacity of the mind to intensify human experience—nothing, for Sappho, is more virtuous than this. There is a
continuity in human culture and in the change of values; transformation,
not repression, must be the goal of the radical spirit. Sappho would

transform the love of horsemen and marching men into a more meaningful love. She does not condemn outright the Homeric past, but she does find it inadequate to fill her vision of life.

As Greek culture developed during the Lyric age, certain writers became consciously aware of the contradiction between heroic values and the new individualistic values, and the idea that one must choose between them. Xenophanes (580?-500? B.C.) was half-philosopher and half-poet. For him, wisdom was the highest good, not love or feasting or poetry. When praising wisdom, he also felt compelled first to reject the alternative values of the warrior-hero:

> Better than brute strength
> of men, or horses either, is the wisdom that is mine.
> But custom is careless in all these matters, and there is no justice
> in putting strength on a level above wisdom which is sound.[25]

All the lyric poets did not share these new values. The infinite adaptability of human beings is such that new forms—invented for the purpose of expressing fundamentally different human emotions—can be used to express old, inherited, unchanged values. The challenge to the heroic world-view inherent in the work of Archilochus and Sappho was ignored by some, even though the forms of lyric poetry were now used by all. The fortress erected by Homer stood intact, even though a whole new world grew up around it. Callinus (fl. middle 7th century B.C.) urged his fellow citizens to war, emphasizing the Homeric notions of shame, glory, and the godlike quality of the warrior:

> When a brave man dieth the whole people regretteth him, and while
> he lives he is as good as a demigod; for in their eyes he is a tower,
> seeing that he doeth single-handed as good work as many
> together.[26]

Alcaeus (fl. 630 B.C.) was an aristocrat and a conservative in politics, hostile to the democratic stirrings of the seventh century B.C. Inherited values were the fairest thing in all the world to him. He declared that " 'tis noble to die in war,' "[27] and he wrote:

> The great hall is aglare with bronze armament and the
>   whole inside made fit for war
> with helms glittering and hung high, crested over with
>   white horse-manes that nod and wave
> and make splendid the heads of men who wear them.
>   Here are shining greaves made out of bronze,
> hung on hooks, and they cover all the house's side. They

are strong to stop arrows and spears.
Here are war-jackets quilted close of new linen, with
    hollow shields stacked on the floor,
with broad swords of the Chalkis make, many tunics
    and many belts heaped close beside.
These shall not lie neglected, now we have stood
    to our task and have this work to do.[28]

The feeling in this poem is lyric, not epic; the shining arms have become a metaphor for, as well as an instrument of, courage. The moral intention, however, is identical to the epic; the work to be done is killing others.

The politics of the Lyric Age differed from those of the time of Homer; the city-state was supreme. Unfortunately, this change did not put an end to the possibilities of tyranny. In the fifth century the Peloponnesian War would demonstrate that the city-state could be as destructive to human values as the wrath of Achilles. Tyrtaeus (fl. 650 B.C.) composed verses for the encouragement of the city-state of Sparta, engaged in a war against the Messenians, the outcome of which would result in the permanent enslavement of the Messenians and the creation in Sparta of a garrison state. This was no war of liberation against Persian imperialism; the purpose for which Tyrtaeus' audience fought was the enslavement of Greeks by Greeks.

Tyrtaeus uses the new antithetical approach to reject more peaceful pursuits and to opt for bloody warfare. He will not praise a man for prowess in the race or wrestling, nor for his stature or strength; he cares not for his good looks or wealth or suaveness of tongue; greatness in kingship cannot compare with warlike strength:

...for a man is not good in war if he have not endured the sight of
bloody slaughter and stood high and reached forth to strike the foe.
This is prowess, this is the noblest prize and the fairest for a lad to
win in the world.[29]

Callinus, Alcaeus, and Trytaeus lived in the seventh century B.C., at the beginning of the Lyric Age, close to the time of Homer. In the fragments of poetry left to us from the sixth century there is much less incitement to war. It is difficult to draw any firm conclusions from such a small amount of evidence, but it may be that—at least in poetry—the belief in heroic values amongst the poets was progressively diminishing.

It was of great significance for Greek culture that, although some lyric poets created a radical break with heroic values, this new world-view was not accepted by all. The profound revolution in values brought by the lyric poets succeeded only in part.

SHAME AND GUILT: GLORY AND CONSCIENCE

In the sixth book of the *Iliad,* when Hektor meets his wife Andromache on the ramparts of the city, and she expresses to him her fears
that he will be killed and Troy destroyed, she pleads with him not that he
should return Helen and make peace with Achaians—nothing as
shameful as that—but that he withdraw from fighting on the plain and
assume a defensive stance to protect the city. "Draw your people up by
the fig tree, there where the city is openest to attack, and where the wall
may be mounted," she counsels him. [VI, 433-434.]
Hektor cannot do it. He tells her:

> "I would feel deep shame
> before the Trojans, and the Trojan women with trailing garments,
> if like a coward I were to shrink aside from the fighting;
> and the spirit will not let me, since I have learnt to be valiant
> and to fight always among the foremost ranks of the Trojans,
> winning for my own self great glory, and for my father."
>
> [VI 441-446]

Shame, not conscience, is the instrument of moral control in a culture
with no true sense of individuality. What matters most for the Homeric
hero is what other people think of him. To go against the opinion of
others results in sharp feelings of shame, and shame is the power that
makes everyone conform. There are rewards for conforming; there
always are in all cultures; for the Homeric hero the chief reward is the
praise received from others—glory.

When Dodds discusses the development of Greek society from a
Shame Culture to a Guilt Culture,[30] his emphasis lies primarily on the
negative aspects of morality, on the aspects of control and prohibition.
One may view the same problem from its positive side. Guilt is the
negative part of conscience. Conscience has a positive human value. It
urges us to do what is right as much as guilt forbids us from doing what is
sinful. In addition to talking of the development of Guilt Culture from
Shame Culture, one can look at the problem, with equal profit, as a
development from a Glory Culture to a Conscience Culture.

When we read the lyric poets, who are merciless in their attacks on
shame, we find almost no sense of guilt. What we do find is the constant
expression of individual conscience. Individuality—impossible for
Hektor and all the heroes of the *Iliad*— is in lyric poetry congruent with
the expression of individual conscience. The sense of guilt, and its particularly Greek manifestion in the idea of *hybris,* does not become important in literature until the fifth century B.C., in the writings of Pindar
and Herodotus. It is also a significant motivating force in tragedy, but in

the writings of the lyric poets it hardly exists, because their emphasis is on the positive aspects of control. When they dissent from the concept of glory, the lyric poets do not reject the idea that there must be a reward for moral behavior. The reward is internalized. Morality itself becomes the reward, and conscience replaces glory as the highest human value.

Many thoughtful critics of Greek lyric poetry have observed that individuality is an essential aspect of the lyric world-view. Bowra writes: "For Sappho finds the criterion of what should most matter not in tradition or convention or law [e.g., the opinion of others] but in her own feelings. Archilochus had done the same, and though his feelings took him in a very different direction, he resembles Sappho in his attachment to them and his firm conviction that nothing in the world is more important."[31]

Individuality has its genesis in negation and dissent; individualism results only from a separating-out from the group, from society as a whole. Jane Harrison was one of the first to observe this when, in discussing Greek religion, she wrote: "We are still apt to put the cart before the horse, to think of the group as made up of an aggregate of individuals rather than of individuals as a gradual segregation of the group....[T]he essence of the sense of self is separateness, or consciousness of the severance of one self from other selves, and of that self as subject and distinct from objects. Now primitive consciousness for the most part lacks this sense of segregation...[32]

Erich Neumann expresses the same idea in psychological terms: "And when we scrutinize the acts upon which consciousness and ego are built up, we must admit that to begin with they are all negative acts. To discriminate, to distinguish, to mark off, to isolate oneself from the surrounding context—these are the basic acts of consciousness."[32]

Thus it is that the negative stance, the antithetical approach, is so important in Greek lyric poetry. Its purpose is the liberation of "I" from the mass. Unlike the epic poet, the lyricist speaks with his own voice because "I" is the ultimate subject of all lyric poetry. Individuality cannot thrive unless an attack is made upon that which would suffocate it—the sense of shame which made it impossible for Hektor to try to control his own life.

The lyric dissent from heroic values, therefore, inevitably included a pervasive attack upon shame. Archilochus thought it no disgrace to admire an ugly captain, to leave his shield in the fighting, or to praise the life-preserving, inglorious hedgehog:

> The fox knows many tricks, the hedgehog only one.
> One good one.[34]

Even Alcaeus, the defender of old values, was not unaffected by the new spirit. He fought the Athenians at Sigeum, dropped his weapons, ran away, and sent a poem to his friend that echoed the words and feelings of Archilochus:

> Alcaeus is safe; his weapons are not. The Athenians
> hung them up in the temple of the grey-eyed goddess.[35]

A central assumption of the shame-view is that certain feelings are too private to express publicly. The lyric poets insisted that any human emotion was a proper subject of poetry. It was one thing for Homer to tell of the sexual passion of Paris or Zeus; it was a far different thing for Archilochus to describe his own feelings when caught up in the madness of love:

> Here I lie mournful with desire,
> feeble in bitterness of the pain gods inflicted upon me,
> stuck through the bones with love.[36]

Similarly, Praxilla (middle fifth century B.C.) fears no opprobrium when she talks of death in the most intense, personal manner:

> Loveliest of what I leave behind is the sunlight,
> and loveliest after that the shining stars, and the moon's face,
> but also cucumbers that are ripe, and pears, and apples.[37]

Anacreon had no fear even of sacrilege in his praise of love; when asked why he did not write hymns to the gods, he answered: "Because our loves are our gods."[38] He also shamelessly expressed an interest in erotic feelings, in that which is specific in sexual passion: "Nay, pledge me, friend, thy slender thighs..."[39]

The Homeric hero can never admit his powerlessness. His pretense is always that he is in control of his own life, even when it is obvious to us that this is not so. Death, for instance, against which all are helpless, is conquered by him—he thinks—through the glory that lives after him. For the lyric poet, there is no ignominy in admitting that one is powerless in the face of certain passions. Sappho declares her helplessness before the force of love:

> When I look on you, Brocheo, my speech comes short or fails me quite, I am tongue-tied; in a moment a delicate fire has overrun my flesh, my eyes grow dim and ears sing, the sweat runs down me and a trembling takes me altogether, till I am as green and pale as the

grass, and death itself seems not very far away...[40]

Loneliness is the price we pay for leading our own lives. No one in the *Iliad* is lonely; the communal sharing of emotions prohibits the emergence of such a feeling. Only Helen is in any sense alone, but she is a stranger in the land. For Sappho there is no shame in publicly singing of a desolate situation:

> The moon is gone
> And the Pleiads set,
>   midnight is nigh;
> Time passes on,
> And passes; yet
>   Alone I lie.[41]

The assault on shame inevitably involved an attack on the opinions of others. Instead of revering public opinion as a god, and attempting to make all their actions conform to what was expected by others, the lyric poets announced not only that did they not care what others thought, but that for the most part others' opinions were worthless. Theognis declared: " 'Tis painful for a wise man to say much among fools, or yet to hold his peace, for silent he cannot be."[42] Archilochus was of the opinion that most people do not know how to live: "No man, Aesimides, would enjoy very many delights who heeded the censure of the people."[43] When the common morality is immoral, individual conscience can only be maintained by appealing to a higher morality than that held by most people. In western cutlure, no concept has been more important to the development of conscience than this ideal. From Antigone and Amos to Tom Paine, the demands of freedom and morality have been based on the idea that there is a higher good than that which public opinion asserts is correct. In Greek culture, this discovery belonged to the lyric age. Ibycus wrote: "I fear I may buy honour among men at the price of sin before the gods."[44]

This struggle between shame and glory, on the one hand, and guilt and conscience, on the other, remains crucial in our culture today. In the United States, the argument over the war in Vietnam took precisely this form. The proponents of the war emphasized the attitudes of shame and glory—we have never lost a war before; we must have peace with honor; it would be shameful if such a little country should force a powerful country to retreat; the colors of our flag do not run. And finally the old Homeric notion of the importance of the "interests" of the glorious dead reappeared, when the argument was made that we could not leave the war because it would be disloyal to the 50,000 who had already died.

Those who opposed the war asserted the claims of conscience and guilt—it was unconscionable to go on murdering people in wholesale fashion; the napalming of whole villages was a form of barbarism; the war was immoral.

It seems clear that what happened in the seventh to the fifth centuries B.C. in Greece was not the transformation of a shame and glory culture into a guilt and conscience culture, because that transformation was never completed by the Greeks nor by any culture that developed after Greek culture. A shame and glory culture was transformed into one in which shame and guilt, glory and conscience, would coexist and struggle against each other. In cultural terms, the final resolution of that conflict has yet to be accomplished.

These categories of human feeling and action—shame, guilt, glory, conscience—can also be analyzed with reference to the developing individual psyche. In our culture, shame is an instrument of control and discipline over small children. The child of two, three, and four years old has no conscience. Such a child, Freud asserts, is made to do what the parents think is proper because the child fears punishment and wishes to be loved by its parents; conscience has no part in it. Like the Homeric hero, the child conforms to the wishes of others in order that it may have the pleasure of their approval. It does no harm to a small child in our culture to assert that it should be ashamed of a certain action.

When the child grows to six or seven years of age, one no longer uses the power of shame to make it conform; the phrase "You should be ashamed" becomes an insult, an implied assertion that the child is behaving in a manner appropriate to a much smaller child. A child of this age now has an internalized sense of what is right and wrong; the most effective way of disciplining him or her is by appealing to this internalized sense. Although the conscience of a seven-year-old has not the power of an adolescent or adult conscience, its existence is manifest. A seven-year-old has the capacity, however undeveloped it may be, of feeling guilt in regard to an action that has resulted in harm to others.

The Homeric heroes were not children; they were grown men living in a complicated society which they had created and which they controlled. The glory they strove for was not something available to a four-year-old child. However, the culture they lived in had institutionalized the concept of shame as an overriding instrument of moral control; their feelings of guilt were feeble and the demands of conscience were heard only at a distance. They continued to live in adult years, in large part, under a system of values appropriate to a small child.

The moral revolution that takes place somewhere between shame and guilt, between glory and conscience, between the ages of four and seven has been identified as the Oedipus complex, and its resolution leads to the birth of the super-ego. Homer retreated not only from the aggressive implications of Oedipal revolt, but from the moral implications as well.

The tragic poets had the courage and the moral insight not to withdraw from the ambiguities implicit in this revolution. The immediate way to tragedy was prepared by the lyric poets, not by Homer. Achilles was not the model of the tragic hero. With his petulant, petty, personal revolt against Agamemnon—a quarrel with no moral content—he could not become the prototype of Prometheus, Antigone, or Oedipus the King. The first Promethean figure in Greek culture was not Achilles but Archilochus—arrogant, shameless, disdainful of the opinions of others, convinced that his own moral conscience had more value than all the tyrannical power in the world.

THE FORMS OF INDIVIDUALITY

Intimately related to the idea of individuality, two concepts appear to be of particular importance: the memory of childhood, and the soul and its ambivalences. Each of these seems to be essential to the existence of the larger form of individuality; each was intrinsic in the lyric world-view; each of these smaller forms—like the greater form of individualism—represents a break with the Homeric past.

The Memory of Childhood. It seems true that all people individually, and all cultures, have a need for organizing a sense of the past. No culture we know of, no matter how primitive, fails to possess a group of stories that relate events that happened at an earlier time.

Until the birth of lyric poetry, this need for an organized sense of the past was satisfied by myth and heroic legend. All epic poetry—the *Iliad* included—not only takes place in the past, but has as its essential subject those days long ago when men were larger, braver, and more glorious than they are today.

The lyric poets did not transcend this human need for history. What they did was to create a radically new way of fulfilling that need. For them the memory of childhood replaced the mythic and heroic past. The recollection of one's own personal, private history replaced the cultural past of myth and heroic legend.

So successful were the poets in their search for the personal past that they were able to recall the very beginnings of consciousness. Not only childhood, but the pleasures and pains of infancy as well were subject to recollection. In one fragment, Anacreon writes: "Mild-eyed, like a suckling fawn that is afraid when he is left by his horned mother in the wood."[45] Sappho gives us an image of sweet reunion and then relates that feeling to the prototype of all such reunions:

Evening star that bringest back all that lightsome dawn hath scattered afar, thou bringest the sheep, thou bringest the goat, thou bringest her child home to the mother.[46]

Even anger, Sappho feels, can be dealt with by recalling the affections of childhood: "...yet I am not resentful in spirit, but have the heart of a little child."[47]

Sappho was not content merely to sing of love. In the recollection of childhood, she discovers its origin and its power: "And I have flown [to you] like a child to its mother."[48] When her heart is divided and she fears she may not take what her desire tells her she must, she encourages herself by recalling the unambivalent personal past:

> Yet I have hopes I shall...refuse nothing I wish for if the gods but offer it me; for when I was a child I should never have been so dull as to disdain my dear mother's offer of a pretty toy. And I pray the gods give me the opportunity to take what I long for now, seeing that I have done them all such honour in my songs and dances.[49]

In a similar fashion the sorrow of unrequited love makes Alcman remember when he was a child: "I will lie an idle ball."[50]

This memory of childhood is necessary for the creation of individuality. If everyone partakes of an identical sense of the past, then all values will be held in common. One must have one's own individual history before one can dissent from the values that all share.

The Soul and its Ambivalences. Bruno Snell describes the invention of the concept of soul during the lyric age: "The first writer to feature the new concept of the soul is Heraclitus. He calls the soul *psyche;* in his view man consists of body and soul, and the soul is endowed with qualities which differ radically from those of the body and the physical organs. We can safely say that these new qualities are irreconcilable with the categories of Homer's thought; he does not even dispose of the linguistic prerequisites to describe what Heraclitus predicates of the soul. The new expressions were fashioned in the period which separates Heraclitus from Homer, that is to say the era of the lyric. Heraclitus says (fr. 45): 'You could not find the ends of the soul though you travelled every way, so deep is its *logos.* '

This notion of the depth or profundity of the soul is not unfamiliar to us; but it involves a dimension which is foreign to a physical organ or its function. To say: someone has a deep hand or a deep ear is nonsensical....In Heraclitus the image of depth is designed to throw light on the outstanding trait of the soul and its realm: that it has its own dimension, that it is not extended in space. To describe this non-spatial substance we are of course obliged to fall back on a metaphor taken from space relations...Not Heraclitus but the lyric poets who preceded him were the first to voice this new idea, that intellectual and spiritual matters have 'depth.' Archaic poetry [i.e., lyric poetry] contains such words as...'deep-pondering'...'deep-thinking'...'deep knowledge'...'deep pain'...In these expressions, the symbol of depth always points to the infinity of the intellectual and spiritual, which differentiates it from the physical.

"Homeric speech does not yet know this aspect of the word 'deep.' It is more than an ordinary metaphor; it is almost as if speech were by this means trying to break through its confines, to trespass on a forbidden field of adventure."[51]

Once this new concept of the soul was discovered, its unique properties could be explored. The soul was no monolithic entity; it has two parts, or three, or several. The different aspects of the soul might easily be in opposition to each other. The lyric poets discovered that, in making "I" the subject of poetry, there were many different "I's" within the *psyche*, a concept that was to be rediscovered by all lyric poets. When the Greek lyric poets invented this new concept of the soul, they discovered ambivalence. Snell writes that Sappho and Anacreon felt that the ambivalence inherent in all feelings could not be explained by an oscillation of feelings or by an alternation in time, "but that the present moment contains the seeds of discord." He cites Anacreon, who wrote:

> Again I love and love not, I rave,
> nor do I rave[52]

Sappho had also written: "I know not what to do; I am in two minds..."[53] In the concept of "bitter-sweet" Sappho invented a way of talking simultaneously about both valences of an ambivalence:

> Love has unbound my limbs and set me shaking
> A monster bitter-sweet and my unmaking.[54]

This conscious concern with ambivalence represented a sharp break with epic ideas of motivation. Homer, Snell says, was no more capable of representing a tension within the soul than anyone could conceive of a tension within the hand or the eye. Homer could not say "half-willing, half-unwilling"; for him any contradiction in motivation comes about when two different organs of the body desire opposite things. Homer says: "he was willing but his *thymos* [breath, spirit] was not." As a result of this mode of thought, Snell concludes, "there is in Homer no genuine reflexion, no dialogue of the soul with itself."[55]

Such a dialogue between the poet and his own soul is precisely what we do find in the lyric poets. The soul may make demands which the conscious ego cannot fulfill. Theognis talks to his own soul as one would urge a child to curb its appetites: "I cannot furnish thee, my soul, with all things meet for thee: be patient; thou art not the only lover of things beautiful."[56] When Freud used metaphor to describe the conflict in the psyche between conscious and unconscious impulses, he compared the unconscious to a horse and the conscious to its rider, and cautioned that sometimes it is wiser for the rider to let the horse take the two of them where it wills. Theognis used the same image and, being a poet and not an analyst, gave voice to the horse: "I am a fair and champion steed, but my rider's a knave, and this grieveth me much; often have I almost taken the bit between my teeth, cast my evil rider, and run away."[57]

One important result of this recognition of the divided self is that the poet is now willing to take responsibility for his or her sorrows. The universal human impulse, when faced with unhappiness, is to find someone to blame for one's condition. Sappho knew that others were not responsible for her griefs; it was something within her, something that was, and was not, herself:

> Be still, my Soul; not for me canst thou send forth with swift thoughts hymn-outwelling an Adonis-Song whose beauty shall please the Goddesses. For alas! thou art made dumb by man-dishonouring desire and whelm-the-Heart Aphrodite; and wit-destroying Persuasion's ewer of gold hath poured its suave nectar upon thy understanding.[58]

To be an individual did not mean to be a person impelled in one direction, unambivalent. Individualism meant the recognition of many selves within the self. The great struggle of life was no longer between huge heroes battling each other or the arbitrary willfulness of the gods. The great battles of the world now took place within the divided soul of one's self.

THE FAILURE OF NEW VALUES

The new soul, the new individualism, the attack on heroic values, the fresh clarity with which life was viewed also yielded a new way of perceiving the inadequacies of human existence. The sorrows that had beset Achilles, Hektor, and Priam were not replaced by human felicity. New griefs replaced old sorrows.

Having carved their individualism out of the monolith of shame culture, the lyric poets had no wish to live alone. They sought the private reciprocations of friendship and love as a replacement for the communal approval they had rejected. Immediately they discovered that friendship will not hold, that love will not last. Love and friendship give one no more control over life than had heroic values. Writing of one, or of both, Alcman plaintively asks: "And prithee who may read with ease the mind of another?"[59]

Theognis climaxes a list of life's disappointments with the failure of loyalty:

> Ah, blessed and happy and fortunate is he that goeth down unto the black house of Death without knowing trouble, and ere he have bent before his foes, sinned of necessity, or tested the loyalty of his friends.[60]

Theognis does not actually say that this test of loyalty will result in the failure of friendship; there is the possibility that loyalty tested may prove adequate. However, since the uncertain test of friendship follows a list of certain disasters, Theognis is creating a tension in the poem by making us come to the conclusion which he himself will not directly give. In doing this, he also renders insight into something that, at first, is not a subject of the poem: the desire to preserve the illusion of loyal friendship. Friendship, untested, is fine; better it should remain untested.

In the private world of the lyric poets anger becomes personal, not communal. Some of the finest lyrics of Archilochus express his intense hatred of someone who has treated him disloyally:

> ...and may he have upon him much tangle of the surges, and his teeth chattering, as he lies on his belly like a dog, helpless on the edge of the surf, spewing out the wave. This I fain would behold, because he wronged me and trod a covenant underfoot, he that once was my friend.[61]

A manner of dealing with woe, which was totally absent in the high aristocratic life of the *Iliad,* is urged upon us by the lyric poets—to drown oneself in wine. Alcaeus' non-solution to the sorrows of life reads:

> To woe the heart must not give in.
> In grief's no help. One medicine,
>   my friend, alone is fit —
>   wine —, and get drunk on it.[62]

The illusion that wine will solve life's problems is, for Alcaeus, a deliberate, self-conscious distortion of the truth. It is a far different thing from the belief of the Homeric hero that he is actually in control of his life. It is painful, and necessary, to admit that happiness is one of the most fragile things in the world. Such an admission may be tragic, not cynical, if it strengthens the human capacities to understand and endure. This wisdom comes only with suffering; it takes a different kind of courage from that of heroism in battle. Theognis prepared the way for the tragic view when he wrote: "Never boast thou, Cyrnus, in assembly; for no man living knoweth what a night and a day have to accomplish for us."[63]

In the end, we are all powerless against death. Neither the old heroic notions of glory and ritual burial nor the new values of individuality and conscience have any power to make old age sweet. In the face of its finality, nothing works:

> My temples have grown grey and my crown bare and white; graceful youth is no longer with me, and my teeth are the teeth of an old man. There is left me but a short span of sweet life. And so I often make my moan for fear of the underworld. For dire is the dark hold of death, and grievous the way down thither; and more, tis sure that once down there's no coming up. [Anacreon][64]

The lyric poets rejected the heroic value system, finding it inadequate both as explanation and as guide to life. In its place they erected a radically new view of the world, but this new understanding did not bring felicity. The time had come, consciously and forcefully, to raise the question of why there is so much suffering and sorrow in the world. That question was to become a central interest of the tragic world-view.

VI
Tragedy: The Heroic
Struggle Against Injustice

The tragic form returns, after the critical revelations of the lyric age, to a particular human problem raised by the *Iliad:* how one should behave in the face of legitimate authority—that which holds power, regardless of its morality. The radical moral experience of the lyric poets had given a new courage to Greek culture, a courage that could be used to go back and reopen questions that Homer had either answered badly or left unanswered. What are the consequences of submission or revolt in the presence of unjust authority? Are these two responses the only possible ones in this circumstance?

Legitimate authority may exercise its power either in a just or in an unjust manner. When legitimate power lacks justice, a critical moral problem presents itself. As we have seen, Homer was not oblivious to this situation. He gave us many powerful scences of tyrannical gods, of despotic political or social power, of autocratic parents. We know what his answer was: it is hard to curb one's anger and submit, but it is preferable, by far, to the terrible consequences of revolt. His aim was to reduce the concept of justice to that of legitimacy. The tragic poets could not accept this moral compromise. The perception of the disastrous gap that may, and does, exist between justice and legitimate power gave birth to the tragic form.

Tragic poetry returned not only to the problems of epic poetry, but also to its particular literary forms. Like the epic, and unlike the lyric, tragedy is dramatic; moral and literary concerns are expressed through the actions of characters. More importantly, the tragic form resurrects the central concern along with the hero. The argument that the *Iliad* is the direct ancestor of tragedy and that Achilles is the prototype of the tragic hero has some validity in respect to this concept of heroism. In both the epic and tragedy, the hero is larger, braver, cleverer, or angrier than most ordinary men. He or she responds to life and its problems with a passion and a power that most people do not possess, and struggles—to the death, or to disaster—against forces in the universe against which most men are content to remain passive. In tragedy, however, the hero may also be wiser and more just than most men.

In the Greek universe there are only three forms of legitimate authority: the gods, social and political power, and parents. Each might be a source of either just action or tyranny. Homer deals at length with the power of the gods and society; he speaks very little of the tyranny of parents. The tragic poets placed the conflict between power and just actions in the heart of the family. The most powerful tragedies are family stories. Aristotle says that when an enemy is killed or an unrelated person, the effect may be pitiful, but not profound. "But when the tragic incident occurs between those who are near or dear to one another—if, for example, a brother kills, or intends to kill, a brother, a son his father, a mother her son, a son his mother, or any other deed of the kind is done—these are the situations to be looked for by the poet." [*Poetics,* XIV, 4][1]

By locating the conflict between justice and tyranny, between *eros* and hatred, within the family the tragic poets raised the question of whether we might not find in such a place the origin of all tyranny. Tyrannical gods and despotic societies may be born in the same place where we are all born. Unjust parents, the tragic poets imply, may be not only one form of tyranny but *the* form.

In the discussion of the quarrel between Achilles and Agamemnon, a definite effort was required to see that this struggle for power was symbolic of the family situation, that it involved Oedipal aggression. With tragedy, no such seeking for this truth behind appearances is required. In the first six plays to be discussed—those tragedies in which the dramatist was most committed to exploring the heroic struggle for justice—one man kills his father and marries his mother; one father condemns to death his sister's daughter, only to have his own son draw a sword in an attempt to kill him; one son kills his mother and her lover after the mother has cruelly murdered her husband; one demi-god revolts against the king of the gods and is painfully tortured. The great moral power of tragedy arises from the circumstance that it insists on discussing morality in terms of the family, where morality—and immorality—have their origin.

Prometheus Bound and the *Oresteia* of Aeschylus, and *Antigone* and *Oedipus the king* of Sophocles, share a common view of heroism. In each play the hero is a victim of the injustice of either a parent or some authority figure. None of the heroes passively accepts victimization, nor does any of them strike back merely for the purpose of personal revenge; in these plays the hero is willing to revolt against an unjust authority, and legitimizes this revolt by an appeal to morality and justice. In every one of these plays the tragic struggle results from the fact that legitimate authority is tyrannical; the hero suffers because he must either submit to this tyrannical authority or rebel against it and pay in profound unhappiness for his revolt.

For the purpose of contrast with the hero, the tragic poet, in every one of these plays presents us with a passive person, an ordinary man who is content to obey legitimate authority without raising the question of whether that power is just or not. This character is always more concerned with personal happiness than with virtue, and knows that the hero will suffer for his morality. The hero remains morally exemplary because the cause for which he struggles is not merely personal. Achilles also suffers as a result of his struggle against Agamemnon for the right to possess legitimate power. Achilles is condemned by Homer, but he may also be condemned by us, for a different reason: his rebellion has no moral content. We weep for Prometheus, Orestes, Antigone, and Oedipus not only because we pity their suffering, but because we identify with the cause for which they struggle.

The tragic poets, unlike Homer, insist that we must have the courage to act out Oedipal drives in an imaginative way, making us witness to dramas in which the characters rebel and assert themselves, refusing to submit. They unconsciously recognize what Freud made conscious: that conscience is involved with this imaginative capacity to revolt. No matter how much the tragic hero may suffer for his rebellion, no matter how much it may appear that the forces of injustice have won out in the end, great tragedy, paradoxically, leaves us with a sense of reconciliation and moral order.

This sense comes not only from Aristotle's *catharsis*—the purging of the emotions through pity and fear—but because we are left at the end of a tragedy with something more than we started with. After all the terror of revolt, punishment, and death, somehow our sense of conscience has been strengthened. In spite of the fact that the surface of the play may be a story of how the virtuous suffer in the cause of justice, we are left at the end with a deep confirmation of the moral order of the world. This ambiguity can be explained by the fact that the tragic form deals not only with the pristine Oedipus complex of rebellion against the parents, but with the whole psychological development of the complex as well, including, most importantly, its resolution in the formation of conscience.

Not every Greek tragedy, not every tragic hero, can be understood in these terms. The meaning in Sophocles' *Ajax* or Euripides' *Bacchae,* for example, is not to be explained as an heroic struggle against injustice. Nevertheless, this theme runs all through Greek tragedy. In the *Ajax,* Teucer argues: "A man may have some boldness in the right." [1125][2] And in the *Ion* of Euripides, Creusa cries:

> Unhappy women! Where shall we appeal
> for justice when the injustice of power
> is our destruction?
>
> [252-254][3]

Though the heroic struggle against injustice does not subsume all Greek tragedy, it represents one important form. It is undeniable that *Prometheus Bound, Antigone, Oedipus the King,* and the *Oresteia*—taken together—are a high point of the tragic form and of any literature ever created. The extraordinary power in these plays lies in their attempt to answer the question of how we shall find conscience and moral order in a world where legitimate power is destructive of both.

PROMETHEUS BOUND

Zeus had planned to destroy the whole race of mortals. Prometheus, alone, saved mankind from destruction, brought fire from heaven to mortals below, and gave to people all the arts of civilization. "One brief word will tell the whole story: all the arts that mortals have come from Prometheus." [504-506][4] In punishment for this rebellion, Zeus has Prometheus chained to a bare rock, high in the mountains, where the latter is visited by Oceanos, who offers advice and friendship, and by Io, who was loved by Zeus, and is now condemned by Hera's jealousy to wander the world, fleeing from the maddening stings of a gadfly.

Prometheus boasts to Io and the Chorus that Zeus will someday be overthrown, that he knows the circumstances under which this shall happen, but will not reveal them. Hermes, ambassador from Zeus, appears to demand that Prometheus tell all he knows. Otherwise, Prometheus will have his liver eaten daily by a great bird and he will be cast down to "lightless Hades and the shadows of Tartarus' depths." [1028-1029] Prometheus refuses; the new punishment begins as the play ends.

No more profound symbol of the discrepancy that exists between legitimate power and justice may be possible than that which declares the King of the gods a tyrant, recently enpowered, a law unto himself. Precisely such a symbol lies at the center of this play. Speaking of Zeus, Prometheus declares:

This is a sickness rooted and inherent
in the nature of tyranny:
that he that holds it does not trust his friends.

[226-227]

The system of tyranny ignores the laws of justice and puts in their place private drives for power. Prometheus describes the justice of Zeus as "a thing he keeps by his own standard" [189], and the Chorus laments:

This is a tyrant's deed; this is unlovely,
a thing done by a tyrant's private laws...

[402-403]

Prometheus Bound is the first play of a trilogy; the two remaining plays are lost to us. Most scholars agree that Aeschylus reconciled the tyrant Zeus and the rebel Prometheus, and thereby reconciled Zeus to justice, in the two lost plays. Aeschylus prepares us for this transformation in the first play when he insists that the tyrannical stance of Zeus results, in part, because he is new to power: "For the mind of Zeus is hard to soften with prayer, and every ruler is harsh whose rule is new." [33-34] Zeus himself has been in rebellion; he has seized legitimate authority from another; not, however, in the interests of justice, but merely in the interest of ego-centered force. He is a tyrant because he sees no connection between virtue and authority:

For new are the steersmen that rule Olympus:
and new are the customs by which Zeus rules,
customs that have no law to them,
but what was great before he brings to nothingness.

[147-151]

In the beginning of the play, Might, Violence, and Hephaistos enter with Prometheus and shackle him to the mountain. Prometheus says nothing until they leave, but we know that he hears all they say to each other. Hephaistos has no stomach for his job, expressing reluctance and sympathy for the condemned Prometheus. In the middle of this prologue, there is a significant interchange between Might and Hephaistos that gives Aeschylus' insight into the motives that drive Prometheus:

Might: There is nothing without discomfort except the overlordship of
the Gods. For only Zeus is free.
Hephaestus: I know. I have no answer to this.

[49-51]

Prometheus has an answer: if the power that rules is unjust, freedom lies in the capacity to revolt. One may suffer deeply as a result of rebellion, but such an act puts the lie to the remark that "only Zeus is free." Revolt can only serve the cause of freedom when it is instigated for the sake of justice and love. With Prometheus, there is never any question that such is the case. In the first lines of the play, Might explains: "this is the sin for which he must pay the Gods the penalty—that he may learn to endure and like the sovereignty of Zeus and quit his man-loving disposition." [9-11.]

In Prometheus' first speech, he echoes these words:

> You see me a wretched God in chains,
> the enemy of Zeus, hated of all
> the Gods that enter Zeus's palace hall,
> because of my excessive love for Man.

[120-123]

After the action of the play has run its course and Prometheus is condemned to suffer even greater tortures, the play closed with lines that emphasize this central concern:

> O Holy Mother mine,
> O Sky that circling brings the light to all,
> you see me, how I suffer, how unjustly.

[1090-1092]

The evidence that this play deals with the ambiguities of the Oedipus complex is unequivocal. Directly when the play begins we are told that the power in the world is not only a god, not only the highest god, but a *father*. Might declares: "Hephaestus, it is you that must heed the commands the Father has laid upon you..." [3-4], and in his reply Hephaestus announces that "it is a dangerous thing to treat the Father's words lightly." [15-16] If one insists on seeking a metaphysical explanation of this play, as Kitto did when he interpreted the trilogy as a contest between Power and Order (Zeus) and Intelligence (Prometheus),[5] if one insists in reducing Aeschylus' moral insight to the notion that the conflict of intellectual ideas causes human suffering, one must still explain why Aeschylus represents Power and Order as a *father*. It would seem closer to the truth to state that Aeschylus recognized that more human suffering is caused by fathers than by metaphysical deities.

The Oedipal implications in the play are reinforced by its structure. The Oedipus Complex has two valences: one of force and one of sexual power. Two victims of Zeus' treacherous behavior are personified in the play: Prometheus and Io. Prometheus suffers from Zeus' unjust use of force; Io from his sexual tyranny. Taken together, they represent the ways in which a father may misuse his legitimate power. After Io appears, Prometheus makes the connection between their experiences, reiterating the word "tryant" in respect to the father of the gods:

> Do you now think this tyrant of the Gods
> is hard in all things without indifference?
> He was a God and sought to lie in love
> with this girl who was mortal, and on her
> he brought this curse of wondering: bitter indeed
> you found your marriage with this suitor, maid.
>
> [734-738]

The introduction of Io allows for another parallel: a mother may bring as much suffering to a daughter as a father to a son. Zeus is the cause of Io's misery, but Hera is the instrument. The Chorus laments:

> Never, never may you see me,
> Fates majestic, drawing nigh
> the bed of Zeus, to share it with kings:
> nor ever may I know a heavenly wooer:
> I dread such things beholding
> Io's sad virginity
> ravaged, ruined; bitter wandering
> hers because of Hera's wrath.
>
> [894-900]

The two themes of sexual tyranny and force come together when Prometheus tells Io what is to befall her and her descendants. Six generations after her, fifty Egyptian maidens, her progeny, will flee to Argos in order to avoid unwanted marriages with their kinsfolk. Forced to receive such husbands, they will kill the men in the dark. The thought of such a grand revenge causes Prometheus to disgress and state his own desires for vengeance:

> Each wife shall rob her husband of his life
> dipping in blood her two-edged sword: even so
> may Love come, too, to my enemies.
>
> [863-865]

Prometheus will have his revenge on Zeus, who will be punished as a consequence of sexual excess. Zeus will be dethroned by a son yet to be born, just as he overthrew his own father. Prometheus' vindication must await "a son mightier than his father." [768.]

Yet shall this Zeus, for all his pride of heart
be humble yet: such is the match he plans,
a marriage that shall drive him from his power
and from his throne, out of the sight of all.
So shall at last the final consummation
be brought about of Father Kronos' curse
which he, driven from his ancient throne, invoked
against the son deposing him...

[907-914]

As a final confirmation that the play is dealing with the consequences of Oedipal revolt, the punishment that Zeus metes out to Prometheus includes a powerful metaphor for castration:

Then Zeus's winged hound, the eagle red,
shall tear great shreds of flesh from you, a feaster
coming. Unbidden, every day: your liver
bloodied to blackness will be his repast.

[1022-1025]

The demonstration that this play involves a central concern with the problems of Oedipal revolt is not an attempt to reduce the play to a mere psychological tract. The only way that such a reduction is possible is when the argument reduces the Oedipus complex itself to narrow, limited drives, stripped of all its moral implications. Aeschylus' purpose is not only to tell us that those who revolt against their fathers suffer fears of castration, as true as this may be. Aeschylus' aim is to give us insight into the nature of justice and morality, and if he insists that we cannot understand these without comprehending what we today call the Oedipus complex, he does not become less of a moralist. What greater moral purpose can be served than that which would give us understanding into the psychological origin of morality?

The Oedipus complex need not be a castastrophe. We are not all condemned to live lives haunted by fears of castration and impotence, or by irreconcilable guilt. The crucial issue for the child caught in this absurd human situation is the behavior of the father. If the father is a tyrant, living by his own laws, unconcerned with human love, then the child has only two options: to submit to tyranny and remain a child, or to revolt and have his liver eaten every day of his life. The father, happily, may not be a tyrant, may care deeply for love and justice, and may help the child work through this temporary psychological situation so that it may succeed in internalizing its own conscience.

Most fathers are both tyrannical and loving. The typical human family situation is one of neither intense love nor all-pervading tyranny; the typical situation is ambivalent. Since the love that most people receive from their parents is ambivalent, the morality that they carry through life has the same ambivalent quality.

The tyrant-father Zeus is the symbol of all tyrannical fathers; more accurately, he is a symbol of that tyrannical part that exists in all fathers. Against such injustice, Aeschylus tells us, there can be only one moral stance if we are to grow up and become truly adult: revolt. Near the end of the play, Hermes, child and lackey of Zeus, comes to demand that Prometheus tell what he knows of Zeus' eventual overthrow; Prometheus refuses:

> Hermes: It seems you will not grant the Father's wish.
> Prometheus: I should be glad, indeed, to requite his kindness!
> Hermes: You mock me like a child!
> Prometheus: And are you not
>   a child, and sillier than a child...
>
>   [984-987]

No one who is the son of a completely tyrannical father will have the courage and the morality necessary for revolt. Only the child who has been loved in large part will have the strength to rebel against the tyranny in his own life. Prometheus' belief in justice could only exist if he had, in some ways, received justice and love from others. This insight keeps the tragic form from becoming an expression of human despair, no matter how much the tragic hero may suffer. This kind of tragic hero has the courage to attempt to transform the world. That he ultimately fails is an indictment not of justice, but of that world. No matter how much he suffers, he reaffirms in us our belief in the possibilities of moral order.

The heroism of the hero is underlined by the poet when he shows us those who are content to submit and who urge Prometheus to do the same. The old Homeric virtue of wrenching one's heart to obedience is preached by characters who might like more justice in the world but are unwilling to take on the pain that the struggle for justice entails. Prometheus' first visitor is his old friend Oceanos, whose advice echoes all the pious sentiments in the *Iliad:*

> You are not humble, still you do not yield
> to your misfortunes, and you wish, indeed,
> to add some more to them; now, if you follow
> me as a schoolmaster you will not kick
> against the pricks, seeing that he, the King,
> that rules alone, is harsh and sends accounts
> to no one's audit for the deeds he does.
>
>   [322-328]

The exchange between Hermes, the preacher of accommodation, and Prometheus is the climax of Prometheus' resolve and heroism:

> Prometheus: Be sure of this: when I set my misfortune
>   against your slavery, I would not change.
> Hermes: It is better, I suppose, to be a slave
>   to this rock, than Zeus's trusted messenger.
> Prometheus: Thus must the insolent show their insolence!
>
> [966-970]

Dissenting from the Homeric value system which preached that Oedipal revolt brings only disaster, Aeschylus insists that, if legitimate authority is unjust, only rebellion makes one free.

ANTIGONE

After the death of King Oedipus, his two sons, Eteocles and Polyneices, fought for political power in Thebes. Eteocles held power, and Polyneices led an army against Thebes in an attempt to capture the city. Both brothers were killed in the ensuing battle, and their uncle, Creon, assumed leadership of the state. He decreed that the corpse of the traitor Polyneices should remain unburied; death would be the penalty for anyone who disobeyed. Antigone, sister of the slain brothers, ritually buries Polyneices' corpse, and is condemned to death by Creon, despite the arguments of his son, Haemon, who is pledged in marriage to Antigone.

At the urging of the seer Teiresias, Creon belatedly withdraws his sentence of death. Antigone has hanged herself. At her tomb, Haemon draws his sword to kill Creon, fails in the attempt, and kills himself. Eurydice, mother of Haemon, wife to Creon, on hearing this news, takes her own life. Creon is a broken man as the play ends.

The play proceeds on two levels of action and meaning: political and familial. Every character in the play and every significant action share this double aspect. Creon is the political ruler of the state, and he is also the uncle of the girl he condemns to death for insubordination. He prides himself that his political tyranny will be softened by no family considerations. Were the girl his own sister, he would still see that his laws are to be obeyed:

> She is my sister's child, but were she child
> of closer kin than any at my hearth,
> she and her sister should not so escape
> their death and doom.
>
> [486-489][6]

Creon talks much of legitimate political power, and the necessity of all to accommodate themselves to it, but three times in the play he makes reference to the fact that the person who has defied him is a woman, and he tells us that it would be unmanly of him not to respond with force to feminine provocation:

> I am no man and she the man instead
> if she can have this conquest without pain.

[484-485]

The tragic form is sparse and concise, rarely given to repetition of ideas or phrases. That Sophocles has Creon repeat these fears about women three times within the course of the play, despite the fact that women held absolutely no political power in Sophocles' world, indicates that he seeks to examine the psychological motivation of political tyranny. The fear of being thought inadequate to deal with feminine force causes Creon to abandon enlightenment, strengthens his drive toward tyrannical action, and ultimately destroys his life. The first experience that all men have of feminine power is not in the state, which they have created for their own uses, and from which women were, at this time, entirely excluded, but rather in the family, where the mother rules during the child's early years. When Haemon seeks to persuade his father Creon not to proceed with the death sentence, the argument swings with great speed between the modes of political tyranny and family conflicts:

> Creon: Is the town to tell me how I ought to rule?
> Haemon: Now there you speak just like a boy yourself.

[734-735]

This double aspect of family and politics exists also within Antigone's vision of her antagonist. For her, Creon is not only an unjust autocrat, but also her mother's brother and her future father-in-law; after the death of her father and her brothers, he represents the one remaining masculine authority figure in her family. He is the political successor of her father and brother, and the psychological successor as well. She rebels not only against some distant political authority, but also against the closest thing to a parent that she has left in the world.

Similarly, when Creon sends the political miscreant to her death, he is simultaneously killing his son's intended bride. When we first see Haemon, he attempts to persuade the tyrant, just as any political councillor might plead the course of greater justice with his master. When we last hear of Haemon, he has attempted to kill his father.

The recurrent double aspect of the play is underlined by the portrayal of two heroes defying unjust authority and dying for it: Antigone and

Haemon. Haemon is not as important to the action of the play as is Antigone, but his sense of justice betrayed and his willingness to revolt against legitimate authority are as great as hers.

The play begins with concern for politial justice and ends as a family tragedy. If politics were the central concern of the play, the play would end with a destruction of the state; such is not the case. The tragic result of the play is the annihilation of the family of Creon. Sophocles moves us from a concern with social tyranny, in its own immediate circumstances, to a consideration of what may be the cause of all tyranny. To say, as almost everyone has said, that Sophocles is the most "psychological" of all the tragic poets, is not to say that he was, therefore, less concerned with morality than other playwrights. Why is the political world so full of destruction and the degradation of people by other people? If we would answer this question, Sophocles tells us, let us look first to the family.

The existence of these parallel themes makes it possible to read and analyze the play on two levels. On the political plane, there is a very close correspondence to the structure and ideas of *Prometheus Bound.* Creon is a tyrant, a law unto himself, the maker of unjust decrees. Antigone rebels against him in the interest of justice and a higher morality, and pays for that rebellion, in this case, with her life. Exactly as in the situation in *Prometheus,* the rebellious hero is constantly contrasted with those who preach accommodation.

That Creon is behaving like a tyrant, with no respect for ancient laws, is clear throughout the play. We are told that the people in the city are against his decree and sympathize with Antigone. The seer Teiresias, symbol of traditional piety, finally persuades Creon to give way. Creon cannot do so until he gives up the tyrant's arrogance. This birth into freedom he finds painful: "To yield is dreadful." [1095.] It is his own son who most clearly tells him that he is playing the tyrant:

> Haemon: When you conclude unjustly, so I must.
> Creon: Am I unjust, when I respect my office?
> Haemon: You tread down the gods' due. Respect is gone.
>
> [743-745]

Although Antigone's interest in the dead corpse of her brother is deeply personal, she justifies her rebellion not in private terms, but by the general laws of justice:

> Creon: And still you dared to overstep these laws?
> Antigone: For me it was not Zeus who made that order.
>   Nor did that Justice who lives with the gods below
>   mark out such laws to hold among mankind.

Nor did I think your orders were so strong
that you, a mortal man, could over-run
the god's unwritten and unfailing laws.

[449-455]

The proper burial of a man who has been important in society is a religious and social concern, of interest to the whole community. Sophocles, the most conservative of the three tragic playwrights, recalls Homeric matters when he makes the central dramatic issue of the play whether or not Polyneices shall receive ritual burial. Three of the seven extant plays of Sophocles (*Antigone, Ajax, and Oedipus at Colonus*) concern themselves with the circumstances of the death and funeral ritual of a hero. In this play, when Teiresias seeks to persuade Creon, he uses words which anyone with the sense and the courage could have spoken to Achilles:

Why goad him where he lies?
What use to kill the dead a second time?

[1029-1030]

Sophocles gives us the argument between the rebellious hero and the non-heroic, accommodating person at the beginning of the play. Antigone would have her sister Ismene assist in burying the corpse, but Ismene declines to help because of the same notions of submission to legitimate authority with which we are already well acquainted:

So I shall ask of them beneath the earth
forgiveness, for in these things I am forced,
and shall obey the men in power. I know
that wild and futile action makes no sense.

[65-68]

Ismene will not move beyond shame culture, where the opinions of others are all-important. She will not share Antigone's revolt and Antigone's guilt, and she would like to think that it is just to submit to legitimate power:

I shall do no dishonor. But to act
against the citizens. I cannot.

[78-79]

Since this play is particularly about politics, Sophocles goes even further in the analysis of accommodation. After Creon has condemned Antigone to die, Haemon enters to try to dissuade his father. At the beginning

Haemon takes the stance of the good son Diomedes, announcing that his first and last loyalty is to his father, that no marriage will count more with him than filial loyalty. This protestation provokes Creon to deliver one of the longest speeches in the play, a paean to accommodation.

First Creon responds with pious words about how sons should respect their fathers:

> There's my good boy. So should you hold at heart
> and stand behind your father all the way.
> It is for this men pray they may beget
> households of dutiful obedient sons,
> who share alike in punishing enemies,
> and give due honor to their father's friends.
>
> [639-644]

We may note that the psychologist Sophocles has indicated that the first task of dutiful sons is to help punish the enemies of the father. Aggression is an important emphasis in this father-son bond.

Gradually, the speech moves from a discussion about family loyalty to pronouncements about the state. Creon makes the state heir to the old Homeric virtue of courage in battle, as in historical fact it was. He preaches the old value system of the *Iliad,* unchanged and unenlightened:

> The man the state has put in place must have
> obedient hearing to his least command
> when it is right, *and even when it's not.*
> He who accepts this teaching I can trust,
> ruler, or ruled, to function in his place,
> to stand his ground even in the storm of spears,
> a mate to trust in battle at one's side.
> There is no greater wrong than disobedience.
> This ruins cities, this tears down our homes,
> this breaks the battle-front in panic-rout.
>
> [665-774, my italics]

Unlike Homer, Sophocles is not ambivalent about heroic values. All that is good in Creon's life will be destroyed as a result of his commitment to those values. Sophocles' insight drives even more deeply than this. He tells us why Creon, and all those who share this system of values, take the stance they do. Two lines later, Creon concludes this lengthy speech that began with the praise of filial loyalty and became a treatise on the state, with words that explain why men commit themselves to values that are destructive of life:

So I must guard the men who yield to order,
not let myself be beaten by a woman.
Better, if it must happen, that a man
should overset me.
I won't be called weaker than womankind.

[676-680]

In literature—and in history—many have died under this banner.

When we turn from the political to the family aspects of the play, we observe that Sophocles' intention is to develop all the political implications of the play first and then to introduce family considerations, as an explanation of and a climax to what had gone before. It is not until the play is almost half over, at line 568, that we learn Antigone is the intended bride of Creon's son Haemon. In condemning her to death Creon is also taking away his son's future wife.

When Sophocles finally gives us this information, he has Ismene repeat it three times in the space of ten lines, lest we should fail to observe how important it is:

But you will kill your own son's promised bride?

[569]

Dear Haemon, your father robs you of your rights.

[572]

You will take away his bride from your own son?

[574]

We cannot but wonder whether Creon's pleasure in his tyranny is not enhanced because he is doing precisely that. In answer to the last question, he answers: "Yes. Death will help me break this marriage off." [575.] After Haemon and Creon have quarreled irrevocably, Creon will enjoy a double revenge:

Bring out the hateful creature; she shall die
full in his sight, close at her bridegroom's side.

[759-760]

Haemon is no passive creature, content to suffer whatever injustice legitimate authority may perpetrate. He leaves the scene, denying his father this barbaric pleasure.

The play which began as a story of social tyranny reaches its climax of terror with an almost unbearable scene of raw confrontation between father and son. Athene, who had kept sons from drawing their swords against their fathers, is no longer active in the world:

> The boy looked at him with his angry eyes,
> spat in his face and spoke no further word.
> He drew his sword, but as his father ran,
> he missed his aim. Then the unhappy boy,
> in anger at himself, leant on the blade.
> It entered, half its length, into his side.
>
> [1231-1236]

It is all too clear where Creon's tyranny has brought him. When his wife, Eurydice, kills herself she curses him as the killer of her children. At the end, Creon himself becomes heroic when he does not deny what he has done, does not excuse himself with false arguments, and takes full responsibility for the disaster. He cries out to the Chorus: "You see the killer, you see the kin he killed.' [1263]

One great concept draws all the various threads of the play together; one idea of human behavior clarifies the connection between family tyranny and political tyranny—that which is opposite to both—justice. The Chorus pronounces to the broken Creon: "You have learned justice, though it comes too late." [1270] "Yes," he says.

OEDIPUS THE KING

As a young man, in the home of his supposed parents, Oedipus is accused by someone of being a bastard. Although assured by his "parents" that it is not so, he visits the oracle at Delphi to find out the truth. Here he does not learn what he came to learn, but instead he hears the prophecy that he is doomed to kill his father and wed his mother. Determined to avoid that fate, he never returns home. Traveling near Thebes, he quarrels with and kills some men he meets on the road. Passing on to Thebes, he solves the riddle of the Sphinx, thereby ending the oppression of Thebes by this supernatural being. His reward for liberating the city is the kingship and marriage to the widowed queen Jocasta; they have four children together.

Years later, Thebes is again oppressed, this time by plague and barrenness of its soil and women. From messengers he sends to Delphi, Oedipus learns that the killer of the former king Laius still lives in the city and is polluting the land. Determined to do everything possible to find the murderer, Oedipus interrogates the seer Teiresias and an old herdsman who had been witness to the crime. He learns that the king was one of the travelers he killed on the highway years ago. More horrible than this, it is revealed that Oedipus is the son of Laius and Jocasta, who had abandoned him as an infant on a mountain with the expectation that he would die, because of a prophecy that the child would commit parricide and engage in incest with his mother. But he had been kept alive by the herdsman, and given to the king of Corinth, who had raised him as his son. As a result of these revelations, Jocasta hangs herself, Oedipus puts out his eyes and is exiled from the land.

Like all tragic heroes, Oedipus is the victim of injustice—from the gods who would destroy him and from his parents who intended to kill him. It is Teiresias, prophet of the gods, who gives Oedipus the first indication of his true history. Oedipus refuses to listen and accuses the prophet of lying, but Teiresias has no urgent need to convince him.

> It is not fate that I should be your ruin,
> Apollo is enough; it is his care
> to work this out.
>
> > [376-378][7]

When the true story is beginning to be known, Oedipus himself says of the dire prophecy:

> Would not one rightly judge and say that on me
> these things were sent by some malignant God?
>
> > [828-829]

His parents have also played their role. The initial act of aggression between parents and child was not from the hand of Oedipus, but from the parents who planned to destroy him. When the herdsman finally begins to tell the whole story, Oedipus unbelievingly asks: "She was so hard—its mother?" After everything is known, Jocasta dead, Oedipus blind, he can still recall with pain the fact that his parents intended to do away with him:

> > > > Leave me live
> in the mountains where Cithaeron is, that's called
> *my* mountain, which my mother and my father
> while they were living would have made my tomb.
>
> > [1451-1454]

It was this seemingly morally senseless suffering that provoked Freud to call the play "immoral."[8][O'Brien, p. 105] The play is by no means immoral, because Oedipus does not passively submit to doom; he is one of the least passive, most assertive heroes ever created. Seemingly trapped in as tight a doom as ever held anyone, Oedipus can still take pride in controlling what lies in his own hands:

It was Apollo, friends, Apollo,
that brought this bitterness, my sorrows to completion.
But the hand that struck me
was none but my own.

[1329-1332]

And towards the parents who had planned his death, he reacts not with despair and insensibility, but with a passionate desire for revenge:

Give me a sword, I say,
To find this wife no wife, this mother's womb,
this field of double sowing whence I sprang...

[1255-1257]

A hero is judged by the antagonist against which he struggles. The most important antagonist of Oedipus is not a tyrant like Zeus or Creon, not unkind parents or morally senseless gods, but the human desires not to know the truth, not to recall the past, not to remember what has long ago been repressed. Oedipus fights—and conquers—no external foe, but something within himself, and in all of us, that seeks to perpetuate an inner blindness. Like Prometheus and Antigone, Oedipus loses the struggle against unjust authority; like them, he is the conqueror in the struggle that goes on within himself.

The play is not about Oedipus' killing his father and wedding his mother; the play is about Oedipus' finding out that he has done so. Sophocles, if he had wished, could have written a play where the central dramatic events concerned the parricide and the incest. He did not choose to do so, but chose instead to give us a play about insight, memory, the capacity to recall and deal with those things that have previously been repressed.

All art brings to consciousness what has been forgotten, glossed over, sentimentalized, or repressed. "Art is the axe that breaks the frozen sea within us." There is an experience of *catharsis* in every artistic response, not only in the witnessing of a tragic play, which takes place when feelings lost to consciousness are brought to light again and are reconsidered. Much of the power that we feel in any experience of art is the power involved in recollecting what has been forgotten.

Oedipus' great heroism results from his capacity to insist upon insight no matter what the consequences. He has been told by the oracle of Apollo what his destiny is. Yet, when he kills a man old enough to be his father and marries a woman old enough to have given birth to him, he does not ask himself—consciously—if there might not be something more in the situation that he should look into. He makes no conscious connection between the prophecy and the situation in which he finds himself. Unconsciously, he must have suspicions he consciously ignores. Forced to seek the true story behind Thebes' troubles, he must have some premonition of what that truth involves. Yet, when the tale begins to unwind, he is all action: "You have not roused me like a man from sleep." [65.] And further on he says:

> What is it?
> I look at every story.
>
> [292-293]

When he has succeeded in his efforts, he exhibits an extraordinary capacity to take on himself full responsibility. "The horror is mine and none but I is *strong* enough to bear it." [1414][9]

The accommodators in this play preach submission not to some tyrannical legitimate authority, but to repression and forgetfulness of the past. Everyone who has some information that Oedipus lacks—Teiresias, the herdsman, Jocasta—attempts, at some point in the play, to prevent his learning what they know. Jocasta advises him that it is better not to pay much attention to such things:

> Before this, in dreams too, as well as oracles,
> many a man has lain with his own mother.
> But he to whom such things are nothing bears
> his life most easily.
>
> [980-983]

Oedipus himself wavers in his pursuit of the truth. Initially he is all for assertive action, but he withdraws from the pursuit at the first insight that he himself may be involved. Delphi had pronounced that the plague at Thebes resulted from the presence in the city of the murderer of King Laius. Oedipus seeks the help of Teiresias in finding the killer: "You are the land's pollution," Teiresias reluctantly cries out [353]. Oedipus acts as if he didn't hear what the seer said: "I do not grasp it, not so to call it known." [360-361.] Teiresias responds by telling Oedipus directly that he is the murderer of the king. Oedipus responds, "Not *twice* you shall say calumnies like this..." [363-364, my italics], indicating that he did, indeed, hear the seer the first time.

At this point in the play, Oedipus stops searching for insight and seeks the lie instead. When he blocks the truth, he becomes paranoid and tyrannical, acting as furiously as Creon acts in *Antigone*. The seer is lying to him, he insists; Creon has plotted with Teiresias to destroy him and take the throne; the plots of the traitors must be met with speed and force; Creon is condemned to death, with no evidence against him:

Oedipus: You are rogue.
Creon: Suppose you do not understand?
Oedipus: But yet
    I must be ruler

[628-629]

What follows this regression into tyranny is remarkable: persuaded by others to let Creon go, the autocrat gives up his tyranny. For Oedipus, renouncing tyranny and discovering the truth are inseparable, and Oedipus now knows what answers await him. Teiresias had told Oedipus that he was the murderer of Laius and then foretold that Laius' killer will be found to be:

...father and brother both
to his own children in his house; to her
that gave him birth, a son and husband both;
a fellow sower in his father's bed
with that same father he murdered.

[457-459]

Oedipus had lived all his life under the potential doom announced to him at Delphi. Only a madman would not understand what Teiresias had said. Oedipus had tried madness, but renounced it. Reluctantly, but willingly, he gives up the paranoia of the tyrant, knowing full well the consequences of his yielding to reason:

Well, let him go then—if I must die ten times for it,
or be sent out dishonoured into exile.

[669-670]

Sophocles, in this play, as well as in *Antigone,* is searching for the origins of tyranny. In *Antigone,* we were shown that political tyranny has its roots in family despotism. Against both of these, the true hero chooses rebellion. In *Oedipus the King,* tyranny results from a repression of the truth, from the failure to recollect the past. Oedipus rebels not against an external tyrant, but against the tyrant within himself. From the moment that Oedipus renounces the tyrannical stance, he no longer wavers in the search for the truth, and the play builds steadily to a climax of insight and terror.

Now, at every moment at which Oedipus receives a fragment of information, he pushes on for more. He is terrified of what he will find—unconsciously, he knows already what it is—yet he drives forward:

O dear Jocasta, I am full of fears

that I have spoken far too much; and therefore
I wish to see this shepherd.

[767-768]

Jocasta learns the whole truth before he does, and seeks to keep him
from it:

Jocasta: O be persuaded by me, I entreat you;
         do not do this.
Oedipus: I will not be persuaded to let be
         the chance of finding out the whole thing clearly.

[1064-1066]

Oedipus hears the truth, this time to call it known:

Herdsman: O God, I am on the brink of frightful speech.
Oedipus: And I of frightful hearing. But I must hear.

[1169-1170]

Oedipus' fate is to kill his father and marry his mother. That does not
make him a hero. His heroism comes from those things over which the
oracle has no dominion: how Oedipus learns what he has done and how
he responds to that insight. We are all fated not for parricide and incest,
but to have to deal with such desires within ourselves.

We have only two alternative modes of behavior in the face of this. We
may, like Homer, repress the knowledge and stay committed to pre-
Oedipal violence. Similarly, we may, like Oedipus in the first part of the
play, flee from insight and play the tyrant.

Alternatively, like the hero Oedipus we may seek that insight, no matter what the consequences. For the moment, that knowledge may blind
us. There is, however, no sweet road to freedom and morality. There is a
cost we all must pay in order to become adult. Such is the tragic vision.

THE ORESTEIA

The manner in which a child is treated by its parents before the child
arrives at the Oedipal stage will determine whether the child's ego is sufficiently developed to handle that experience, live through it, and
transform it into a positive experience. A healthy ego needs love and a
sense of independence. One of the gravest deterrents that prevents the
parents from giving sufficiently of love and independence is anger. It is
pre-Oedipal aggression, not the circumstances of the Oedipus complex
itself, that makes the complex so problematic. Aggression, from the

child and towards the child from the parents, begins at the very beginning of the child's life. By the time a child is four or five years old, it already has a long history of demonstrating and receiving anger.

This trilogy is much more about pre-Oedipal aggression than the Oedipus complex itself. The dehumanization of people through violence is the true subject of these plays. We are asked to take note of many of the great forms of social and religious aggression: cannibalism, human sacrifice, the primitive religious concept of blood-sucking Furies, and the horrors of warfare. From the personal, family side we are witness to the gross mistreatment of children by their parents, the murder of a husband by his wife, and the revenge slaying of a mother by her son. The dramatic interest of this trilogy—the plot itself—is concerned with the worst things that human beings can do to one another.

The background of the play is the story of the house of Pelops and Pelops' two sons Atreus and Thyestes. Thyestes seduced the wife of Atreus, disputed the throne with him, was defeated, and returned as a suppliant to his brother. Atreus, instead of accepting his brother's supplications, killed all the children of Thyestes, save one, and served them to their father to eat. Learning what had happened, Thyestes fled with his remaining son, Aegisthus.

Years later, Agamemnon, the son of Atreus, spent ten years away from home, leading the Greek armies against Troy. During his absence, Thyestes' son Aegisthus seduced Clytaemestra, Agamemnon's wife. In the first play of the trilogy, Clytaemestra murders Agamemnon when he returns from the war. In the second play, their son, Orestes, at the bidding of the god Apollo, returns from exile, kills Aegisthus, and murders his mother. Immediately thereafter the Furies appear to Orestes, determined to drink his blood and kill him to revenge the slain mother.

Apollo, in the final play, arranges that Orestes shall be tried by a court at Athens, with Athene as chief judge. The vote of the jury is tied; Athene's vote frees Orestes. The Furies threaten to blight the city-state of Attica, but are persuaded by Athene to remain in the city in a place of honor and worship. The trilogy closes with a processional in praise of Athens and the transformed Furies.

No one in fifth-century Athens was a cannibal, but other forms of institutionalized and personal violence were problematic for the culture. Aeschylus' purpose in setting the act of cannibalism as the dark background against which the events of the plays take place is to make a connection between all forms of human aggression, so that none of them may be excused from censure. Aeschylus has no ambivalence about violence. Unlike Homer, he does not sanction one form of aggression because other forms may be worse. Behind human sacrifice, warfare, and murder lies cannibalism. If it is a horror, Aeschylus insists, they are no less so.

The first play, *Agamemnon,* builds slowly to its climax of terror—the murder of Agamemnon. Although we know what is going to happen, we are reluctant to admit that human beings really are capable of doing such terrible things to one another. The long dialogue between Cassandra and the Chorus, more than 250 lines, occupies the central portion of the play, directly before the murder of Agamemnon. Its purpose is to convince us that it is really possible that such a killing will take place. As Oedipus is deaf to Teiresias, so the Chorus, at first, will not hear what Cassandra has to say: that Agamemnon is to be cruelly murdered by his wife.

It is in this dialogue that we have the first mention of the old act of cannibalism, when Cassandra says:

> Behold there the witnesses to my faith.
> The small children wail for their own death
> and the flesh roasted that their father fed upon.
>
> [A. 1095-1097][9]

The Chorus will not hear; they answer her: "We want no prophets in this place at all." [A. 1099.] But Cassandra will not be silenced. For another hundred lines they talk with each other, and the tension mounts. Finally Cassandra will tell them the horrible truth, but first she refers once more to the cannibal feast: "But this is evil, see!" [A. 1214], and then:

> Look there, see what is hovering above the house,
> so small and young, imaged as in the shadow of dreams,
> like children almost, killed by those most dear to them,
> and their hands filled with their own flesh, as food to eat.
>
> [A. 1217-1220]

The Chorus can no longer refuse to see what will happen, but is still incapable of saying it:

> Thyestes' feast upon the flesh of his own children
> I understand in terror at the thought, and fear
> is on me hearing truth and no tale fabricated.
> The rest: I heard it, but wander still from the course.
>
> [A. 1242-1245]

Cassandra answers in words that cannot be misheard. The Chorus, and we, no longer have the option to believe, magically and childishly, that the terrible thing may not happen: "I tell you, you shall look upon Agamemnon dead." [A. 1246]

Aeschylus uses the memory of cannibalism as a hammer to drive into our conscious minds what we are all enormously reluctant to admit: in regard to violence, there is nothing that human beings are incapable of doing to one another.

The theme of human sacrifice is central to the play. Agamemnon, before going to Troy, had sacrificed Iphigeneia, his own daughter, in order that the ships might not be prevented from sailing. Clytaemestra refers to this sacrifice of her daughter as one of the her reasons for killing Agamemnon. Aeschylus understands the connection between human sacrifice and cannibalism. All animal sacrifices to the gods were eaten by the worshipers. The symbolic horror of human sacrifice is that it cannot be eaten. The Chorus makes the first reference to the sacrifice of Iphigeneia early in the play, calling it a "sacrifice unholy, untasted." [A. 151.]

The killing of Agamemnon is performed in such a way that he, too, becomes a sacrificial object. Clytaemestra persuades him to walk into the palace on a crimson carpet, like a prize bull to the altar. After they both have gone in, Clytaemestra comes out to demand that Cassandra enter the palace, that she too may be murdered. Cassandra refuses. Clytaemestra has no time to waste arguing with her; she has murderous work to do:

> At the cental altarstone
> the flocks are standing, ready for the sacrifice
> we make to this glad day we never hoped to see.
>
> [A. 1056-1058]

The blood that is to flow will not be the blood of cattle. Cassandra knows of the death within the house:

> Cassandra: That room reeks with blood like a slaughter house.
> Chorus: What then? Only these victims butchered at the hearth.
> Cassandra: There is a breath about it like an open grave.
>
> [A. 1309-1311]

After the deed is done, Clytaemestra, glorying in her triumph, describes how Agamemnon's blood spattered over her, gladdening her, "as gardens stand among the showers of God in glory at the birthtime of buds" [A. 1391-1391]—like a sacrifice to make the crops grow. She herself tells us that she has sacrificed Agamemnon to the Wrath and Fury of their dead child. [A. 1431-1433.]

For Aeschylus, these horrors of cannibalism and human sacrifice are one with the Trojan War and the sanctified killing by warrior-heroes. Until the plays of Euripides, no more consummate critique of heroic values existed in Greek culture than in the first play of this trilogy. For Aeschylus, all violence is evil; heroic violence has its origins in the same place in the human mind from which springs the desire to eat other people or kill them in order to satisfy some barbaric god. Agamemnon claimed he went to war solely to bring back the adulterous Helen; yet he was willing to kill his own daughter to further the enterprise:

> The sickening in men's minds, though,
> reckless in fresh cruelty brings daring. He endured then
> to sacrifice his daughter
> to stay the strength of war waged for a woman,
> first offering for the ship's sake.
>
> Her supplications and her cries of father
> were nothing, nor the child's lamentation
> to kings passioned for battle.
>
> [A. 222-230]

Clytaemestra learns from beacon fires that Troy has been conquered. Ten years of struggle have been rewarded. The prize that is won:

> Trojans are stooping now to gather in their arms
> their dead, husbands and brothers; children lean to clasp
> the aged who begot them, crying upon death
> of those most dear, from lips that never will be free.
>
> [A. 326-329]

The conquered enemy is not the only one to suffer in this mad enterprise. The Chorus laments the human cost of such heroism:

> Those they sent forth they knew;
> now, in place of the young men
> urns and ashes are carried home
> to the houses of the fighters.
>
> [A. 432-435]

> There by the walls of Ilium
> the young men in their beauty keep
> graves deep in alien soil
> they hated and they conquered.
>
> [A. 451-454]

The great conquering hero Agamemnon returns home to triumph; before he can say a word in praise of his heroism, Aeschylus' Chorus tells him what kind of a man he really is:

But I: when you marshalled this armament
for Helen's sake, I will not hide it,
in ugly style you were written in my heart
for steering aslant the mind's course
to bring home by blood
sacrifice and dead men that wild spirit.

[A. 779-804]

Agamemnon will die not simplistically, as punishment for the evil he has committed, but because he is a willing participant in the great system of human violence. So long as that system prevails, no one is free from evil.

Parallel to these forms of socially institutionalized aggression (cannibalism, ritual sacrifice, warfare) are the forms of personal hatred and evil. These manifest themselves within the family. Agamemnon has sacrificed his own daughter; he brings home a beautiful concubine and demands that she be well treated, oblivious to the potential jealousy of his wife. Clytaemestra has taken a lover in her husband's absence and kills her husband on his return. The lover, Aegisthus, in part is revenging the outrage committed on his father and brothers by his uncle. The central act of the second play is a calculated murder of the mother by her son.

Whereas the first play of the trilogy concerns itself with all forms of violence, *The Libation Bearers* focuses on one particular form of aggression: that between parents and children. By concentrating all his dramatic energy on this one specific form of hatred, Aeschylus is not merely giving us an in-depth study of some arbitrarily chosen form of aggression. He is demonstrating that all forms of aggression, social and personal, have their genesis in that place. In the original act of cannibalism, it was a father and brother who were forced to eat the flesh, but it was children who were killed and eaten.

The theme of such hatred is repeated over and over again in *The Libation Bearers*. Electra discovers a lock of hair offered to the tomb of Agamemnon; it could not have come from her mother, Clytaemestra, she argues:

She never could have cut it, she who murdered him
and is my mother, but no mother in her heart
which has assumed God's hate and hates her children.

[L.B. 189-191]

When Electra and Orestes are reunited, he says to her: "I know those nearest to us hate us bitterly." [234.] She responds by telling him that he is the recipient of all the desire for family love she carries within her:

To call you father is constraint of fact,

and all the love I could have borne my mother turns
your way, while she is loathed as she deserves; my love
for a pitilessly slaughtered sister turns to you.

[L.B. 239-242]

Before Orestes kills Clytaemestra, he pleads not the case for his
father's revenge but for his own revenge for the hatred she has shown
him: "You bore me and threw me away, to a hard life" [L.B. 913]; "I
was born of a free father. You sold me" [L.B. 915]. Orestes has judged
his mother rightly. After Aegisthus is killed and Orestes has not yet appeared to Clytaemestra, she cannot be certain that he will also commit
matricide, but she will not take the chance of trying to find out. Ever
ready for action, she cries out:

Bring me quick, somebody, an axe to kill a man
and we shall see if we can beat him before we
go down—so far gone are we in this wretched fight.

[L.B. 389-891]

He, at least, has the humanity to be ambivalent before he strikes his
mother. She would kill her son as one kills a snake that crosses one's
path.
    Orestes appears before the axe. Clytaemestra, helpless, makes an ap-
peal to the memory of human love:

Hold, my son. Oh take pity, child, before this breast
where many a time, a drowsing baby, you would feed
and with soft gums sucked in the milk that made you strong.

[L.B. 896-898]

Soft gums do not stay that way forever. We have already been prepared
for this appeal, and the response to it. Previously were told that
Clytaemestra dreamed that she gave birth to a snake, laid it in swaddling
clothes, and took it to her breast to suck. Teeth it had: "The creature
drew in blood along with the milk." [L.B. 533] Orestes has easily read
the meaning of the dream:

                    As she nursed this hideous thing
of prophecy, she must be cruelly murdered. I
turn snake to kill her.

[L.B. 548-550]

We all somehow draw in blood along with the milk; somehow we all
turn snake. Nothing happens in the world without a reason. People have

eaten one another and killed one another in bloody warfare. In the image of the snake that tears the nipple, Aeschylus has come as close as art can to giving us the reason.

One concept that runs through all of these acts of aggression, personal and social, is revenge. Atreus revenges himself for Thyestes' seduction of his wife with the cannibal feast. Aegisthus takes vengeance for what was done to his father, Thyestes, by seducing Clytaemestra and plotting the murder of Agamemnon. Clytaemestra kills Agamemnon to revenge her sacrificed daughter. The Trojan War is fought as retribution for the trespasses of Paris and Helen. Orestes murders his mother to avenge his father. The Furies seek the blood and life of Orestes as vengeance for the mother slain. Even the pitiful Cassandra, triple victim of Apollo, the War, and Clytaemestra's hatred, "a small thing, lightly killed" [A. 1326], is powerless to do anything but call out for future vengeance, as she goes to her death:

> I call upon the Son in prayer
> against that ultimate shining when the avengers strike
> these monsters down in blood, that they avenge as well
> one simple slave who dies...

> [A. 1323-1326]

Revenge, no matter how great the justification, is not justice. Justice can put an end to violence; vengeance is a process that has no ending. In the first play of the trilogy, the Chorus raises the question which the last play will attempt to answer:

> Here is anger for anger. Between them
> who shall judge lightly?
> The spoiler is robbed; he killed, he has paid.
> The truth stands ever beside God's throne
> eternal: he who has wrought shall pay; that is law.
> Then who will tear the curse from their blood?
> The seed is stiffened to ruin.

> [A. 1560-1565]

This mad circle of revenge for revenge can be broken only when an avenger appears who is as interested in justice as in vengeance. The character of Orestes, and the circumstances under which he seeks vengeance, elevate the action of the first two plays of the trilogy, making them much more than just the story of human horrors.

The Libation Bearers begins with a dialogue between the Chorus and Electra, who has been sent by Clytaemestra to Agamemnon's tomb with offerings. The Chorus represents the old notion of justice—to strike

back at one's enemy. Electra struggles to elevate the notion of retribution; the Chorus reduces it to its primitive form:

> Electra: What shall I say? Guide and instruct my ignorance.
> Chorus: Invoke the coming of some man, or more than man.
> Electra: To come to judge them, or to give them punishment?
> Chorus: Say simply: "One to kill them, for the life they took."
> Electra: I can ask this, and not be wrong in the gods' eyes?
> Chorus: May you not hurt your enemy, when he struck first?
> [L.B. 118-123]

When Orestes comes, he comes as a killer and a judge. His heroism is
of the same form as that of Prometheus, Antigone, or Oedipus. His
revolt against the injustice of those who hold power involves murdering
his mother. A more terrible act is hard to conceive of, but a mother more
committed to evil is equally unimaginable. A moral person can commit
such an act only in the interests of justice:

> But while
> I hold some grip still on my wits, I say publicly
> to my friends: I killed my mother not without some right.
> [L.B. 1025-1027]

As commanding as Orestes' own motivation, is his instruction by the
god Apollo that he must do the act. When his mother pleads with him
not to, reminds him of the soft gums and the milk, he hesitates and turns
to his friend Pylades for encouragement. Pylades, answering with the only words that he speaks in the play, calls to mind the instructions given by
the god: "What then becomes thereafter of the oracles declared by Lox-
ias at Pytho?" [L.B. 900-901]

In the last play of the trilogy, *The Eumenides,* the principal theme
deals with the nature of justice. Orestes is declared innocent of murder
and freed from the pursuit of the Furies by the vote of the goddess
Athene, who supports the position of Apollo. Orestes has been an instrument of the gods. No one who has Agamemnon for a father and
Clytaemestra for a mother can make himself free. Only a moral, divine
power can liberate one from such parents. In Aeschylus' vision, the only
escape from the revenge circle of killing for killing is the creation of gods
who are able to nurture humankind.

VII
Tragedy: The Origins
of Evil

There is an intellectual, psychological, and moral coherence in the tragic form. Despite the great variety in theme and character, we intuitively sense, when reading tragedy, that there is an organic relationship among all the plays that overrides individual differences. There seems to be a shared world-view, a continuity of moral and psychological insight, in which every play that can be termed "tragic" participates. Since the heroic struggle against injustice does not describe all tragedy, one must search further to find what is universal in all tragic plays.

Every play of the tragic form seeks to answer three fundamental questions about human life:

1. *Why is there so much suffering in the world?*

2. *What shall we, or can we, do about it?*

3. *Where is morality and order in a world full of suffering about which, it seems, we can do very little?*

These are precisely the questions to which all post-magical religions have addressed themselves. The close connection between tragedy and religion arises not only from the fact that the tragic form originated in religious rites, but also because the form addresses itself to the same questions as religion, and in the same way. Insofar as Greek tragedy gives a supernatural, or partly supernatural, explanation to any of these three questions, it remains religious. Euripides is the only tragic poet who seeks a secular answer to these questions. Aeschylus, and Sophocles most especially, not only ask "religious" questions, but also give religous answers. The strain that we feel in Euripides' plays[1] results, to a great extent, from the fact that he continues to ask "religious" questions, as he continues to work within the boundaries of the tragic form, but he refuses to give religious answers.

All of this is not to say that the tragic form holds a monopoly on these interests, that the novel is not concerned with moral order, that lyric poetry does not address the problem of human suffering. What is true is that every tragedy asks not one but *all* of these questions, every tragedy takes these concerns as its central interest, and the manner in which tragedy asks, and answers, these questions defines the tragic form. Somehow, the tragic view seems to be uniquely capable of dealing with the problems of human suffering, of our response to it, and the questions that suffering imposes on the search for moral order.

WHY IS THERE SO MUCH SUFFERING IN THE WORLD?

Tragedy offers a clear and simple answer: Injustice—the evil that people do to one another, the evil that people receive from the gods—is the cause of human suffering. Injustice and evil have only three sources: parents, gods, society. Each of these commands power in the world—each is a legitimate authority. All are shown by the tragic poets to be morally inadequate. The tragic view of the word tells us that human suffering comes from those who should be most loving to us: our parents, our gods, the society in which we live.

The relationship of parent to child is a fundamental of human existence. The gods that people create are reflections and projections of this parent-child relationship. So is the society in which people live, although society is also much more than a reflection and projection of psychological forms. We may start our search for the origins of human suffering with the tragic view of the family. Those who wrote tragedy were not the only ones in Greek culture who observed how cruel parents might be to their children. The *History* of Herodotus is replete with stories of quarrels between men and barbaric revenge. It is remarkable how many of these stories relate that revenge is taken by one man on another by destruction of the *children* of the man who is the object of vengeance. Astyages, king of the Medes and the Persians, had a daughter who married and conceived a child. The king, having had a dream that was interpreted to mean that his grandchild would grow up to displace him as ruler, ordered that the child be destroyed and entrusted the task to Harpagus. The latter refused to kill the infant and gave him instead to a herdsman, who raised him as his own child. Years later the king Astyages discovered the treachery of Harpagus and exacted his revenge, not by killing Harpagus, but by murdering Harpagus' son, roasting his body, and serving the meat to the father to eat.[2]

Similarly, Herodotus relates how the Persian king Cambyses was told by his most trusted counselor Prexaspes that the Persians were saying that the king was too much given to the love of wine. Enraged, the king proved his sobriety by shooting the son of Prexaspes with an arrow, straight into the boy's heart.[3]

The killing of innocent children gives these stories of cruel revenge a poignancy they would not have had if the fathers alone were the victims of vengeance. The circumstances of the stories are particular, but the poignant feeling comes from what is universal. All children are innocent; all children suffer from the cruelty of those who hold legitimate power, kings and parents alike.

Empedocles, a philosopher of the fifth century B.C., in his poem the *Purifications* describes the primal sin and the fall of man. Meat-eating and bloodshed destroyed the time of innocence. For Empedocles there is no disguising the origin of evil:

> The father lifts up his own son, whose form is changed, and sacrifices him with a prayer—infatuate foul! The attendants hesitate to sacrifice the victim that pleads for its life, but the father, deaf to their cries, butchers him in his house and makes ready the evil feast. In like manner the son lays hand upon the father, the children upon their mother; they tear out the life and eat the kindred flesh![4]

Although tinged by exaggeration, this could almost be a scenario for many tragic plays.

Returning specifically to tragedy, the discussion of *The Oresteia, Oedipus the King,* and *Antigone* provided us with many examples of suffering inflicted upon children by parents. It is of value to pursue this line of reasoning further, for I believe it can be demonstrated that recognition of the evil that parents perpetrate upon children is fundamental to the tragic view of life. It is an essential insight not only of these particular plays, but of all tragedy.

Injustice breeds injustice; suffering gives birth to suffering; evil generates evil. Children always do what their parents teach. In *The Libation Bearers* Electra cries out:

> For we are bloody like the wolf

and savage born from the savage mother.

[421-422]⁵

This theme Sophocles expands upon in his play *Electra,* when the heroine explains to her mother:

> I know why
> I act so wrongly, so unlike myself.
> The hate you feel for me and what you do
> compel me against my will to act as I do.
> For ugly deeds are taught by ugly deeds.

[617-621]⁶

When parents will not be real parents, the child's freedom is gone:

> It makes the stoutest-hearted man a slave
> if in his soul he knows his parents' shame.

[*Hippolytus,* 424-425]⁷

The *Orestes* of Euripides is one of the most savage plays ever written, anticipating the Jacobean in its perception of immorality and cruelty. Orestes, having killed his mother, is condemned to death by the citizens of Argos. His uncle Menelaos, refuses to help him escape, although he recognizes the justice of Orestes' cause. Orestes and his friend Pylades murder Menelaos' wife Helen (also sister to Orestes' mother) in revenge, take their child hostage, and threaten to kill the girl if they are not allowed to escape.

> Orestes: In the meanwhile
>   I will kill your daughter.
> Menelaos: The mother-killer
>   strikes again!
> Orestes: His father's avenger
>   and betrayed by you.
> Menelaos: Wasn't her death enough?
> Orestes: I can never have my fill of killing whores.

[1586-1590]⁸

The origins of cruelty are not mysterious; the mother-whore makes her son a savage:

> Menelaos: And those who love their mothers?
> Orestes: Were born lucky.
> Menelaos: That leaves you out.

Orestes: Yes. I loathe whores
                                                [1606-1607]

    The story of Clytaemestra and her children is not the only one used by the tragic poets to demonstrate how the injustice of the parents makes children less "human" than they might be. In the *Alcestis* of Euripides, Admetus has been condemned by the Fates to die in the prime of his life. But they will allow him to live if he can find someone to take his place, to die for him. No hero, an average egotist, Admetus asks for volunteers. His aged mother and father, with only a short span of life left to them, refuse. His wife Alcestis offers herself. Admetus should refuse this offer, but he does not.

    Euripides sees clearly Admetus' egotism, but he does not present it as the acme of evil. Most men in Admetus' place would have done the same; Admetus is a perfect confirmation of Aristotle's comment that Euripides showed men as they really are—narrow, self-centered, incapable of loving or dying for anyone. Euripides' deeper interest lies in explaining why men so easily treat others, especially women, as objects, things created for their own comfort. When he addresses this question he confronts us with violence and raw evil. At the center of this play we witness an extraordinarily ugly interchange between parent and child.

    Alcestis has died for Admetus; Admetus' father Pheres comes to share in his son's mourning. Pheres feels no guilt about having refused to die for his son. Why should he? It runs in the family to preserve one's own life and let others die for you. Did not Admetus let Alcestis die for him? When Admetus charges Pheres with egotism, Pheres' answer is prepared:

> You wretch, you dare to call
> me coward, when you let your woman outdare you,
> and die for her magnificent young man? I see.
>
> > [696-698]

> Silence. I tell you, as you cherish your own life,
> all other people cherish theirs. And if you call
> us names, you will be called names, and the names are true.
>
> > [703-705]

    Neither the father nor the son is capable of loving someone else. They deserve each other; they have created each other. Pheres instructs his son that love is impossible in their world: "Do not die for me, I will not die for you." [690] Admetus, like all children, is capable of imitation:

Admetus: I hope that someday you will stand in need of me.
Pheres: Go on, and court more women, so they can all die.

Admetus: Your fault. You were not willing to.

[720-722]

Admetus is helpless; he has been taught by his parents to care primarily for his own survival; love, for him, exists only when it does not threaten life. He can curse the parents who made him so: "Go and be damned, you and that woman who lives with you," [734] but he is incapable of becoming more just than they.

The Chorus pronounces Euripides' judgment that evil is the failure of love:

Too much evil has been said in this speech and in
that spoken before. Old sir, stop cursing your own son.

[706-707]

In the *Hippolytus* of Euripides, the doom of the hero is overdetermined. He is the victim of a flaw within himself, of the vengeance of the goddess Aphrodite, and of a father too ready to assume an attitude of hatred towards his son. Hippolytus is the grown son of Theseus, born of a liaison of Theseus' young days. He disdains the worship of Aphrodite and keeps himself sexually chaste. The goddess of love decides to punish him for rejecting her by making Phaedra, the young wife of Theseus, fall in love with him. Hippolytus spurns Phaedra's love; she kills herself and leaves a note that she has been raped by Hippolytus. Theseus finds his dead wife, and the note, hesitates not a moment in believing that Hippolytus is guilty, and condemns his son to death.

The three causes of Hippolytus' doom—the cruel goddess, the hatred-prone father, and the sexual repression of the hero—are intimately related to one another. Hippolytus' character, and his fate, hold together all three elements. Euripides insists that a connection exists between a father quick to hatred and the conception of a goddess prone to vengeance; there is a link, he also suggests, between sexual repression and cruel parents.

In the first scene of the play, Hippolytus returns from the hunt and deliberately disdains the altar of Aphrodite, keeping all his reverence for the chaste goddess Artemis. His servant reasons with him, attempting to bend his arrogance. In the community of men, the servant argues, one rule holds good: men hate the person who is arrogant and will not be everyone's friend; "affability wins favor." [95]

Servant: Do you think
            that it's the same among the Gods in Heaven?
Hippolytus: If we in our world and the gods in theirs

know the same usages—yes.

[96-97]

The gods behave with senseless cruelty because they act just as people do.

In back of Hippolytus' fear and repression of sexuality there lies a hatred and fear of woman. When he rejects Phaedra's protestations of love, delivered by Phaedra's nurse, he is not content to condemn one wanton woman; half of humankind he curses:

I'll hate you women, hate and hate and hate you,
and never have enough of hating...
     Some
Say that I talk of this eternally,
yes, but eternal, too, is women's wickedness.
Either let someone teach them to be chaste,
or suffer me to trample on them forever.

[664-668]

We cannot know for certain what role Hippolytus' mother has had in creating this feeling. Unlike the case of Orestes, we have no evidence for the actions of the mother, but in this speech of Hippolytus there lies a great congruence of attitude with that of Euripides' Orestes, who cannot get his fill of killing whores. We also know that in folk tales the wicked step-mother is a symbolic displacement of the cruel mother. It is reasonable to assume that the sexually seductive step-mother Phaedra stands in place of Hippolytus' mother, sexually alluring and intensely seductive, who has driven her son to sexual chastity and hatred of all women.

About the cruelty of the father there is no need to speculate. Theseus, directly upon reading Phaedra's note, calls upon Poseidon to kill his son. The Chorus begs Theseus to call back the curse; he refuses:

The mind of man—how far will it advance?
Where will its daring impudence find limits?
If human villainy and human life
Shall wax in due proportion, if the son
shall always grow in wickedness past his father,
the Gods must add another world to this
that all the sinners may have space enough.

Look at this man! He was my son and he
dishonors my wife's bed!

[935-943]

When Hippolytus arrives, he swears a great oath by Zeus and the earth
that he is innocent of the deed. The oath has enormous power; anyone
not bent on destruction would pay attention to the fact that Hippolytus is
willing to utter it. The Chorus leader underlines this: "You have rebutted
the charge by your oath" [1036] but Theseus refuses to be moved. He
will listen to nothing but his own inner desire to strike out at his son:
"Pledges, oaths, and oracles—you will not test them?" [1055], asks Hippolytus. Later, Artemis echoes this charge, emphasizing Theseus' blind
cruelty: "You did not stay for oaths nor voice of oracles ... [O]nly too
quickly you hurled the curses at your son and killed him." [1321-1324]

An interchange between Hippolytus and Theseus reminds us of
Admetus and Pheres, so raw and undisguised is the hatred a father feels
towards his own child:

> Hippolytus: Where shall I turn? What friend will take me in,
>   when I am banished on a charge like this?
> Theseus: Doubtless some man who loves to entertain
>   his wife's seducers welcoming them at the hearth.
> Hippolytus: That blow went home.
>   I am near to crying when I think that I
>   am judged guilty and that it is you who are judge.
> Theseus: You might have sobbed and snivelled long ago,
>   and thought of that before when you resolved
>   to rape your father's wife.
>
> [1066-1074]

But this is not the worst. A hot anger has something redeeming in it: it
comes from frustration of love; it may yet be transformed. From cold
cruelty there is no hope of redemption. Poseidon has answered Theseus'
curse. Hippolytus is dying and the news is brought to the father:

> For hatred of the sufferer I was glad
> at what you told me. Still, he was my son.
> As such I have reverence for him and the Gods:
> I neither rejoice nor sorrow at this thing.
>
> [1257-1260]

King David also condemned his son to death. He knew with certainty of
his son's treachery; even so, he grieved and wept copiously when the deed
was done. In Greek literature, fathers do not respond in such a manner.

Sophocles' *Oedipus at Colonus* is unique among extant Greek tragedy
in that it is a play about epiphany, apotheosis, blessing, and love. The
old, blind Oedipus, led by his daughter Antigone, comes to Attica not so
much to die as to be translated from the earth as a deified hero, and to

give blessing to the land for generations to come. It is a play of religious exaltation. It is also a play of cold hatred.

The mood of reconciliation, between man and man, between god and man, is established early in the play through a discussion of the guilt of Oedipus. It is almost as if Sophocles had been intent, as he neared the end of his life, on being reconciled with his most famous hero. He gives Oedipus a chance to argue, with great force, his own innocence of what he had done. Oedipus does not diminish the horror of his life, but he insists that he is guiltless because he did not consciously, nor deliberately, do what he was suffered to do:

Oedipus:
    I had to face a thing most terrible
        not willed by me, I swear
    I would have abhorred it all.
            *   *   *   *   *
Chorus: You suffered—
Oedipus: Yes, unspeakably.
Chorus: You sinned—
Oedipus: No, I did not sin!
            *   *   *   *   *
Oedipus: Before the law—before God—I am innocent.
                        [521-523; 537-538; 548][10]

Later in the play, Creon arrives from Thebes, and casts old accusations at the former king; Oedipus reiterates his belief in his own innocence:

    No: I shall not be judged an evil man,
    Neither in that marriage nor in that death
    Which you forever charge me with so bitterly.

                                    [988-990]

It is essential that we believe that Oedipus, if not innocent, has certainly been forgiven by the gods, for no one with such pollution still adhering to him could become blessed and a source of grace to the land.

Antigone has cared for Oedipus through twenty years of exile and torment, the very symbol of filial devotion. Ismene, her sister, has also done what she could for her father, and arrives on the scene during the play to bring him news from Thebes. His final words before his apotheosis are of the love there has been between him and them:

    "Children, this day your father is gone from you.
    All that was mine is gone. You shall no longer
    Bear the burden of taking care of me—

I know it was hard, my children—and yet one word
makes all those difficulties disappear:
That word is love. You never shall have more
from any man than you have had from me.
And now you must spend the rest of life without me."

[1612-1619]

The conception that the old Oedipus is endowed with the capacity to
bring grace and blessing is a highly sophisticated, deeply sublimated
transformation of an ancient magical-religious belief that great pollution—and great sacred power—simultaneously exist in the person who
has broken a great taboo. The king who killed his father and conceived
children with his mother—and lived—is a source of blessing:

For I come as one endowed with grace
By those who are over nature; and I bring
Advantage to this race...

[287-289]

As the play is concerned with love and reconciliation, Theseus, the king
of Attica, immediately accepts the truth of Oedipus' assertions: "Your
presence, as you say, is a great blessing." [647.] As Oedipus goes off to
his apotheosis, the last words we hear him say are a benediction:

I pray that you and this land and all
Your people may be blessed: remember me,
Be mindful of my death, and be
Fortunate in all time to come!

[1553-1555]

He leaves this world, not as a man, but as a god:

But some attendant from the train of Heaven
Came for him; or else the underworld
Opened in love the unlit door of earth.
For he was taken without lamentation,
Illness or suffering; indeed his end
Was wonderful if mortal's ever was.

[1661-1665]

No work of Greek tragedy comes as close to the Christian spirit as this
play. It is remarkable how similar are the religious emotions and forms
of *Oedipus at Colonus* to the religious spirit of our own culture. Why is
it, then, that this play of reconciliation and grace is interrupted by two

vicious episodes of scheming, hypocritical, nakedly ambitious politicians—sons coldly disdainful of their father's misery—and of terrible
cursing by a father of his sons?

Many critical writers have been troubled by these scenes, which seem
so much at variance with the predominant spirit of the play. Cedric
Whitman writes: "These two scenes have caused much difficulty. They
seem somewhat extraneous and, in the eyes of many, give the work a
quality of melodramatic pastische."[11] Whitman himself demurs from
this judgment, and does not find the scenes irrelevant. What concerns us
here is the content of these intrusive episodes. What Sophocles gives us in
this "melodramatic pastische" is more evidence of the cruelty to which
children and parents subject each other. The exaltation of grace is flawed
by evil; evil not of some vague metaphysical kind, but evil from parents
and from children grown to power who return injustice for injustice
received.

Eteocles, Oedipus' son, rules in Thebes. His brother Polyneices, desir-
ing the crown, is bringing an army to attack the city. Ismene brings news
to Oedipus that the oracle has declared that victory will belong to the side
that succeeds in bringing the old king to its aid. Creon, agent of Eteocles,
appears in an attempt to win Oedipus over, first by argument. This failing, he takes Ismene hostage, then forces Antigone to go with him, hoping that Oedipus will bow to this show of force. Creon's criminal
behavior is foiled by the power of Theseus.

Oedipus rejects Creon's offer because he knows that the intention is
not to take him home, but to settle him outside the city, and thus to
escape his pollution while preserving the fiction that he has taken
Eteocles' part in the war. The father is not content merely to decline; he
will not stay neutral in the quarrel. He pledges an active hatred against
both sides:

> But you will not have it. What you'll have is this:
> My vengeance active in that land forever;
> And what my sons will have of my old kingdom
> Is just so much room as they need to die in!
>
> [787-790]

Oedipus comes to give grace to a strange land, reserving his hatred for his
homeland and his sons. For all the sense of blessing and reconciliation,
Sophocles was still writing tragedy, and in tragedy evil comes from those
who have the most reason to love.

Oedipus is not angry without reason. During all the years of his exile,
his sons have performed no act of compassion towards him. Had it not
been for his daughters, he would have been alone in the world. Eteocles,
in fact, while ruling Thebes, banished Oedipus from the city, in the ver-

sion of the story that Sophocles uses in this play. It is natural therefore that, as the play drives towards the climax of psychological violence, in the confrontation of Oedipus not with an agent of his son but with one of the sons himself, the great question of forgiveness is raised.

Polyneices approaches; Oedipus refuses to see him. Antigone, who has more right to speak of love and compassion than anyone else, pleads with her father:

> You sired him; even had he wronged you, father,
> And wronged you impiously, still you could not
> Rightfully wrong him in return!
> Do let him come!
> Other men have bad sons,
> And other men are swift to anger; yet
> They will accept advice, they will be swayed
> By their friends' pleading, even against nature.
>
> [1189-1194]

How terrible that Antigone must plead for love against nature! It recalls, for us, Lear's great question: "Is there something in nature that makes these cold hearts?"

Oedipus agrees, for Antigone's sake, to let Polyneices approach. Polyneices echoes his sister's pleas:

> Compassion limits even the power of God;
> So may there be a limit for you, father!
>
> [1268-1269]

Oedipus will not answer. Polyneices pleads his case. Finally Oedipus responds. It were better had he remained silent. The old hero, soon to become a god, one who brings great blessings to the land of Attica, can find in his nature only hatred towards his son:

> Now go! For I abominate and disown you!
> You utter scoundrel! Go with the malediction
> I here pronounced for you: that you shall never
> Master your native land by force of arms,
> Nor ever see your home again in Argos,
> The land below the hills; but you shall die
> By your own brother's hand, and you shall kill
> The brother who banished you. For this I pray.
> And I cry out to the hated underworld
> That it may take you home; cry out to those
> Powers indwelling here; and to that Power

Of furious war that filled your hearts with hate!

[1383-1393]

All this is not melodrama; it is a scene full of terror, full of hatred and cruelty and the failure of love and compassion. No discussion of whether or not Polyneices deserved Oedipus' curse can disguise what really matters in this scene: that a father and a son confront each other with such hatred.

If Sophocles "interrupts" a play seemingly about apotheosis, blessing, and love with two episodes such as these, it is not a mistake or a weakness in the play. He does so because he cannot conceive of a world in which this kind of hatred and cruelty, and this kind of inability to forgive, do not exist. By establishing the *locus* of cruelty between a father and his sons, Sophocles makes the story as universal as any story can be. We have all been children; most people become parents. That hatred which will not go away, no matter how blessed becomes the land of Attica, lies within us. When the tragic form sees that suffering comes from evil, and that evil comes from parents, that is only half of what it comprehends. It also sees that we incorporate the hatred we received from our parents within ourselves; we become the parents who breed evil. That is the true terror in the tragic vision. "Terror is the feeling which arrests the mind in the presence of whatsoever is grave and constant in human sufferings and unites it with the secret cause."[12] In Greek tragedy, the terror is there, but the cause of suffering is not secret.

A remarkable thing happens to Polyneices after his father prays for his death: he becomes a Homeric hero. His father's hatred leaves him emotionally impoverished, incapable of reconciling himself with the human being who fathered him. He must content himself with the "virtues" of the warrior-hero: shame at cowardice and love of death in battle. We witness his Hektorization in this exchange between him and Antigone:

Antigone: Withdraw your troops to Argos as soon as you can.
           Do not go to your own death and your city's!
Polyneices: But that is impossible. How can I command
           That army, even backward, once I faltered?
Antigone: Now why, boy, must your anger rise again?
           What is the good of laying waste your homeland?
Polyneices: It is shameful to run; and it is also shameful
           To be the laughing-stock to a younger brother.

[1416-1423]

It is human to love what is inevitable, no matter how terrible it may be. The worst horror in Oedipus' curse is not that Polyneices is to die, but that he is condemned to love that death:

> Antigone: Sweet brother! You go with open eyes to death!
> Polyneices: Death, if that must be.
> Antigone: No! Do as I ask!
> Polyneices: You ask the impossible.
>
> [1440-1442]

Sophocles is a great psychological playwright because he addresses himself to the origins of human behavior. Polyneices is shown not only as a Homeric hero, not only as the kind of person who would resort to heroic values in times of stress; Sophocles also gives us the reasons why Polyneices becomes a warrior-hero. He gives us insight into the cause of the whole heroic world-view. It is the failure of love in a fundamental situation of love—between father and son—that gives rise to the dread of shame and the love of killing. The father's curse makes the son a lover of death.

We turn now, in the search for the origins of suffering, from natural to supernatural parents—to the gods. We will find the gods no more moral than the people who created them. In the Greek mind, the gods were certainly a source of legitimate power; with rare exceptions, in tragedy, that power is a cause of evil and suffering rather than love and justice.

The argument has previously been made that one cannot understand *Prometheus Bound* and *Oedipus the King* without recourse to the conception that the gods are a source of suffering. Like the theme of unjust parents, this idea is not confined to a few plays; it is a major preoccupation of all Greek tragedy. In *The Trojan Women* of Euripides, Poseidon addresses the goddess Athene:

> This is a springing change of sympathy. Why must
> you hate too hard, and love too hard, your loves and hates?
>
> [67-68][13]

In the same play, the deep-suffering Hecuba calls out to these unreliable supernatural beings: "O gods! What wretched things to call on—gods—for help." [469.] In that nakedly cruel play *Orestes,* Euripides has the criminal hero piously invoke the god:

> Hail, Apollo,
> for your prophetic orcales! True prophet,
> not false!
>   And yet, when I heard you speak,
> I thought I heard the whispers of some fiend
> speaking through your mouth.
>
> [1666-1669]

All this may be dismissed as the ranting of the atheist Euripides, but what do we make of the speech that closes *The Women of Trachis*—a play written by the devout Sophocles on the senseless death of Heracles?

> You see how little compassion the Gods
> have shown in all that's happened; they
> who are called our fathers, who begot us,
> can look upon such suffering.
> No one can foresee what is to come.
> What is here now is pitiful for us
> and shameful for the Gods...
>
> [1266-1272]

Are we really reconciled to the basic goodness of divinity when the speech ends:

> You have seen a terrible death
> and agonies, many and strange, and there is
> nothing here whichis not Zeus.
> [1276-1280][14]

It was, undoubtedly, a comfort for Sophocles that he could continue to believe in that order in the world which was called "Zeus," in spite of the fact that this being could look upon human suffering with such little compassion. Sophocles and Euripides differed on the question of whether one should remain pious towards the gods, but they were in total agreement about the fact that much of human suffering comes from these deities.

Dionysius, in Euripides' *Bacchae,* arranges matters so that Pentheus is torn apart by the maddened worshipers of the god. His mother, a member of that troop, brings on stage the severed head of her son, glorying in the kill. Dionysius' vengeance has been taken because people in Thebes denied his divinity and his power. Was it justice, what the god wrought?

> Cadmus: We have learned. But your sentence is too harsh.
> Dionysius: I am a god. I was blasphemed by you.
> Cadmus: Gods should be exempt from human passions.
>
> [1346-1348][15]

The tragic poets did not invent the conception of gods who destroy human life for a minor fault or sin. As far back as Homer, Hera was ready to eat Priam and his children raw. It is important to ask what make a culture conceive of divinity in this manner. What is the experience of

legitimate power, in such a culture, that it cannot conceive of power
without cruelty? Hera and Dionysius did not exist, but the world-view
that produced such a conception of divinity was a powerful reality within
the Greek cultural form.

Euripides' *Heracles* begins with the hero absent from home on one of
his labors. His family—wife, children, father—reside in Thebes. In his
absence there has been a revolution in the city; the old authority has been
overthrown by an upstart tyrant, Lycus. Since Heracles' family is related
to the dispossessed rulers of the city, Lycus plans to destroy them so that
they cannot ever take vengeance on him. Assuming that Heracles will
never return, Lycus is arrogant in his cruelty.

Before the murders can be accomplished, Heracls returns, kills Lycus,
and saves his family. All this would be mere melodrama were it not for
the insight that Heracles receives in regard to the situation. He realizes
that in pursuing his heroic life he has neglected his family and endangered
their existence. He renounces heroism in order to become a loving father:

> What should I defend if not my wife and sons
> and my old father? Farewell, my labors!
> For wrongly I preferred you more than these.
> They should have died for me, and I should die
> in their defense. Or is this bravery,
> to do Eurystheus' orders and contend
> with lions and hydras, and not to struggle
> for my children's lives? From this time forth,
> call me no more "Heracles the victor."

                                                              [574-582][16]

This perception that heroic values are incompatible with real family affection leads to one of the few moving scenes of love between a father
and his children in the whole corpus of Greek tragedy. Heracles "sets
down his bow and club and takes his children by the hands."

> Here, I'll take your hands and lead you in my wake,
> like a ship that tows its little boats behind,
> for I accept this care and service
> of my sons. Here all mankind is equal:
> rich and poor alike, they love their children.

                                                              [630-634]

During the time when Heracles' family is in danger of extinction,
Euripides constantly raises the question of how the gods, especially Zeus,
could permit such a thing to happen, considering that Heracles is Zeus'
son. Amphitryon, Heracles' mortal father, blasts the king of the gods:

For nothing, then, O Zeus, you shared my wife!
In vain we called you partner in my son!
Your love is even less than you pretended;
and I, mere man, am nobler than you, great god.
I did not betray the sons of Heracles.
You knew well enough to creep into my bed
and take what was not yours, what no man gave:
What do you know of saving those you love?
You are a callous god or were born unjust!

[339-347]

Heracles' melodramatic return at the last possible moment his wife takes as indication of Zeus' concern for justice: "He comes to rescue us and Zeus comes with him." [521-522.] This sentiment the Chorus echoes after Lycus is killed:

What lying mortal made the fable
That mindless tale
That slander on the blessed?
Who denies the gods are strong?

[757-758]

The Chorus rejoices that Zeus' paternity of Heracles is proved by the rescue of his family—suddenly the thunder crashes, a horrible image of Madness is seen on the roof of the palace. Hera, out of jealousy and hatred of Heracles, has sent Madness to destroy his world. Having saved his children from Lycus' cruelty—all praise the justice of Zeus—Heracles will himself murder those children of his and his wife—by the mad justice of Hera. Even Madness cannot understand this senseless brutality:

Madness: I would place you on the better path: you choose the
        worst.
Iris: Hera has not sent you down to show your sanity.

[856-857]

Helpless in the face of such suffering, the Chorus can only cry out: "O daughter of Zeus, what do you do? You have brought upon this house ruin that reaches to hell...!" [907-908.]

Hera's revenge is satisfied when Heracles kills his own sons. In his madness, he conceives that he is murdering the sons of Eurystheus—avenging himself on the man who hated him and set him so many terrible tasks. Hera's vengeance and Heracles' delusional vengeance are both wrought on children. It is reminiscent of all the

stories told by Herodotus wherein the death of children satisfies adult
revenge. Family cruelty and the cruelty of the gods are united. " 'You are
their father! Will you kill your sons?' " [975.] The Queen of the gods insists upon it! All gods are symbolic projections of what people think their
parents are, or should be. A people can believe in gods so cruel only if
they have experienced cruelty at the hands of persons in authority. If the
experience of family life contradicted such notions of brutality, cruel
gods would cease to reign.

What is so terrifying in this play is that a man who has just uttered
some of the most loving, most sane sentiments in all of Greek literature
suddenly runs mad. After three hundred years we finally get an answer to
Hektor on the battlements with his wife and son. Heracles not only rejects the heroic value system, as Archilochus and others had done, but he
also goes far beyond it. He puts in its place a conception of the world
which is far more loving: he will be a father, a husband, a loving son to
his old father. He knows that he cannot have both heroic values and a
true family life. Hektor had chosen death. Heracles chooses life—and
goes mad.

It is as if Euripides conceived of Heracles as a symbol of the great
moral struggle within Greek culture. The culture would rather run amok
than abandon heroic ideals and seek love instead. The Peloponnesian
War would demonstrate that Greek culture would never abandon the
heroic world-view. Twenty years after this play was written Greece was
morally exhausted.

After Heracles comes to grief, Euripides continues to inquire into the
role of the gods in human suffering. "O Zeus, why have you hated him
so much, your own son?" [1086-1087], cries the Chorus, but Amphitryon wonders if the gods even care: "Even a god would weep, if he
knew it." [1115.]

In the face of such divinities, the courageous thing for people to do is
to take responsibility for their own lives and their own sufferings:

> Amphitryon: O Zeus, do you see these deeds Hera has done?
> Heracles: Is it from *her* hate our sufferings come?
> Amphitryon: Let the goddess go. Shoulder your own grief.
>
> [1127-1129]

At first it seems that Heracles is capable of seeing human suffering in
human terms only, that he is capable of rejecting the whole divine
machinery as he rejected the whole heroic system. He says to his father:

> Then Zeus—whoever Zeus may be—begot me
> for Hera's hatred. Take no offense, old man,
> for I count you my father now, not Zeus.
>
> [1263-1265]

Such complete liberation, however, was not possible, neither for Heracles nor for Euripides. The temptation to understand suffering by blaming someone outside oneself was too great. Heracles will not let the goddess go. He denies her morality but he cannot deny her reality. He needs someone to blame; someone not himself must have caused his misery:

> Let the noble wife of Zeus begin the dance,
> pounding with her feet Olympus' gleaming floors!
> For she accomplished what her heart desired,
> and hurled the greatest man of Hellas down
> in utter ruin. Who could offer prayers
> to such a goddess? Jealous of Zeus
> for a mortal woman's sake, she has destroyed
> Hellas' greatest friend, though he was guiltless.
>
> [1303-1310]

Such hatred from the gods implies that no one is free of their unjust, legitimate authority. Euripides saw their authority as profoundly immoral, but it still held dominion over Heracles, over Euripides, over all of Greek culture.

The *Hippolytus* of Euripides illuminates further this discussion of suffering that comes from the gods. The play begins with a prologue delivered by Aphrodite, wherein she tells us exactly what is to happen in the play, and why. Hippolytus, she says, has blasphemed her, "counting me the vilest of the Gods in Heaven." [13.] She does not begrudge him the pleasures he takes with Artemis and the hunt, "But for his sins against me I shall punish Hippolytus this day." [21.] She will arrange that Hippolytus' father will be the instrument of her vengeance: "Father will slay son with curses—this son that is hateful to me." [44.]

From one point of view, we may argue that Hippolytus gets what he deserves. By denying the demands of sexuality, he is living only half a life. Repression of a basic human drive could lead to terrible consequences, in Euripides' view; it was a theme he returned to in *The Bacchae,* the last play he wrote. But what of Phaedra? She is certainly innocent of such repression; she has not offended the goddess Aphrodite in any way. Is it right that she also die as Aphrodite relentlessly pursues her vengeance on Hippolytus? Aphrodite does not ignore this problem; her callousness in this regard is almost more terrifying than her hatred for Hippolytus:

> Her suffering does not weigh in the scale so much
> that I should let my enemies go untouched
> escaping payment of that retribution

that honor demands that I have.

                                                                    [48-50]

Hippolytus' servant vainly tries to persuade his master to give some honor to Aphrodite. Failing in this attempt, fearing that Hippolytus may suffer for such irreverence, the servant asks the goddess for mercy:

> You should grant forgiveness
> when one that has a young tempestuous heart
> speaks foolish words. Seem not to hear them.
> You should be wiser than mortals, being Gods.

                                                                [116-120]

We already know how this call for mercy will be answered. This conception of the gods as merciless, incapable of forgiving the trespasses of their worshipers, is not peculiar to the irreverent Euripides. In all of classic Greek literature there is not one instance of a mortal who offends the gods, realizes his mistake, asks for mercy, and receives it. Nothing is as certain in the world-view of this culture as the fact that any offense against the gods is certain of punishment. Oedipus, in *Oedipus at Colonus,* receives a kind of mercy and forgiveness from the gods, but he had merely transgressed an impersonal taboo; he had not blasphemed any particular god. Once a god's honor is slighted, there can be no forgiveness. Mortals were striving to liberate themselves from shame culture; the gods did not even make the attempt.

Euripides knows what kind of gods people ought to have. Euripides' pessimism comes from the fact that he knows what ought to be and has lost hope in its possibility. As Hippolytus goes out to his death, the Chorus sings:

> The care of God for us is a great thing,
> if man believe it at heart:
> it plucks the burden of sorrow from him.
> So I have a secret hope
> of someone, a God, who is wise and plans;
> but my hopes grow dim when I see
> the deeds of men and their destinies.

                                                              [1102-1108]

It is not true that Euripides portrays the gods as bringing no comfort of any kind. Artemis has been helpless to prevent Hippolytus' catastrophe—the law of the gods is that no god can interfere with the vengeance of another. She will, however, make sure that Hippolytus has not died in vain; she brings him the comfort which shame culture reveres—vengeance; he may die in peace knowing his death will be avenged:

> Theseus: A god tripped up my judgement.
> Hippolytus: O, if only men might be a curse to Gods!
> Artemis: Hush, that is enough! You will not be unavenged,
> Cypris shall find the angry shafts she hurled
> against you for your piety and innocence
> shall cost her dear.
> I'll wait until she loves a mortal next time,
> and with this hand—with these unerring arrows
> I'll punish him.
>
> [1414-1421]

Thus it is, after a father's curse kills his innocent son, these gods restore order to the world.

Those plays in which the role of the gods is essential to the action—*Hippolytus, Heracles, The Bacchae, Alcestis*—are among the most powerful plays that Euripides wrote. There is something in the symbolic conception that suffering comes from divinity which brings it close to the heart of the tragic view of life. When outside agents who are neither gods nor parents are the cause of suffering, it requires a great leap of the moral imagination to say that these should have been loving and compassionate, instead of tyrannical, towards their victims. The Greeks who conquered Troy were not expected to be merciful to their enemies. Jason, who originally married Medea for his own convenience, does not disappoint us when he throws her over for an even greater advantage. The gods, however, should bring love and compassion. They are not mere mortals; their morality and their capacity to love are supposed to be greater than those of a Jason or an Odysseus.

When gods become the source of our suffering our outrage knows no bounds. Gods who should be loving but who bring hatred and cruelty instead are a perfect symbol of the essential reality of the family situation. Our first experience with evil does not come from the Jasons of the world. It comes from those who have most reason to love us, from those on whose love we are most dependent; it comes from our parents. It is for this reason that the gods—no gods—who bring hatred and cruelty are such a powerful symbol of moral disorder.

We have been taught by critics, ancient and modern, to expect such irreverence from the greengrocer's son Euripides. From the devout Sophocles, priest of Asclepius, we are supposed to look for a far different attitude. It is true that these two playwrights do not share an identical attitude towards divinity, but if we examine closely the plays of Sophocles we find that some of his gods carry standards of morality no more elevated than those of the gods of Euripides. Divinity in Sohpocles' dramas may be as cruel and vindictive as Euripides' Aphrodite. We have already observed Teiresias' proclamation that Apollo will accomplish Oedipus' ruin. It is instructive to look at Sophocles' *Ajax.*

After the death of Achilles, the leaders of the Greek army balloted to determine who should be awarded his armor as recognition for valor and honor. Ajax was convinced that the award should be his. The leaders of the host thought otherwise and gave the prize to Odysseus. Enraged, Ajax sets out to kill Menelaos, Agamemnon, and Odysseus; Athene brings madness on him and he succeeds only in slaughtering some livestock, whom he mistakes for the leaders of the army. Coming to his senses, he carries a burden of unendurable shame and goes off to kill himself.

A goddess with the power to make a man mad and cause him to slaughter horned beasts instead of men could also have used that power to convince him to give up his anger. In the first book of the *Iliad* this very goddess did exactly that. But Athene has no love for Ajax. Odysseus is her favorite, and she can show her love for one hero only by spending her hatred on the other. Joyful at Ajax's humiliation, she encourages Odysseus to enjoy the same revenge:

> Athene: What are you afraid of? He was only a man before.
> Odysseus: Yes, but he was my enemy and still is.
> Athene: But to laugh at your enemies—
>   What sweeter laughter can there be than that?
>
>   [78-79][17]

For Ajax there is no question about the origin of his suffering: "... the martial goddess, daughter of Zeus, cruelly works my ruin." [401.] His wife, Tecmessa, also knows the power of Athene:

> Tecmessa: Even in what we suffer I see the gods' hand.
> Chorus: Yes, but they have given an overload of grief.
> Tecmessa: I think Pallas, the dreadful goddess, has bred
>   This pain, perhaps for her favorite, Odysseus.
>
>   [950-955]

Athene's power to make men mad is not peculiar to her. All insanity, we are told, comes from the divine parents:

> For never, son of Telamon, of your own heart's prompting,
>   Would you so far have strayed
> To fall upon the flocks. Yet frenzy comes
> When the gods will.
>
>   [181-185]

When Ajax gives up reverence for the gods, he does not exhibit the kind of bitter hatred that we find in Euripides, but there is the same sense of profound betrayal: "Don't you know by now that I owe the gods no service any more?" [589-590.]

What has Ajax done that has brought upon him such hatred from the goddess? Of what great sin is he guilty that his whole life comes to ruin in one night and a day? Sophocles, feeling the necessity to explain, has the seer Calchas interpret for us this divine justice. When Ajax left home, his father cautioned him: "Resolve to win, but always with God's help." [765.] The hero answered that anybody could win with divine aid; he was determined to triumph without that assistance. Some time later, during the fighting, Athene urged him on. He answered "with words to shudder at, not to speak" [774]:

'Go stand beside the other Greeks; help them,
For whole I bide, no enemy will break through.
These were the graceless words which won for him
The goddess' wrath; they kept no human measure.

[775-778]

Hybris, we may say, and diminish our understanding with a slogan. Far better to ask what experience of human life causes a people to adopt the concept of *hybris*—the notion that the gods would destroy the life of a noble hero because he has the human power to assert his independence. The gods are jealous, frightened, and angered that people should strive to live adult lives, free from dependency. Such a view of the world can arise and be maintained only if parents behave towards children in exactly that manner. The gods do not exist; they take their shape from the shadows of our parents that fall on our lives. The human suffering that comes from these shadow-gods turns out to be of the same order as the suffering that comes to children from those who hold legitimate power over them.

The third great category of legitimate power conceived by the tragic poets as a source of suffering is human society. "[S]ociety may be no less corrupt than 'the gods' and as unjust in the necessities it imposes."[18] In Greek tragedy all human misery that comes neither from the gods nor from the parents comes from persons politically empowered. Euripides' *Medea* may be read as pure domestic tragedy, but even here Jason leaves Medea in order to attain greater social power. In Euripides' *Orestes* the failure of Menelaus to aid Orestes is one of the causes of suffering, but it is Menelaus' political and military power that Orestes requires. The tyranny of human society is a major tragic theme.

In Greek culture warfare was the great crime of society. Each of the tragic poets attacks this form of institutionalized violence without confu-

sion or ambivalence. We have already looked at Aeschylus' assault on
warfare in the *Agamemnon*. In *Ajax* Sophocles has his Chorus proclaim:

> Whoever it was that first revealed to Hellas
> Their common scourge, detested arms and war,
> I curse him. Would the large air first had taken him
> Or else the impartial house of Death. Generations
> Of toil he made for us. Ah,
> There indeed was a harrier of men!
>
> [1192-1194]

What fell on Athens, perhaps ten years after these words were written,
was a plague of imperialism, aggressive warfare, and senseless killing.
Most of the plays of Euripides were written during the Peloponnesian
War. He could not escape, and had no desire to, the horrible implications of what that war was doing to the moral cohesion of the city:

> Mindless, all of you, who in strength of spear
> and tearing edge win your valors
> by war, thus stupidly trying
> to halt the grief of the world.
> For if bloody debate shall settle
> the issue, never again
> shall hate be gone out of the cities of men.
> By hate they won the chambers of Priam's city;
> they could have solved by reason and words
> the quarrel, Helen, for you.
> Now these are given to the Death God below.
>
> [*Helen*, 1151-1161][19]

Many people contend that it is impossible to write great political
literature. "Mere" politics, we are told, does not lend itself to the great
purposes of art. Such argument pays no attention to the fact that
Euripides did write great political drama. Political art must be more than
just a denunciation of horrible deeds. For the artist it is not enough to
condemn acts of social violence, the Athenian genocide against the island
of Melos (416-415 B.C.), or the destruction of millions in concentration
camps. The artist must make a connection between acts of horror and
something within us. The perception that, although we could never actually do such deeds, still there exists a perpetrator of genocide within
ourselves—nothing is more appropriate to the artistic vision. Euripides
was writing his plays for those who had ordered the doing of the deed.
The artist can certainly begin to address the question of why society is a
bringer of suffering, a source of evil. Society, exactly like parents or the

gods, should give us sustenance, purpose, and love. Why then, does it bring misery? The *Hecuba* of Euripides is representative of a series of plays that attempt to answer this question.

The play is set in Thrace. The victorious Greek army is on its way home from Troy. All the men of Troy, and all of the sons of Priam, save one—Polydorus—are dead, and the Trojan women have been enslaved by the Greeks. As if to prove that in regard to cruelty and killing men are insatiable, the Greek army decides that Polyxena, daughter of Priam and Hecuba, is to be sacrificed to the ghost of Achilles. Victory and glory for heroes can come only with slavery and sorrow for others:

> Polyxena: I was born to freedom and I die a slave.
> Hecuba: Fifty children I once had, and all are dead.
> Polyxena: What message shall I take to Priam and Hector?
> Hecuba: Tell them this: I am the queen of sorrow.
>   [420-423][20]

One of Euripides' purposes was to unmask the slogan of "political necessity" that had been used at Athens during the Peloponnesian War as the banner under which the grossest cruelty was committed. In the play, Odysseus is representative of the politician who does not come out and say that he is pursuing a certain course because he loves killing, but rather hides his destructive drive behind the screen of rational policy. Arriving on the scene to explain to Hecuba why her daughter must be killed, he begins: "But let me review the facts," as if he were discussing the annual budget and not the taking of a human life. He continues: "By majority vote the Greeks have decreed...your daughter, Polyxena, must die as a victim and prize of honor for the grave of Achilles." [219-222.] Euripides knew that "by majority vote" a people could decide to commit genocide. Ever rational, Odysseus gives Hecuba sound advice: "Nothing you do or say can change the facts. Under the circumstances, the logical course is resignation." [228-229.] This is not the first time we hear submission to unjust legitimate authority preached as the wisest course.

Hecuba knows that rational considerations have had nothing to do with the decision to destroy her daughter:

> O gods, spare me the sight
> of this thankless breed, these politicians
> who cringe for favors from a screaming mob
> and do not care what harm they do their friends,
> providing they can please a crowd!
>
> Tell me,
> on what feeble grounds can you justify
> your vote of death?

    Political necessity?
    But how? And od your politics require
    the shedding of human blood upon a grave,
    where custom calls for cattle?

                             [255-263]

If it is politics that dictates such actions, it is clearly a politics of cruelty.

These politicians are exactly like the parents and the gods of tragedy: the concept of mercy is unknown to them. Hecuba will not resign herself even though she is helpless. Human decency, she hopes, may yet change the course of things:

    But I implore you,
    Odysseus, be merciful, take pity on me!
    Go to the Greeks. Argue, coax them, convince them
    that what they do is wrong. Accuse them of murder!
    Tell them we are helpless, we are women,
    the same women whom they tore from sanctuary
    at the altars. But they pitied us, they spared us then.
    Plead with them.
    Read them your law of murder. Tell them how
    it applies to slave and free without distinction.
    But go.

                             [286-293]

We know just how effective the call to mercy can be in Greek tragedy, and in Athenian politics. When the time came for the human sacrifice, Achilles' son was ambivalent about doing the deed. "Torn between pity and duty," the pity quickly dissolved. He "slashed her throat with the edge of his sword. The blood gushed out, and she fell, dying, to the ground..." [565-568.]

In the Athens of Euripides' day the sophists and rhetoricians had taught people how to argue rationally the cause of cruelty. Odysseus feels the necessity of arguing rationally with Hecuba the reasons why her daughter must be sacrificed: "Allow me to observe, Hecuba, that in your hysterics you twist the facts." [298-299.] Odysseus had given his word that when Troy was taken Hecuba's daughter would be a living prize for the best soldier. He cannot help it if that soldier is now dead and the daughter must die in order to be with him. "Besides, there is a principle at stake," [307] and cities will come to ruin if it is neglected. If the most exceptional man receives no more honor than the ordinary soldier, who then will gladly die for his country? The politics of warfare may occasionally require that innocent people suffer, but what is that compared to the health of the state?

What this argument defends, what the sophistic politics of Athens reverenced, were the old Homeric values of honor and killing. The sophists were supposed to have liberated the Athenians from a blind commitment to inherited values. In fact, what they did was enable people to argue slickly a defense of the oldest values in Greek culture:

> Would we fight or would we look to our lives,
> seeing that dead men get no honor?
> > No:
> for my lifetime give me nothing more than what I need;
> I ask no more. But as regards my grave,
> I hope for honor, since honor in the grave
> has eternity to run.
>
> > > [316-320]

One great illusion of Athenian politics in the last half of the fifth century was that the progress of reason had left people free to choose any life they pleased. The truth was that they were under as great a compulsion as they had ever been. Their only choice was either to reject heroic values and move forward morally or to continue the sins of their forefathers and defend their actions with the only thing that was really new: facile argumentation. Euripides knew, and history proved, that in reality they had no choice.

In the midst of all the cruelty and suffering that people bring to other people, Euripides has Hecuba deliver an extraordinary speech, a soliloquy on the nature of good and evil that comes as close to the deep Shakespearean view of the world as anything in the whole of Greek tragedy. It is a speech similar to those passages in *Lear* in which Lear has the imaginative and moral strength to generalize from his own condition and ruminate on all the evil and suffering in the world. In Hecuba's speech, Euripides' insight goes deep into the human condition; it is no longer a question of "power," or "necessity," or "compulsion," words which give insight and yet hide the true nature of things. It is simply a question of good and evil, of love and hatred. Everything else is symbolic of these moral categories:

> But human nature never seems to change;
> evil stays itself, evil to the end,
> and goodness good, its nature uncorrupted
> by any shock or blow, always the same,
> enduring excellence.
>
> > Is it in our blood
> or something we acquire? But goodness can be taught,

and any man who knows what goodness is
knows evil too, because he judges
from the good.

But all this is the rambling nothing
of despair.

[596-604]

After the sacrifice of her daughter, Hecuba has yet another sorrow to
endure. During the course of the war, Priam had sent their son
Polydorus and a large quantity of gold to Polymestor, the king of
Thrace, for safekeeping. After the sacrifice of Polyxena, Polydorus'
body is found washed up by the sea. Polymestor has murdered him to get
the golden horde with which he had been entrusted.

This new suffering cracks Hecuba's spirit. Her life is reduced to
nothing but an overwhelming desire to be revenged on Polymestor.
Human cruelty needs a victim; the suffering of the victim turns him or
her into a victimizer, determined to hurt back what has given hurt. No
law of human nature is more fundamental than this. If people, organized
together as society, practice cruelty against others, may it not be that
they also are revenging themselves against someone who gave them
hatred instead of love? If Hecuba, in her state of despair, held political
power, what outrages might we not expect from her? The lust for
vengeance causes Hecuba to abandon other human desires:

Agamemnon: What can I do to help you Hecuba? Your freedom
is yours for the asking.

Hecuba: No, not freedom.
Revenge. Only give me my revenge
and I'll gladly stay a slave the rest of my life.

[754-757]

Hecuba's situation is clear. What is more difficult to see is that the
facile, easy-talking, corrupt politician Odysseus has also sold his
freedom for revenge and cruelty. He has political power and, therefore,
the illusion of freedom. But he is not free, any more than the demagogic
political leaders of Athens were. They were living their lives under the
compulsion to choose evil instead of good. Having rejected love, they
were slaves of "necessity." We know the cause of Hecuba's suffering
and her lust for vengeance. We don't know why Odysseus, or Athens,
chose cruelty, but we may use Hecuba's experience to help us understand. He who is hurt, when he gets power, hurts back. Unlike Hecuba,
he may displace his vengeance and commit cruelty against someone who

was not the source of his own suffering but one thing is certain: cruelty breeds cruelty. When we observe Odysseus or Athens committed to a course of human destruction, we may surmise the cause.

VIII
Tragedy: The Failure
of Reconciliation

Every Greek tragic hero is a victim: no tragic hero is the prime mover in his own tragedy. Even Prometheus—the most assertive of heroes—is no exception to this law of tragedy. Prometheus brings fire and the arts to mankind in defiance of the edict of Zeus, but the play is not about Prometheus' actions to save humankind; it concerns itself with the way in which Prometheus responds to Zeus' tyranny and cruelty. The original tragic agent is always someone who is not the hero.

The manner of the hero's response to the suffering and injustice brought by others determines the answer to the second great question that all tragedy raises: *What shall we, or can we, do about all the suffering in the world?*

No tragic hero remains passive in the face of injustice. However, all do not respond identically. In Greek tragedy there are three characteristic responses that the hero makes:

1. The assertive hero responds to suffering by seeking justice, not mere revenge. His or her response is never merely personal, but is always generalized as a struggle for justice.

2. The passive-reactive victim is vulnerable because of a fault within himself or herself. The injustice of others touches this fault and tragedy results. The passive-reactive victim does, ultimately, respond aggressively to the situation, but can only do so with a demand for revenge, a wish to hurt back those who have caused suffering. Such a hero makes no

distinction between vengeance and justice.

3. The powerless victim—usually a woman, an old man, a child—suffers through no fault of his or her own. He or she is the victim of injustice in the political world. Such people seek a pitiful revenge. There is no terror in their vengeance; it is merely the last illusion that conceals their total impotence.

The hero who struggles for justice (e.g. Prometheus or Antigone) is distinguished from the passive-reactive victim (Medea or Ajax) by the stance he takes towards revenge. The passive-reactive victim does strike back at those who bring suffering, but he or she is incapable of sublimating the desire for vengeance into a general call for justice. The heroism of such heroes results from the fact that they do not passively submit. Nevertheless, they all fail to make of their situations something more than personal vindication. Medea, Ajax, Euripides' Orestes, Oedipus at Colonus, Phaedra—all react aggressively against those who have hurt them, but there is something profoundly pessimistic, as well as tragic, in their stories. Their answer to the question of what can be done about human suffering seems to be that all we can do is take vengeance on those who torment us. After they take their revenge, the world remains unchanged. Temporarily the score may be evened, but the cruel game goes on.

Euripides' *Medea* is a play about the passive-reactive hero. When Jason went in search of the golden fleece, he succeeded in his efforts only with the help of Medea, who had fallen in love with him. They married, had two children together, and they reside in Corinth when the play opens. Jason has succeeded in winning the love of the daughter of Creon, king of Corinth; he divorces Medea and intends to marry the princess. Betrayed in her love, Medea kills Jason's intended bride by magical arts and murders their children as a final act of revenge against her husband.

Like most tragic heroes, Medea's suffering does not come from some distant foreign source; it comes from the person who is closest to her. She has left her family and her homeland to be with this man whose cruelty she must now suffer. Jason's actions are not only aggressive and self-seeking, they are acts of betrayal:

And she herself helped Jason in every way.
This is indeed the greatest salvation of all—
For the wife not to stand apart from the husband.
But now there's hatred everywhere, Love is diseased.

[13-16][1]

Since "betrayal" describes those situations in which those who should bring love bring suffering instead, all the cruelty that comes from gods and parents can be subsumed under that word—all tragic heroes, except

those victims of war or political tyranny, are betrayed. In this play, the
theme of betrayal is constantly before us:

> Is it not an example of overconfidence
> Or of boldness thus to look your friends in the face,
> Friends you have injured—no, it is the worst of all
> Human diseases, shamelessness...

[469-472]

> Medea: O God, you have given to mortals a sure method
>   Of telling the gold that is pure from the counterfeit;
>   Why is there no mark engraved upon men's bodies,
>   By which we could know the true ones from the false ones?
> Chorus: It is a strange form of anger, difficult to cure,
>   When two friends turn upon each other in hatred.

[516-521]

Jason is the prime mover in Medea's tragedy, and Jason's treachery
touches a fault in her, a fault which will consume her life. Medea is
capable of an uncontrollable, almost insane, rage. This anger is reactive,
not primary; it needs a betrayal of love to set it in motion. A victim of
cruelty, she will perpetrate greater cruelties than anyone else. Her nurse
knows Medea's nature; her wish is that the power of aggression may be
displaced, and thereby rendered harmless:

> She'll not stop raging until she has struck at someone.
> May it be an enemy and not a friend she hurts!

[94-95]

Medea is not a man, however. She cannot go off to war and destroy the
lives of others to comfort her rage. Women have their own mode of
vengeance against the husbands who oppress them; the objects of
revenge are always close at hand:

> Chorus: But can you have the heart to kill your flesh and blood?
> Medea: Yes, for this is the best way to wound my husband.

[816-817]

No one commits an act of cruelty, not even reactively, unless he or she
can take pleasure in the suffering of the victim. Medea has suffered. She
strikes back at the source of her unhappiness. That is only human. It is
human also to love the suffering of one's enemies. Medea encourages the
messenger to deliver in great detail the story of how Jason's intended

bride and the bride's father were destroyed:

> Do not be in a hurry, friend,
> But speak. How did they die? You will delight me twice
> As much again, if you say they died in agony.
>
> [1133-1135]

Anger, hatred, cruelty—take these subjects away and the tragic form would cease to exist. Medea herself tells us clearly why people suffer:

> I know indeed what evil I intend to do,
> But stronger than all my afterthoughts is my fury,
> Fury that brings upon mortals the greatest evils.
>
> [1078-1080]

Here, as so often happens in Greek literature, vengeance is wreaked upon children who are innocent of any cruel action themselves. We all grow to adulthood only by incorporating into ourselves what has been done to us. If we have been loved, we incorporate that love and become capable of loving as well. If we have suffered hatred, we incorporate that hatred and become a hater as well as someone hated. The victim of cruelty so easily becomes a perpetrator of evil because of this process of incorporation. Only the unconscious memory of one's own childhood experiences with cruelty could make one conceive that the most appropriate way to revenge oneself on one's husband is to kill one's children. Medea is incapable of distinguishing the hatred she feels for her husband from the emotions she experiences with her children. Husband, children, father, mother—all merge together in her mind. She kills them all, and herself, when she destroys her own children. Only unconscious recollection of the past could drive her to such excess:

> Ah, I have suffered
> What should be wept for bitterly. I hate you,
> Children of a hateful mother. I curse you
> And your father. Let the whole house crash.
>
> [111-114]

Injustice plays an enormous role in this play, but where is justice? In Euripides' mind, there is no confusion between revenge and justice. It is difficult to find meaning and order in a world in which the "hero" seeks only vengeance. The passive-reactive hero in Greek tragedy cannot by himself or herself restore moral order to the world. If that order exists, it resides only in the conception of the playwright who sees cruelty and suffering as the basis of evil. The passive-reactive hero leaves us with a gnawing intimation of pessimism: is there really so little we can do about human suffering except to hurt those who have hurt us?

Medea is representative of the whole class of passive-reactive tragic heroes. Each play wherein the central character assumes this stance is tinged with pessimism. In all cases the pessimism results from a single cause: the failure of the hero to transform his or her motivations beyond revenge. Sophocles' *Ajax* is a play built around four incidents of vengeance. The original act of injustice occurred when the Achaians denied Achilles' armor to Ajax. The first act of vengeance is Ajax's attempted killing of the Achaian leaders. The divine justice of Athene knows no higher conception; she avenges herself on the pitiful hero for the irreverence he has shown to her. After Ajax is dead, Agamemnon insists on taking his revenge on the dead corpse by denying it proper burial. The central act of the play, Ajax's suicide, is itself an act of masochistic revenge. Frustrated in his attempts to hurt those who have wounded him, Ajax can satisfy his vengeance only by killing himself. He will make them pay for what they did to him by acting out the fantasy of suicide, which every child, at some time or other, has contemplated in an attempt to return hurt to the parents. This is a play full of suffering and the failure of revenge to restore order.

Euripides' *Orestes* is a disturbing play because we have no sympathy, no pity, for the hero. In the cases of Ajax and Medea we sympathize with their sufferings; we are even forced to feel the legitimacy of their desires for revenge because we care about them. Orestes, in Euripides' play, is such a mean, despicable character that we watch his actions with a fascinated curiosity, without any human sympathy. However, Orestes' situation and his reactions to it are similar to the situations of Ajax and Medea. Orestes is the victim of injustice from the one person who could help him, his uncle Menelaos. His response to his victimization is to bring down with him the man who could have prevented his death:

> I have to die. Very well then,
> but above all else I want my death
> to hurt the man I hate. He betrayed me,
> he made me suffer, so let him suffer now
> for what he did.
>
> [1163-1167][2]

Oedipus at Colonus is a near-saint. In regard to his sons, who have betrayed him, he is one with the criminal Orestes:

> They see both me and you; and they see also

that when I am hurt I have only words to avenge it!

[872-873][3]

This man is blessed by the gods; his words have power. When he curses his sons and predicts that they shall kill each other, the words become instruments of destruction. He is translated to heaven, happy in the knowledge that his revenge will be accomplished.

So various are the characters of these passive-reactive heroes: the gangster Orestes; the near-crazed Medea who does not deserve her suffering; the aged, pitiful Oedipus moving toward his apotheosis; the warm, full-bodied Ajax who makes us weep at his death. How identical are their responses to their own suffering. All are victims of betrayal; all respond with the same impulse: kill, kill, kill!

The third type of tragic hero, the powerless victim, differs from the passive-reactive hero in respect to the degree to which he contributes to his own tragedy. The powerless hero, caught in a political situation in which he exercises no control, is doomed to suffer the cruelties of those in power. The passive-reactive hero also is not the original agent in his tragedy, but responds with greater cruelty, and greater injustice, than was originally directed at him. The powerless hero makes a pitiful attempt at revenge, but his reactive cruelty never matches the immorality of those in power.

The passive-reactive hero always has a fault of character that causes an overreaction to the injustice done. It was unjust of Jason to abandon Medea, but the killing of their children is hardly a response of equal violence. It may have been unjust of the Achaians to award Achilles' armor to Odysseus, but Ajax's attempted killing of Agamemnon, Menelaus, and Odysseus is a far greater act of violence. Oedipus' sons should have honored him in his lifetime, but his curse that they should kill each other goes far beyond that neglect.

It is not inevitable that Medea, Ajax, Oedipus, and Orestes must respond in the way they do. Something within their own characters makes them answer injustice with accelerating violence. That fault of character also keeps each of them from going beyond revenge towards a generalized notion of justice.

The powerless hero also responds with a call for vengeance, but helplessness makes this revenge a pitiful thing. Hecuba, whose daughter and grandson have just been cruelly murdered by the conquering Greek army, tries to find some comfort by calling on Menelaus to kill Helen for her adultery. It is a pitiful call for revenge, and holds no terror for us. The vengeance of Medea, Ajax and Oedipus are full of horror and are central to the action in their respective plays.

In the case of the powerless victim, no fault of character in the hero expands the tragic consequences. All the fault lies in those who exercise the tyranny. The plays concerned with the powerless hero are essentially political, directing our interest at those who hold social power and exercise it cruelly. We do not blame Hecuba for the way in which she responds to her situation. No matter what she might do, she could not come close to equaling the cruelty of Odysseus.

Of the Greek tragedies that have survived, the plays of Aeschylus are primarily concerned with the assertive hero who seeks justice; the plays of Sophocles treat of the assertive and of the passive-reactive hero; the dramas of the helpless hero, political tragedies, were written by Euripides alone. His tragedies deal with the passive-reactive and the helpless heroes. This development of the tragic form is a descent into pessimism. It is a troubling journey from Prometheus to Hecuba, from Oedipus the King to the old man at Colonus. Something had cracked in Athenian culture. The optimism of Aeschylus, his hope that people, with the aid of religion and culture, could succeed in controlling their own lives with justice, had disappeared. Political developments in Athens proved that such optimism was unfounded. Homer's view had triumphed. The tragic hero, faced with injustice and cruelty, could do nothing but call for more injustice and more cruelty.

All the tragedies of the powerless hero are alike. The patterns are almost identical: the victims of the political violence of warfare suffer; fresh cruelties are perpetrated by those in power; the victim responds to this new cruelty with the call for vengeance; the pitiful revenge may or may not be accomplished—it makes no difference to the moral impact of the story.

The Trojan Women takes place shortly after the city has been sacked. The men of Troy are dead or in exile; all the women and children are captives. Each of the women will be sent into slavery to serve one of the Greek heroes. Cassandra has been given to Agamemnon to be his concubine. In the midst of her wretchedness, she can still take pleasure in the fact that she shall be avenged when Agamemnon is killed by his wife:

> If Loxias
> is Loxias still, the Achaeans' pride, great Agamemnon
> has won a wife more fatal then ever Helen was.
> Since I will kill him; and avenge my brothers' blood
> and my father's in the desolation of his house.

[356-360][4]

Three times within the space of 150 lines she exults in the vengeance she will take on her captor. Unlike Medea or Ajax, her life is not consumed by this lust for revenge. Her life has already been consumed by the cruelties of the conquering Greek army. In the little that is left to her there is room only for the emotions of vengeance:

You beneath the ground, my brothers, Priam, father of us all,
I will be with you soon and come triumphant to the dead below,
leaving behind me, wrecked, the house of Atreus, which destroyed
    our house...

[459-461]

Her mother, Hecuba, is not reduced to this minimal condition until the
Greeks reveal that there is nothing they will not do in the service of cruelty. Hecuba's daughter Polyxena is sacrificed on the grave of Achilles.
Her grandson Astyanax, child of Hektor, is thrown from the walls of the
city to his death.

Stripped of all freedom, impoverished of any hope of happiness,
Hecuba is left with one human emotion—revenge. She is powerless to
hurt those who are the cause of her misery, but she must hurt something.
Helen, she conceives, is the original cause of all her suffering. If she can
persuade Menelaos to kill Helen, as punishment for Helen's adultery, her
life will still have some "meaning." "Kill your wife, Menelaos, and I will
bless your name." [890.]

It is the most pitiful, the most impotent, vengeance imaginable. Helen
is not the cause of the barbarism of the Greeks. Menelaus will not
become the instrument of Hecuba's sick revenge. Even were he to do
such a monstrous thing, it would not change Hecuba's condition. As the
play ends, the city of Troy is burning, Hecuba is led away: "O shaking,
tremulous limbs, this is the way. Forward: into the slave's life."
[1327-1330.]

From all these passive-reactive and powerless tragic heroes we learn an
enormous amount about the causes of human suffering. When faced
with the question of what we can do about all this evil, however, the
answer is deeply clouded. Certainly, neither the terrible vengeance of
Medea nor the pitiful revenge of Hecuba can restore order to the world.
The Greek tragic view seems to be telling us that in regard to human suffering there is very little, if anything, that we can do.

*Where is morality and order in a world full of suffering
about which, it seems, we can do very little?*

There is a universal human inclination to impose some kind of moral
order on the universe. Inherent in the value system of every culture is the
conception that human life makes sense, has meaning, no matter how
much evil or suffering that life may entail. In most cultural circumstances, this certification of meaningful order is the work of religion.
Clifford Geertz writes: "Thus the problem of evil, or perhaps one should

say the problem about evil, is in essence the same sort of problem of or about suffering. The strange opacity of certain empirical events, the dumb senselessness of intense or inexorable pain, and the enigmatic unaccountability of gross iniquity all raise the uncomfortable suspicion that perhaps the world, and hence man's life in the world, has no genuine order at all—no empirical regularity, no emotional form, no moral coherence. And the religious response to this suspicion is in each case the same: the formulation, by means of symbols, of an image of such a genuine order of the world which will account for, and even celebrate, the perceived ambiguities, puzzles, and paradoxes in human experience. The effort is not to deny the undeniable—that there are unexplained events, that life hurts, that rain falls on the just—but to deny that there are inexplicable events, that life is unendurable, and that justice is a mirage."[5]

Since tragedy is a literary form committed to exploring the origins of evil and suffering, it inevitably must confront the problem of moral order. There seems to be no question that Aeschylus and Sophocles were convinced that the world portrayed in their dramas contained an inherent conception of order. These poets seemed certain that we can be reconciled to life, albeit one full of disorders. The "religious" essence of tragedy lies in that reconciliation.

With Euripides, however, such is not the case. If he is profoundly "irreligious," if his dramas put an enormous strain on the tragic form, it is not merely because he may question the existence of the gods, or if they do exist, their morality. His atheism goes far deeper than a concern for the gods. His perception of the possibilities of human evil is so sharp and clear that it forces him to question one of the bases of religious and cultural life: the assumption of a meaningful moral order. "I am in love, it seems," says his character Amphitryon, "with what cannot be." [*Herakles*, 318.[6]]

There is a terrifying speech that Hecuba delivers. Her son has been murdered; Agamemnon appears and offers his compassion and aid. She begins with a statement about justice and meaning:

> But the gods are strong, and over them
> there stands some absolute, some moral order
> or principle of law more final still.
> Upon this moral law the world depends;
> through it the gods exist; by it we live;
> defining good and evil.

[*Hecuba*, 799-802][7]

It is a revolutionary statement of morality, radical not only for Greek culture but for any culture until the twentieth century. We are startled that Hecuba and Euripides have, seemingly, gone beyond any previous conception of morality. What we find, however, as the speech develops, is not that Hecuba is intent on organizing the world on a new principle. She is intent in asserting the ancient law of retribution against those who have caused suffering. Instead of driving forward to a new order of meaning, she uses these grand words to reassert the old morality of the heroic world. She wants Agamemnon's aid in killing the murderer of her son:

> Honor my request,
> Agamemnon.
> > Punish this murder.
> > > Pity me.
> > > > [806-807]

The great principle of morality that defines good and evil, to which even the gods are subordinate, turns out to be the ancient law of vengeance. We have been cheated of our hopes. A new order of meaning seems impossible. Euripides, it turns out, is also in love with what cannot be.

All three tragic playwrights agreed that the gods are a source of suffering and evil for human beings. All disagreed as to how we should respond to that fact. Sophocles believed that, no matter what the gods may do, we should still reverence them, that ultimately they are the source of moral order. His faith was strong; the evidence in his plays may lead us to a different conclusion. Euripides believed either that the gods do not exist or that if they do exist they can never be the ground of meaning. Aeschylus, believing that the gods bring suffering and disorder, felt that only the transformation of the gods can resolve this dilemma.

G. M. Kirkwood writes that Sophocles "keeps himself within the confines of the traditional mythological setting in a way that is foreign to Aeschylus with his creative use of myth and to Euripides with his critical use of myth."[8] The same may be said of the attitudes of the playwrights towards the gods: Sophocles is traditional, Aeschylus creative, and Euripides critical.

In the case of Sophocles, we are torn between admiring his faith, so stubbornly held in the face of a mass of contradictory evidence that he himself presents, and criticizing his naivete. Critics have wrestled with this problem, which can only be solved by perceiving the contradiction that exists in his view of the world. "But we must remember," writes Bernard Knox, "that for Sophocles and his contemporaries gods and men were not judged by the same standards. The Christian ideal, 'Be ye therefore perfect, even as your father in heaven is perfect,' would have made little or no sense to a fifth-century Athenian, whose deepest religious conviction would have been most clearly expressed in opposite terms: 'Do not act like a god.' Sophocles clearly admires the attitude of Odysseus [when he urges the proper burial of Ajax], but we must not therefore assume that he criticizes the attitude of Athena [who has brought Ajax to destruction]. She is a goddess, and her conduct must be examined in a different light."[9]

Euripides was also a fifth-century Athenian. He had no hesitation in asking his audience why it was that gods and men were not to be judged by the same standard.

E. R. Dodds, without accepting this contradiction, observes the same schizoid propensity in Sophocles' religious thought: "First, he did not believe (or did not always believe) that the gods are in any human sense 'just';

"Secondly, he did always believe that the gods exist and that man should revere them."[10]

The problem with this kind of blind faith is that it can only exist by suspension of the faculties of criticism. It accepts what is as good and keeps us from transforming the gods or their worshipers. "Sophocles did not share Aeschylus' belief in a Zeus who worked through the suffering of mankind to bring order out of chaos, justice out of violence, recon-ciliation out of strife....The Olympian gods in Sophoclean drama are enigmatic, masked figures whose will humanity can for the most part only guess at, and only identify with justice by a kind of heroic, defiant faith."[11] This kind of mysticism cannot transform the world, and no world has ever been in as great a need of transformation as the morally divided culture of fifth-century Athens.

Euripides, when he rejects either the existence of the gods or, at the very least, their capacity to impose moral order, is faced with an awful question: if the gods are incapable of giving meaning to the world, can that meaning come from humankind alone?

> O Zeus, what can I say?
>   That you look on man
> and care?
>   Or do we, holding the gods exist,
> deceive ourselves with unsubstantial dreams
> and lies, while random careless chance and change
> alone control the world?
>
>   [Hecuba, 468-472]

"Random careless chance" is precisely what the human drive for moral order denies. If the gods care not for justice, and if there is such a thing, it can only come from people in their relationships to one another. Euripides writes:

Do you think that deeds of wrong fly up on wings to heaven, and then someone writes them on tablets of Zeus, who looks upon the record and gives judgement upon men? Why, the whole heaven would not suffice for Zeus to write man's sins thereon, nor Zeus himself to consider them and send a punishment for each. No; Justice is here, close at hand, if you will but see it. [*Melanippe,* frag. 506][12]

Euripides knew that the gods had failed. The evidence of the human world gave him little hope that people were capable of replacing the gods in the role of bringers of justice. He never quite loses his faith that human beings can create their own order and meaning, but his uncertainty continually undermines his optimism. One of the great tensions in the plays of Euripides arises from the strain of a man desperately trying to believe something he knows may not be true. We cannot correctly describe the plays of Euripides as "pessimistic," but a constant gnawing doubt runs through them. Hera and Zeus had failed; could one really look to the genocidal polity of Athens for meaning and order?

Aeschylus belongs to an older, more optimistic time. When he died, nearly seventy years old, the Peloponnesian War was more than twenty years' distant. The terrible political conflicts that were to rock Athens had not yet begun. Aeschylus had enormous pride in what Athens had achieved and faith in what it would achieve in the moral sphere.

The last play of the *Oresteia* trilogy, *The Eumenides,* has as its central theme the power of culture to transform human experience. Orestes has been caught in a tight trap. He has avenged his father by killing his mother, at the urging of the god Apollo, who has promised Orestes eventual absolution and safety. No sooner is the killing done than the Furies arrive to avenge Clytaemestra by drinking Orestes' blood and taking his life. Apollo is incapable, by himself, of fulfilling his promises to Orestes. The Furies do not accept the dominion of Apollo over them; they will avenge the spilling of kindred blood no matter what that god may say or do.

Apollo directs Orestes to go to the altar of Athene at Athens as a suppliant. The Furies agree that Orestes shall be tried by a court in that city with Athene as the chief justice. The jury's vote as to Orestes' innocence or guilt is tied; Athene breaks the tie in Orestes' favor, freeing him to return home absolved of his crime.

The Furies will not relent. No longer capable of wreaking their vengeance on Orestes, they promise to blight the land of Athens. Athene persuades them to forego this revenge, but only after she has promised them great honor and privilege in the religious life of Athens. Offerings for children and the marriage rite will belong to the Furies; no family will prosper without their consent. They will be transformed from powers of vengeance into a source of benefit and blessing. They consent. The play ends with a grand processional in praise of the city, of moral order, of the transformation that Athene has wrought.

Orestes, in order to grow up and become adult, in order to assert his individual independence, was forced to kill his mother. After doing so, he was plagued by all the primitive fears that beset anyone who would leave the security of the family and strike out on his own. To believe in the morality of the Furies is to stay a child. To disregard those primitive fears is impossible: they will demand their due. Orestes, alone, is incapable of resolving this great human problem. Only the development of culture, Aeschylus insists, with its great power to transform primitive experience, can make Orestes free.

What we witness in this play is not only the metamorphosis of the primitive Furies, but the transformation, as well, of the Olympian gods. Apollo and Athene, always acting as agents of Zeus, are far different from the gods of Homer, who knew nothing of justice. In the plays of Aeschylus the gods become what they so rarely were in Greek culture, what gods should be: loving and concerned above all with justice. Aeschylus' moral vision was extraordinary. If the gods have been a source of cruelty and injustice, then the continuing drive towards moral order demands that the gods themselves be transformed into the bringers of that order. Aeschylus' vision was far in advance of the culture in which he lived. The pagan world had to wait almost eight hundred years before the new gods would come.

Aeschylus' vision was wonderfully accurate. The Christian-Hebrew God who overthrew the Pagan gods was a god of love and mercy and justice. He was capable of transforming the world. No one in all of Greek culture had a moral imagination as close to the Biblical as did Aeschylus. Just as Athene was born full-blown from the head of Zeus, so Aeschylus gave birth, in his own head, to a merciful, loving, monotheistic god: "Zeus is Aither, Zeus is earth, Zeus is heaven; Zeus is all, and whatever is beyond the all." [Frag. from *The Daughters of the Sun.*[13]]

A true reconciliation that can restore the moral order of the world requires that the person or god who is a source of power, and who has been the cause of injustice and evil, renounce cruelty and perceive that only love and justice can give meaning to the world. The victimizer must yield. The father who has unjustly condemned his son to death must observe that he has destroyed the moral basis of the world; the god who punishes a hero for a minor fault must bring mercy and forgiveness instead of retribution; the hero who reacts to the injustice done to him with the barbaric call for vengeance must forswear revenge. Without this kind of action no true reconciliation is possible; without this sort of insight, no matter what happens, we are left with the intimation that the world makes no sense.

Such a profound moral reconciliation seems alien to the Greek tragic view. In extant Greek tragedy it happens convincingly only once. In *Antigone,* Creon, who has been the source of evil, recognizes what he has done; he sees that he has unnecessarily destroyed his family and his life. Creon knows how difficult it is for the tyrant, bent on destruction, to change his course: "To yield is dreadful..." [1095], he announces before he forsakes his tyranny. When Creon's insight finally does come, it is too late; his son, niece, and wife are all dead as the result of his actions. We admire his heroic capacity for insight, but we are left at the end of the play not with a feeling of reconciliation and order, but with a terrifying feeling of the waste of human life.

In other literature, true reconciliation is possible. In the Bible it happens often: when Esau is reconciled to Jacob after Jacob has stolen his birthright, and when Joseph, holding great power, renounces the temptation to take revenge against his brothers. In the tragedy of *King Lear,* Lear has been the source of evil towards Cordelia, who, in turn, directs her anger toward him and causes him great suffering. Each has been a victim, each a victimizer of the other:

> *Lear.*   Come, let's away to prison.
> We two alone will sing like birds i' the cage.
> When thou dost ask me blessing, I'll kneel down
> And ask of thee forgiveness.
>
> [V, iii, 9-12]

The Greek tragic poets did attempt to write plays in which the final moments of reconciliation and forgiveness were as convincing as the scenes of Joseph and his brothers and of Lear and Cordelia. In my view, all these attempts failed. Something in the Greek mind seemed to withdraw when faced with the problem of making people love each other after they had held each other in hatred. The hatred in these plays is always believable; the love which is supposed to conquer the hatred is vague or spoiled.

The Greek tradition of the failure of reconciliation goes back to the beginning of things, to Homer. When Priam goes to the hut of Achilles to bring back the corpse of his son Hektor, our great wish that Achilles should voluntarily forswear hatred is disappointed. Achilles gives back the body under compulsion, and he cuts short the feelings of pity and affection he feels for Priam, insisting that the old man not push him so hard or he might become angry enough to defy the gods and refuse Priam's supplications. When the tragic poets attempt to go beyond this reconciliation-under-compulsion and give us a true scene of the triumph of compassion, whatever it was that made Homer incapable of such feelings still held dominion over the playwrights. The scenes do not work; love does not hold; the world refuses to be ordered.

In addition to *Oedipus at Colonus*, wherein Sophocles' great hymn to reconciliation is tainted by the clash of arms and the father's fatal curses against his sons, there are three plays—*Heracles* and *Hippolytus* of Euripides, and the *Eumenides* of Aeschylus—in which the tragic poet makes an attempt to order the world through forgiveness and love, and fails in the attempt.

In *Heracles*, after the hero has been maddened by Hera and killed his wife and children, there are three ways that he may respond to what has happened: he may kill himself; he may decide to live with an almost unendurable shame; he may live and reject the notion of shame because he is not reposnsible for the murders. It is a measure of his heroism that he chooses the last alternative, and yet that profound reconciliation to life is clouded by a strange interchange among Heracles, Theseus, and Heracles' father that keeps us from enjoying a final sense of triumph over evil.

Theseus' love for and friendship with Heracles is the crucial element that keeps the hero from taking his own life:

Theseus:	Why does he hide his head beneath his robes?
Amphitryon:	Shame of meeting your eye,
	shame before friends and kin,
	shame for his murdered sons.
Theseus:	I come to share his grief. Uncover him.

[1199-1202]

Theseus' friendship is so strong that it disregards old, primitive concepts of uncleanliness:

Heracles:	Away, rash friend! Flee my foul pollution.
Theseus:	Where there is love contagion cannot come.

[1123-1234]

Like Ajax, Heracles conceives of death as the only means to end his shame. "What will you do? Where does your passion run?" Theseus asks him. "To death: to go back whence I came, beneath the earth." [1246-1247.]

Unlike Ajax, Heracles is not alone in his grief. Theseus' arguments and love prevail:

Even in my misery I asked myself,
would it not be cowardice to die?

The man who cannot bear up under fate
could never face the weapons of a man.
I shall prevail against death. I shall go
to your city. I accept your countless gifts.

[1347-1352]

The decision to live is not enough. Heracles must also face the question
of how he is to live with what he has done. He must decide whether or
not he is guilty of murder, whether or not Hera's madness has destroyed
all meaning in his life. Are all the acts of heroism he has accomplished
rendered meaningless, and is his whole sense of identity destroyed by one
hour of madness? Euripides' craft is such that in nine lines he has
Heracles raise and answer these questions:

O my weapons, bitter partners of my life!
What shall I do? Let you go, or keep you,
knocking against my ribs and always saying,
"With us you murdered wife and sons. Wearing us,
you wear your children's killers." Can that be worn?
What could I reply? Yet, naked of these arms,
with which I did the greatest deeds in Hellas,
must I die in shame at my enemies' hands?
No, they must be bourne; but in pain I bear them.

[1377-1385]

When we compare the situation of Ajax with that of Heracles, we see
how assertive of life Heracles' actions are. Both heroes are driven mad by
a goddess, but Heracles' slaughter of his wife and children is certainly
more terrible than Ajax's murder of the cattle. Both heroes conceive that
the acts of madness have rendered all their previous heroism meaningless. Ajax makes a long speech in praise of life, convinces others that
he has decided to live, and goes off to kill himself as a final act of revenge
against his tormentors, human and divine. Heracles decides that the
greatest heroism is to live without the great burden of shame and thus he
diminishes Hera's barbaric revenge.

Why, then, does Euripides spoil this act of triumph in the last scene of
the play? Theseus, the savior of Heracles, the bringer of love, refuses to
understand the full emotional possibilities of Heracles' life and reduces
his courage to that of the warrior-hero. We have observed how Heracles,
in the middle of the play, rejects the heroic world-view and determines to
be a loving father, son, and husband. In the last scene, as Theseus is
leading Heracles off to Athens, Heracles returns to these feelings. He
longs to go back to whatever is left of his family. Theseus cannot understand and sets upon these feelings the mark of weakness:

Heracles:	Theseus, turn me back. Let me see my sons.
Theseus:	Is this a remedy to ease your grief?
Heracles:	I long for it, yearn to embrace my father.
Amphitryon:	My arms are waiting. I too desire it.
Theseus:	Have you forgotten your labors so far?
Heracles:	All those labors I endured were less than these.
Theseus:	If someone sees your weakness, he will not praise you.

[1406-1412]

Theseus refuses to comprehend the moral impact of Heracles' wish, and Theseus has the power in the situation. "Then you will say my grief degrades me now?" asks Heracles. Theseus is incapable of understanding or answering such a question. "Forward!" he barks. "Farewell, father!" answers the submissive Heracles. "Farewell, my son," replies the helpless Amphitryon. [1417-1418.]

Theseus has forced Heracles to choose between Theseus' friendship and the "weakness" of his love for his father. We do not get the final embrace between father and son. Throughout the whole of extant Greek tragedy we have waited for that embrace. Oedipus in Colonus had rendered curses instead. Euripides takes us as close to it as we are ever to come—and then denies us. Friendship is possible, we are told, but between father and son no absolute love can exist. "The gulf [between people]," says Arrowsmith, "seems to close only to widen out again."[14] Reconciliation is an illusion.

Hippolytus is another play wherein we are brought to the very threshold of true reconciliation only to be denied entrance to that place at the very last moment. After Theseus' curses have brought Hippolytus to the point of imminent death, Artemis appears to the father and reveals to him that his son was guiltless of the imputed crime, that Theseus has rashly brought death to Hippolytus without having made any attempt to test the evidence.

Artemis intends to be the instrument of reconciliation between father and son. "Son of old Ageus," she exhorts, "take your son to your embrace. Draw him to you." [1431-1432.[15]] Theseus does lift his son up, but in the exchange of words that passes between them Theseus does not ask his son for forgiveness. He wishes to be cleared of the pollution of murdering his son, but the manner in which he requests acquittal has the same egocentricity and coldness that has characterized Theseus' relations to Hippolytus from the beginning:

Theseus:	Alas, what are you doing to me, my son?
Hippolytus:	I am dying. I can see the gates of death.
Theseus:	And so you leave me, my hands stained with murder.

Hippolytus: No, I free you from all guilt in this.
Theseus: You will acquit me of blood guiltiness?
Hippolytus: So help me Artemis of the conquering bow!
                                                              [1446-1451]

Even with his son dying, Theseus' primary concern is with what that
death is doing to *him*. His last words to his child are: "Dear son, bear up.
Do not forsake me." [1456.] We cannot weep for a father who, even in
the teeth of death, cannot ask forgiveness. What an enormous distance
there is between this "reconciliation" and Lear's "When thou dost ask
me blessing, I'll kneel down and ask of thee forgiveness."

What is so striking in this failure of reconciliation is that Euripides has
brought us so close to the transformation and then denied it. Theseus
knows he has done wrong; the goddess urges him to embrace his son and
instructs Hippolytus that he must forgive his father, but from Theseus
the words will not, cannot, come. It is as if, for Euripides, such a true
reconciliation is unimaginable.

Bernard Knox has pointed out that, at the very moment at which Hippolytus forgives Theseus, Euripides is undercutting the pardon. "As he
forgives his father he calls to witness his sincerity 'Artemis of the conquering arrow'....The epithet is not ornamental; it recalls vividly
Artemis' announcement of her intention to repay, twenty-five lines
before,—'with these inescapable arrows...I shall punish another.' Hippolytus calls to witness his act of forgiveness the goddess who cannot
herself forgive."[16]

We have no difficulty believing in the hatred and cruelty exhibited in
this play—Aphrodite's for Hippolytus, Phaedra's for Hippolytus,
Theseus' for his son. When Artemis declares that she will revenge Hippolytus by destroying some favorite of Aphrodite, we do not in the
slightest question her intention. The reconciled love between the father
and the son is not believable. It closes the play in a manner that is merely
acceptable.

Euripides could see that true forgiveness, real reconciliation, and unambivalent love are necessary, but he could not enter that place. With all of
Greek culture, he shared in the profound failure of love.

Though the *Eumenides* of Aeschylus expresses the moral ideas that
culture can be transformed only by a transformation of the gods and that
only a transformation in culture can solve individual moral and
psychological problems, the play is not a philosophical or religious
treatise. There is a question as to whether the play works as drama, as
literature. Is the transformation that happens within the play believable? Is
Aeschylus successful in creating an objective correlative of his great
cultural insight?

In my view, these questions must be answered in the negative, and other readers have made the same judgment. Jan Kott writes: "But in the final part of the *Eumenides* there is no longer any human drama; discussion is carried on by ideas dressed in costume."[17] Kitto expresses essentially the same feelings: "Aeschylus treats his dramatic material as it were externally. There is no presentation of an inner drama of the mind, of an agony in the hero's soul, but a conscious manipulation of the material in the interest of the dramatic theme which Aeschylus wishes to present through it...The difference in tone between this strong intellectual drama and pure tragedy is felt when Clytaemestra's ghost appears. Here alone we feel that complete engagement of a tragic personality whose general absence leaves the *Eumenides* as great a play as any, but different."[18]

Aeschylus was capable of accomplishing extraordinary things in his other plays, all of which worked as drama. If, in this case, there is a strain between the ideas of the play and its literary form, if the play does not work as a play, it is important to try to discover why. It makes no sense to ascribe this failure to a weakness of craft, to argue that even the greatest dramatists are entitled to off-days. The two plays that precede the *Eumenides, Agamemnon* and *The Libation Bearers,* are powerfully successful and represent two of the highest points of western literature. It is equally certain that Aeschylus cared passionately about the ideas expressed in *Eumenides*; they were not something he casually threw in in order to meet the deadline for the competition. For us the play has an enormous moral power, even though it does not succeed as drama. Failure of craft will not answer the question.

Two explanations seem resasonable: either the tragic form is incapable of expressing this kind of reconciliation and transformation, or else there was something in Aeschylus that did not finally believe that such a transformation was possible. The examples provided by Shakespeare indicate that the first argument will not hold. In regard to the second explanation, it is one thing to know what culture must do to save itself; it is quite another to believe that culture will, indeed, do it. The brilliance of Aeschylus' moral insight gives the play the power it has; his lack of faith makes it impossible for him to create a believable work of art out of such ideas.

The weakness of the play results from the character of Athene. Since Athene's role in the ultimate transformation is essential, this flaw is fatally damaging to the success of the play. Within Athene we observe no conflict, no struggle, no triumph of just actions over the temptation to do otherwise. The agony in the soul which Kitto found absent from the play should have been present within this goddess. Everything Athene does to effect Orestes' reconciliation is too easy. The absence of struggle leaves us without a feeling of triumph.

Orestes has become a mere pawn in a game played by supernatural beings. From his character the play cannot take shape. Apollo is believable in his role as Orestes' advocate, but he by himself has not the power to free his charge. Athene has that power. She takes the most important actions of the play, but we do not care about her. We have cared for Clytaemestra, as horrible as she is—which is why the appearance of her ghost can give some body to the play. What Athene does is profoundly liberating, and yet we do not love her for it.

Our failure to relate emotionally and dramatically to Athene results from the fact that her reasons for voting for Orestes' freedom are paltry. For the play to have a great moral impact, we must be passionately convinced of the necessity of Orestes' being judged guiltless. Athene's reasons for freeing him must be the dramatic climax of our belief in his innocence. Instead, we are left with an explanation of her motivations that reminds us of the narrow, self-centered gods of Homer rather than the glorious moral gods that Aeschylus believed must rule the world.

Apollo, in his defense of Orestes, touches on deep psychological, moral, and social problems. Where, he asks, were the Furies after Clytaemestra murdered Agamemnon? If they are so intent on punishing murderers and preserving justice, why then had they no concern for Clytaemestra's slaughter of her husband? "Then what if it be the woman and she kills her man!" [211][19] he challenges them. "Such murder," they answer, "would not be the shedding of kindred blood." [212.]

Is it worse to murder a mother than to kill a husband? Since most people are not faced with such alternatives in their lives, that is obviously not what Aeschylus is asking. The question that the play really addresses is whether the inherited ties of kinship are more important than the freely chosen bonds of marriage. Does the family one leaves or the family one creates require one's greatest loyalty? One of the most significant steps in the development of culture has been the transformation of the foundations of social cohesion from narrow kinship solidarity to the political solidarity of the society as a whole. Parallel to this, one of the most important psychological steps in the growing independence of a person is the transformation of psychological commitment from the family which raised him or her to the new family created by marriage. To insist, as the Furies do, that killing a person of kindred blood is worse than killing a spouse is to preserve the primitive notions of society and love and to reject the drive towards individuality.

Apollo's answer is of enormous importance: Orestes must be freed because an independent, freely chosen marriage must replace primitive conceptions of loyalty:

You have made into a thing of no account, no place,
the sworn faith of Zeus and of Hera, lady
of consummations, and Cypris by such argument
is thrown away, outlawed, and yet the sweetest things
in man's life come from her, for married love between
man and woman is bigger than oaths, guarded by right
of nature. If when such kill each other you relent
so as not to take vengeance nor eye them with wrath,
then I deny your manhunt of Orestes goes
with right. I see one cause moves you to strong rage
but on the other clearly you are unmoved to act.
Pallas divine shall review the pleading of this case.

[213-224]

These are not merely "ideas dressed in costume." The interchange between Apollo and the Furies has dramatic impact. The idea is of enormous human importance, and it dramatically gives meaning to everything that has happened to Orestes. However, when Pallas divine comes to review the case the play collapses. Compared to the passion of Apollo's pleading, Athene's judgment seems written by a man who would criticize, not exalt, the goddess:

This is a ballot for Orestes I shall cast.
There is no mother anywhere who gave me birth,
and, but for marriage, I am always for the male
with all my heart, and strongly on my father's side.
So, in a case where the wife has killed her husband, lord
of the house, her death shall not mean most to me.

[735-740]

How lucky for Orestes that he found a narrow, petty judge who would relate to matters of high justice on the basis of personal bias. If Athene had had a mother, was Orestes then to be condemned? We cannot know what relevance the particular circumstances of Athene's birth have to the extraordinary moral crisis in which Orestes finds himself.

The failure of this play is consistent with the inability of any Greek playwright to give us one consistent, believable play that ends with a true reconciliation. This want of success is at one with the failure of Greek culture to develop the conception of a god of love who is capable of forgiving us for our sins. Tragedy—the greatest expression in Greek culture of moral compassion and the absolute necessity of human love—ultimately fails to reconcile us with life. It leaves us with the suspicion that, no matter how necessary such a reconciliation may be, it is, ultimately, not possible. All the great insights into the causes of human suffering seem to lead to a cure of which human beings cannot avail themselves. Even the tragic playwrights, it seems, were in love with what could not be.

IX
Politics Imitates Art: Thucydides

If a man writes a history of his time so obscure and enigmatic in its approach that a debate rages for 2400 years as to what his true attitudes towards the problems of his age were, a question of importance equal to that of what he really meant deals with what he may have been hiding. David Grene writes that it is difficult to say of Thucydides: "He believed this or that politically"; or "He is shocked by this or that."[1] We cannot know for certain Thucydides' real beliefs about democracy, the inevitability of the war, the responsibility of Athens for its own destruction; we do not know what his moral positions were concerning the great Mitylenean, Melian, and Plataean debates. When a man writes about the most important issues within his own culture in a manner that is "hard, obscure, complex, and ambiguous,"[2] we may assume that this lack of clarity represents a defense against some human feeling that must be repressed. In the attempt to find out not only what Thucydides meant, but also what he was hiding from himself and his audience, we may learn a great deal about the critical situation of Greek culture at the end of the fifth century B.C.

On many things Thucydides does express his opinion openly, without obscurantism. He does not claim that the scientific historian should be without opinions about what he describes. The book abounds with Thucydides' personal attitudes towards men and the events they create. Such being the case, it becomes even more important to discover why, in other equally important circumstances, he leaves us at a loss as to what he felt.

The *History* does not abjure psychological considerations in the interest of "scientific" sociology, and it does not speak only of economics, politics, and social relationships. Some of the finest passages in the book result from Thucydides' brilliant analysis of the motives that drive men. He readily discusses fear, the lust for power, vanity, ambition, the pursuit of honor, self-preservation, the desire to rule rather than be ruled. Certain psychological motives are excluded from consideration, however, almost to the point of taboo, as factors that motivate men: pity, compassion, sympathy, morality, the love of human beings for one another. Only the negative side of psychology has any interest for him.

If Thucydides' value system (more accurately, lack-of-value system) were unique to him, the pursuit of what he really felt would be a biographical activity only. However, all the evidence we have points overwhelmingly to the fact that Thucydides' view of the world was held by many, if not most, people within Greek culture of his time. If we read Euripides with Thucydides in mind, it is remarkable how many passages may be regarded as specific refutations of the views expressed by Thucydides. It is almost as if Euripides intended to answer the historian, point by point, in regard to moral considerations. When we realize that it was impossible that Euripides should have read the *History,* we recognize that what the playwright was arguing with was not the specific views of one man but the moral disease that had infected the city he loved.

When a man deliberately obscures his own position, we may gain insight into what is going on in his mind by looking at a person he admires. Thucydides' great hero is Pericles. If Pericles had not died two years after the war started, he tells us, the world would have remained safe for Athenian imperialism and the tragedy of Athens would never have happened. The myth of Pericles—more enduring than the myths of Apollo and Athena, since it is still believed in our own time—is the creation of Thucydides. We may comprehend the historian through his vision of this political savior.

The funeral oration of Pericles-Thucydides has been held up to us, by some, as a great moral document, comparable in its lasting value to the plays of Aeschylus or the dialogues of Plato. The modern version of the myth of Pericles-Thucydides runs as follows: "That was the ideal which the great leader of the Athenians expounded, with the full majesty of language, in order to make them at the critical juncture fully aware of the supreme values for which they were fighting, and to turn them into passionate 'lovers' of their country. But Thucydides did not mean it to be valid for the Athenians alone. Spiritually as well as politically, he envisaged Athens as the centre of a historical sphere of influence. He saw it as exercising a vast intellectual stimulus, not only on itself but on the entire Greek world. 'To sum up, I call the whole city of Athens the school of Greek culture'...In this realization of the spiritual hegemony of Athens—a realization fully worthy of the greatest Greek historian—Thucydides' creative insight first recognized the fact that Attic culture was to have a far-reaching historical influence, and the problems which that fact involved. Thereby the Greek ideal of culture, which had attained a new breadth and sublimity in the age of Pericles, was charged with the utmost possible historical life and meaning. It became the complete expression of the noble influence which the Athenian people and the Athenian state exercised through their intellectual and spiritual life upon the rest of their world, and which led other nations to live and to create as they had done.''[3]

Such encomia make one rush back and read the speech again. We find, indeed, that Pericles did say that Athens was the school of Hellas; it had earned the right to instruct others:

> ...this is no mere boast thrown out for the occasion, but plain matter of fact, the power of the state acquired by these habits proves. For Athens alone of her contemporaries is found when tested to be greater than her reputation, and alone gives no occasion...to her subjects to question her title by merit to rule. Rather, the admiration of the present and succeeding ages will be ours, since we have not left our power without witness, but have shown by it mighty proofs; and far from needing a Homer for our panegyrist, or other of his craft whose verses might charm for the moment only for the impression which they gave to melt at the touch of fact, we have forced every sea and land to be the highway of our daring, and everywhere, whether for evil or for good, have left imperishable monuments behind us. Such is the Athens for which these men...nobly fought and died; and well may every one of the survivors be ready to suffer in her cause.
>
> [Book II, XLI][4]

> *Do not be so certain that power*
> *is what matters in the life of man; do not mistake*
> *for wisdom the fantasies of your sick mind.*
>   [Euripides: *Bacchae*, 310-312][5]

This funeral oration was delivered over the bodies of men killed not in a war of liberation against the Persian who sought to destroy Greek liberty, but in a battle to save the imperial state of Athens, a state that Thucydides has Pericles himself describe as a "tyranny" [Book II, LXIII], in a moment of hypocritical candor. Who needs a Homer—with his fantasy violence and fictional destruction—when the killing of Greeks by Greeks goes on every day? Who needs the legendary heroism of the past when the present gives such opportunity to satisfy blood-lust? Such was the great ideal of Greek culture expounded by Pericles: that one could live without all the "charming" poets when real life was so full of the degradation of one human being by another. Having incorporated the Homeric world-view into himself, Pericles no longer had need of its creator.

The schoolmaster of Hellas goes on:

> No, holding that vengeance upon their enemies was more to be desired than any personal blessings, and reckoning this to be the most glorious of hazards, they joyfully determined to accept the risk, to make sure of their vengeance and to let their wishes wait...Thus choosing to die resisting, rather than to live submitting, they fled only from dishonour, but met danger face to face, and after one brief moment, while at the summit of their fortune, escaped, not from their fear, but from their glory.
>
> [Book II, XLII]

> *Until he spoke—*
> *that hypocrite with honeyed tongue,*
> *that demagogue Odysseus.*
> *And in the end he won,*
> *asking what one slave was worth*
> *when laid in the balance*
> *with the honor of Achilles.*
>
> [Euripides: *Hecuba,* 131-136][6]

All this may produce in us the eerie sense of *déja vu.* We have heard all this before: that the power to dominate and kill men is the greatest proof of manliness, that enacting vengeance against one's enemies is a great virtue. We imagine that next we will be told that glory represents the highest ideal of mankind, that man can achieve no greater goal than to die gloriously in battle and be honored by his fellow-killers when he is dead. We are not to be disappointed in our expectations:

> For heroes have the whole earth for their tomb; and in lands far from their own, where the column with its epitaph declares it, there is enshrined in every breast a record unwritten with no tablet to preserve it, except that of the heart. These take as your model, and judging happiness to be the fruit of freedom and freedom of valour,

never decline the dangers of war....And surely, to a man of spirit, the degradation of cowardice must be immeasurably more grievous than the unfelt death which strikes him in the midst of his strength and patriotism!

[Book II, XLIII]

I think that the plausible speaker
Who is a villain deserves the greatest punishment.
Confident in his tongue's power to adorn evil,
He stops at nothing. Yet he is not really wise.

[Euripides: *Medea,* 580-583][7]

Thucydides, Pericles, and Werner Jaeger are all correct in their views: Athens was the school of Hellas. It was a catastrophe, not a triumph. What Pericles taught was the old, untransformed Homeric morality. In spite of the great wisdom of the lyric and tragic poets, despite the growth of moral insight that would culminate in Socrates and Plato, the lust to annihilate reigned supreme. The morality of Euripides had become part of a sub-culture. The culture itself was in love with death. F. E. Adcock said it succinctly: "...if Athens was the school of Greece, she was a hard school and taught much that was evil."[8]

Although Thucydides does reveal his own position concerning morality, throughout most of the book it is not his intention to do so. He expends an enormous amount of energy trying to keep that position hidden. His most consistently held view is that morality does not exist. He prides himself on being the creator of "value-free" history and sociology. He is the great ancestor of all those analysts of society who attempt to understand human culture without giving any power to moral values.

In the human condition, amorality is as impossible as asexuality. An individual may achieve a state of asexuality, but only as the result of enormous repression of an instinctual drive. It is not different with morality. A moral position is an imperative of every psyche. If it does not consciously exist, it is legitimate to inquire why it has been repressed. We can observe in Thucydides that the pretense of amorality only covers a commitment to immorality. Lusting for violence, feeling both shame and guilt about that lust, he insists on a double denial; he denies that he has either that lust or a super-ego which condemns it. He must deny the existence or conscience, because if it exists, his own immorality is revealed.

Thucydides' position placed him at the center, not on the fringes, of his society. In the last thirty years of the fifth century, Athens was in a condition of acute psychological and moral crisis. The old optimism of Aeschylus and Sophocles was gone. People no longer believed in the infinite perfectability of the human condition: "This change, the greatest, probably, which has ever passed over a society in so short a space of time...in thirty years changed the best Athenians from impulsive enthusiasts into morose psychologists..."[9]

Greek scholars have attempted to answer the pressing historical question of why such a sudden change occurred. Like Thucydides, most have excluded from their explanations the very factor that answers the question: the conflict concerning moral values. This extraordinary reversal of world-view is laid at the door of a handful of teachers of rhetoric. "It was due, say all moderns, to a deep-rooted and wide-spreading spiritual movement: it was due to the Sophists."[10] To argue that the Sophists were the *cause* of the Athenian moral crisis, rather than one of its most dramatic symptoms, is equivalent to arguing that tuberculosis is caused by the fever which accompanies it.

It is true that the Sophists held amoral reason and rationality to be the highest good; it is true that they taught people, especially the young, "to make the worst argument seem the best;" it is a fact that Plato's moral ire is directed against these teachers of amorality. But one cannot argue that the Sophists created the Athenian imperial state—a tyranny over Greece. The Sophists did not make the Peloponnesian War "inevitable," nor did they drive the Athenians into the suicidal mission to Sicily. The Sophists did not cause the Athenian genocide against Melos and Scione.

The crisis in Athenian culture at the end of the fifth century cannot be understood without reference to the commitment to sadistic violence that had dominated Greek culture since the time of Homer. "The new rationalism did not *enable* men to behave like beasts—men have always been able to do that. But it enabled them to justify their brutality to themselves, and that at a time when the external temptations to brutal conduct were particularly strong."[11]

What was new in the situation was not that the temptations to sadistic violence were stronger at the end of the fifth century than at any other time in Greek history. What was unique at that time was the fact that the commitment to brutality was being attacked by a revolutionary moral view with such power that it forced the old Homeric morality to defend itself with any weapon that was at hand. If amoral rationality could permit sadistic violence to exist, that weapon was used, or else one could claim, as did Thucydides, that morality or immorality were figments of the imagination, that they held no power to motivate men. Sophistry became the rage in Athens because, for the first time in Greek culture, people felt the necessity of defending an immoral position which had always been taken for granted.

The attack on the Homeric view of violence, beginning with the lyric poets, reached a powerful climax in the work of the tragic playwrights. The moral split in Greek culture, which had maintained the Homeric view side by side with its critics, could no longer be maintained. The culture had to choose: Homer or Archilochus. It could no longer have both. The moral insights of an Aeschylus could not tolerate the ambivalence of Homer. If we have no god of love, Aeschylus proclaimed, then let us create one and end senseless brutality. The lust to annihilate had become critically problematic for the culture. The old moral compromise no longer possible, confrontation was inevitable.

In that confrontation, the defenders of Homeric violence were forced to resort to subtle, hypocritical arguments for their position. The destruction of the entire populations of Greek cities was accomplished under the banner of "wise political precaution."

> *My policy, old man, is not mere cruelty;*
> *call it caution. I am well aware*
> *that I killed Creon and usurped his throne.*
> *It does not suit my wishes that these boys*
> *go free to take their grown revenge on me.*
>   [Euripides: *Heracles* 165-169][12]

A man of Pericles' sensibility could no longer go out and kill, as Hektor and Achilles had, for the mere pleasure and glory of killing. Too "civilized" for that kind of behavior, the Athenians invented the notion of "political necessity" to disguise, even from themselves, their bloodlust.

> *Tell me,*
> *on what feeble grounds can you justify*
> *your vote of death?*
>   *Political necessity?*
> *But how? And do your politics require*
> *the shedding of human blood upon a grave...?*
>   [Euripides: *Hecuba,* 259-263]

The defenders of Homeric violence unconsciously knew that the radical moralists were right. Thucydides, deep in his psyche, recognized that what he preached was evil, but he was incapable of accepting the new moral position. Caught in this binding psychological trap, he created a defense that has been adopted by all the practitioners of *realpolitik,* amoral politics, and "value-free" intellectual endeavors: there is no evil—there is no good—all that motivates men is fear or power or ambition or political necessity. Praise is due the man who knows what he wants and knows how to get it. Condemnation is due those who get carried away by their emotions and lose their advantages.

Morality, that is a matter for school teachers or women.

Thucydides' history is the tragic story of how the defenders of sadistic violence won the great confrontation in Athenian culture. The plays of Euripides demonstrate how a proponent of the radical moral view felt himself becoming more and more isolated. Euripides' anger is directed at a society which is going mad, a situation in which he is helpless.

A detailed analysis of the History will demonstrate, I believe, the truth of these propositions.

THUCYDIDES' ANALYSIS OF SOCIETY

It is to Thucydides' lasting credit that he attempts to analyze all cultural behavior from a psychological point of view. He is deeply concerned with matters political, economic, and social, but, in the final analysis, when he attempts to explain *why* history took the course it did, his explanation is always in psychological terms. He has no doubt that what motivates men to action also motivates history.

He is keenly alert to the magical wishes of humankind—people tend to believe that what they want and what is are identical:

> The secret of this was their general extraordinary success, which made them confuse their strength with their hopes.
>
> [Book IV, LXV]

> ...for it is a habit of mankind to entrust to careless hope what they long for, and to use sovereign reason to thrust aside what they do not fancy.
>
> [Book IV, CVIII]

His psychology has a pessimistic bias, and he is most perceptive when revealing people's vices:

> Indeed it is generally the case that men are readier to call rogues clever than simpletons honest, and are as ashamed of being the second as they are proud of being the first.
>
> [Book III, LXII]

His analysis of people's reactions to the plague, and war in general, reveals how stress brings out the worst in them. He is keenly aware of those situations of psychological stress that cause people to regress and act with egocentricity and cruelty. He has no interest in examining what social conditions bring out the best in people, and he has no awareness that he might have been living in a particularly terrible time, from which it was dangerous to generalize. The Thirty Years' War, the Jacobean Terror, the purges of Josef Stalin, and the operation of the concentration camps were all critical phenomena of human history, but they are not the whole of that history. Decent, honest human behavior hardly exists in the pages of Thucydides.

> *But human nature never seems to change;*
> *evil stays itself, evil to the end,*
> *and goodness good, its nature uncorrupted*
> *by any shock or blow, always the same,*
> *enduring excellence.*
>
> [Euripides: *Hecuba,* 596-600]

Fear is a fundamental category in Thucydides' psychological analysis. Fear drove the Athenians to create an empire so that they would not be dominated by others; fear of future revolts made the Athenians commit genocide against reluctant or rebellious allies; fear drove the Spartans to war against Athens; fear forced the Athenians to invade Sicily in a suicidal expedition:

> "Now, as we have said, fear makes us hold our empire in Hellas, and fear makes us now come, with the help of our friends, to order safely matters in Sicily, and not to enslave any but rather to prevent any from being enslaved. Meanwhile, let no one imagine that we are interesting ourselves in you without your having anything to do with us, seeing that if you are preserved and able to make head against the Syracuseans, they will be less likely to harm us by sending troops to the Peloponnesians."
>
> [Book VI, LXXXIII-LXXXIV]

> *I killed him, and I admit it.*
>   *My action, however,*
> *was dictated, as you shall see, by a policy*
> *of wise precaution.*
>   *My primary motive was fear,*
> *fear that if this boy, your enemy, survived,*
> *he might someday found a second and resurgent Troy.*
> *Further, when the Greeks heard that Priam's son*
> *was still alive, I feared that they would raise*
> *a second expedition against this new Troy,*
> *in which case the fertile plains of Thrace*
> *would once again be ravaged by war...*
>
> [Euripides: *Hecuba,* 1137-1143]

In the first book of his history, Thucydides addressed himself to the problem of the true causes of the war. In his view, psychological considerations played the crucial role; the psychology of fear made the war inevitable:

> The Lacedaemonians voted that the treaty had been broken, and that war must be declared, not so much because they were persuaded by the arguments of the allies, as because they feared the growth of the power of the Athenians, seeing most of Hellas already subject to them.
>
> [Book I, LXXXVIII]

> *Achaeans! All your strength is in your spears, not in*
> *the mind. What were you afraid of, that it made you kill*
> *this child so savagely? ...*
>
> * * *
>
> ... I despise the fear
> which is pure terror in a mind unreasoning.
>
> [Euripides: *Trojan Women,* 1157-1166][13]

Related to fear, in a way that Thucydides hints at but never tries to explain, is a whole set of psychological drives: self-interest, ambition, honor and power. The implicit assumption in Thucydides' psychology is that the drives to power and domination are universal in all men, to a greater or lesser degree; such being the case, men become natural enemies to one another, since one man's or one nation's power can only be increased at the expense of another's freedom. War between nations, then, becomes inevitable. The wise man, the man worthy of admiration, is he who recognizes that this is so, proceeds with intelligence and caution in the pursuit of power, and does not get carried away by passion into doing things that are destructive to his own cause. Pericles and Thucydides were two such men, in the opinion of the historian.

Thucydides has no quarrel with Athenian imperialism. He does not believe that the war against the Peloponnesians was a mistake. Writing of his hero, he states: "For being the most powerful man of his time, and the leading Athenian statesman, he opposed the Lacedaemonians in everything, and would have no concessions but ever urged the Athenians on to war." [Book I, CXXVII.] He reiterates, and emphasizes, this point when he gives these words to Pericles:

> "It must be thoroughly understood that war is a necessity; but the more readily we accept it, the less will be the ardour of our opponents, and that out of the greatest dangers communities and in-

dividuals acquire the greatest glory.... We must not fall behind...but must resist our enemies in any way and in every way, and attempt to hand down our power to our posterity unimpaired."

[Book I, CXLIV]

After Pericles died, two years after the war began, the "democratic rabble" in Athens increasingly took control of the government, Thucydides tells us, and the intelligent war-imperial policy of Pericles was thrown to the winds. It was this that brought Athens down, in Thucydides' view—not the original commitment to violence—which is an unavoidable, even heroic aspect of human psychology.

When the war between Athens and Sparta began, Argos (a strong Peloponnesian power) was neutral because she had a thirty-year treaty of peace with Sparta. During the course of the Peloponnesian War that treaty ran out, and Argos "naturally" entered the war on the side of the Athenians: "Argos came in to the plan the more readily because she saw that war with Lacedaemon was inevitable, the truce being on the point of expiring; and also because she hoped to gain the supremacy of Peloponnese." [Book V, XXVIII.]

This passage is cause for wonder. For thirty years two powerful, neighboring states are kept at peace by a scrap of paper, and—suddenly—war is inevitable. It is important to observe that in Thucydides' psychology war is *always* inevitable, because the human drive for supremacy is inevitable.

One of Thucydides' methods of disarming the reader, and destroying morality as a basis of human actions, is to have the tyrants admit openly and freely that tyrants are exactly what they are. It is a virtue, Thucydides feels, not to make a pretense of caring about moral considerations. It is not a condemnation of tyranny, but a praise of honesty. "For what you hold," he causes Pericles to say, "is, to speak somewhat plainly, a tyranny; to take it perhaps was wrong, but to let it go is unsafe." [Book II, LXIII.]

In a similar fashion he has the Athenians preach to the Lacedaemonians:

"It follows that it was not a very wonderful action, or contrary to the common practice of mankind, if we did accept an empire that was offered to us, and refused to give it up under the pressure of three of the strongest motives, fear, honour, and interest. And it was not we who set the example, for it has always been the law that the weaker should be subject to the stronger."

[Book I, LXXVI]

Having excluded all moral considerations, Thucydides' psychology is a closed system. The insatiable drive towards power on the part of some, and the fear of others that they will be dominated, perpetuates forever the necessity of killing. His first book is devoted to examining the causes of the war; his psychology gives a "rational" answer: "The real cause I consider to be one which was formerly most kept out of sight. The growth of Athens, and the alarm which this inspired in Lacedaemon, made war inevitable." [Book I, XXIII.]

> *O witless mortals! Richly you deserve*
> *Your many woes; you listen not to friends,*
> *But to your interests. Cities! You might use*
> *Reason to end your troubles; but with blood,*
> *Not words, you ruin your affairs. — Enough!*
>   [Euripides: *Suppliant Women,* 745-750][14]

Having embraced *realpolitik,* Thucydides decided that war was inevitable, and assumed that he had come to the end of explanations. However, it may be asked whether it was true that the war could not have been avoided and if, having begun, it was destined to become a duel to the death. "When war is described as 'inevitable', we may be almost certain that its causes are not known."[15]

One of the most important causes of an "inevitable" war may be the fact that people have decided on its inevitability. "For it began now to be felt that the coming of the Peloponnesian war was only a question of time..." [Book I, XLIV.] We have all lived, during the past thirty years, under the threat of catastrophic war, with the power, ambition, and interests of two formidable nations poised against each other. As yet, that "inevitable" war has not come. There is no question that the most dangerous people in both camps are those who are convinced that war is destined. When General Curtiss LeMay urged us to "Nuk the Chinks" as the only tactic that would settle matters in Southeast Asia, he undoubtedly did so under the conviction that, war being inevitable, it was to our advantage to strike first. Those who decide that war is inevitable, before every means to prevent a confrontation has not been taken, do so because they love death and killing. For Thucydides, as for Athens and Sparta, war was inevitable because they were in love with it.

Thucydides' own recital of the facts contradicts the assumption that war could not have been avoided. One of the immediate causes of the war was a conflict between Corinth (an ally of Sparta) and Corcyra (a neutral state that possessed the third-largest fleet in Greece) over the city of Epidamnus. Corinth refused to settle the argument peacefully; the Corcyraeans sought an alliance with Athens. The latter accepted the alliance even though it was an undeniable provocation of Sparta, because the Athenians wanted the help of the Corcyraean navy in the coming "inevitable" war. Thucydides tells us:

> When the Corcyraeans heard of their preparations they came to Corinth with envoys from Lacedaemon and Sicyon, whom they persuaded to accompany them, and bade her recall the garrison and settlers, as she had nothing to do with Epidamnus. If, however, she had any claims to make, they were willing to submit matters to arbitration of such cities in the Peloponnese as should be chosen by mutual agreement [note that the Corcyraeans are willing to submit the quarrel for arbitration by the allies of *Corinth*], and that the colony should remain with the city to whom the arbitrators might assign it. They were also willing to refer the matter to the oracle at Delphi....The answer they got from Corinth was, that if they would withdraw their fleet... from Epidamnus negotiation might be possible; but, while the town was still being besieged, going before arbitration was out of the question. The Corcyraeans retorted that if Corinth would withdraw her troops from Epidamnus they would withdraw theirs, or they were ready to let both parties remain *in status quo,* an armistice being concluded till judgment could be given.
>
> Turning a deaf ear to all these proposals, when their ships were manned...the Corinthians sent a herald before them to declare war, and... sailed for Epidamnus to give battle to the Corcyraeans.
>
> [Book I, XXVIII-XXIX.]

> *Mindless, all of you, who in strength of spears*
> *and the tearing edge win your valors*
> *by war, thus stupidly trying*
> *to halt the grief of the world.*
> *For if bloody debate shall settle*
> *the issue, never again*
> *shall hate be gone out of the cities of men.*
> *By hate they won the chambers of Priam's city;*
> *they could have solved by reason and words*
> *the quarrel, Helen, for you.*
> *Now these are given to the Death God below.*
> [Euripides: *Helen,* 1151-1161][16]

The story of the Corinthians and the Corcyraeans is just one of several sets of circumstances in Thucydides' history in which offers of arbitration and efforts for peace are trampled upon. The war was inevitable only in the psyches of the men who made it.

THE EXORCISM OF MORALITY

In his exclusion of moral considerations, Thucydides goes far beyond the demands of "value free" history. He does not simply state that moral values have no place in "scientific" history, as many historians would do today. He attacks the concept that men are motivated by morality with a cold vehemence, as if he were afraid of some evil that had to be exorcised from his mind and from the state. "Even the most openly brutal book of our time, *Mein Kampf*, is based on some mystical faith in the destiny of Germany and its significance. But Cleon and Diodotus at Athens and Euphemos before the Sicilians, or the Athenian envoys at Sparta, speak openly of their state's imperialism and its cruelty, greed and aggressiveness, merely claiming for all these qualities the sanction of human behavior at any time... Nowhere does Thucydides vouch for the actual existence of a genuine power in the moral issues themselves."[17]

One may argue, in Thucydides' defense, that his purpose was not to have opinions on the behavior of men, but merely to show us men as they truly were, unsentimentalized, to give us the "facts" and let us judge for ourselves, if we insist upon judging. This argument will not hold. Firstly, Thucydides does give his personal opinions about many men and actions throughout the book: about Pericles, Theramenes, Hyperbolus, Nicias, and Cleon; about democracy, the insane violence of the Corcyraean revolution, and the slaughter of the children at Mycalesus.[18] Secondly, any sensitive reading of the *History* will clearly demonstrate that Thucydides admired the amoral attitude that considered problems only from the standpoint of self-interest and thrust aside "sentimental" moral considerations. "To Thucydides the really evil thing about Cleon's argumentation is not...the fact that he can discuss the question of putting several thousand Greeks to death purely from the point of view of Athenian self-interest, without one single hint or suggestion of a higher Justice or Humanity—he himself would have done the same had he spoken in the assembly—it was Cleon's unconscionable and outrageous stupidity.... Nor is the case presented by the Melians in the dialogue cynical. They are both given by Thucydides as pieces of sound and reasoned statesmanship, such statesmanship as Pericles, had he lived to see affairs reduced to such an imbroglio, would have been the first to approve."[19]

If Thucydides was not convinced that Athenian genocide was a moral catastrophe, he can be easily convicted of immorality. If he did think so, but refused to express his opinion, then he is guilty of something much more complicated: repression of his own moral instincts. Morality is never repressed, no matter what people may say, in the interests of "science" or "objectivity." Morality can only be repressed in the service of immorality. Euripides was famous in ancient times for portraying men not as they ideally should have been, but as they actually were. Euripides could be as coldly objective and analytical in his portrayal of the evil that men commit as anybody who has ever written anything. His judgment of evil was never "value-free"; his opinions and moral instincts were never repressed; the evil perpetrated by the city he loved made him sick at his heart.

During the course of the war, Mitylene, a subject state of the Athenian empire, revolted against her imperial masters. The rebellion was put down by Athenian arms, the leaders of the revolt were brought to Athens, and the fate of Mitylene was debated in the Athenian assembly. Democracy is no safeguard against barbarism. The assembly "...in the fury of the moment determined to put to death not only the prisoners at Athens, but the whole adult male population of Mitylene, and to make slaves of the women and children." [Book III, XXXVI.]

> *But let me review the facts.*
> *By majority vote the Greeks have decreed as follows:*
> *Your daughter, Polyxena, must die a victim*
> *and prize of honor for the grave of Achilles.*
>
> [Euripides: *Hecuba,* 219-222]

The Athenians, however, had not yet lost all trace of human feeling. Thucydides, in this single instance in the whole *History,* tells us that pity and sympathy for the victim played a role in human events:

> The morrow brought repentance with it and reflexion on the horrid cruelty of a decree, which condemned a whole city to the fate merited only by the guilty. This was no sooner perceived by the Mitylenian ambassadors at Athens and their Athenian supporters, than they moved the authorities to put the question again to the vote; which they the more easily consented to do, as they themselves plainly saw that most of the citizens wished some one to give them an opportunity for reconsidering the matter.
>
> [Book III, XXXVI]

The historian then proceeds to give us an idealized account of the second debate, wherein the matter was reconsidered and the original decision was reversed, it being decided to execute only the guilty and permit the rest of the city to live. What is remarkable in this account is that Diodotus, who speaks for moderation, and whose humane proposal carries the day, repeatedly emphasizes that sympathy for the victims, human compassion, should play absolutely no role in the decision. He abjures the moral position even though Thucydides himself has told us that they were moral considerations that brought on the reconsideration of the original decision. It is impossible that no speaker in the debate should have touched on matters of justice. Thucydides would have us believe that self-interest was the only "ideal" appealed to:

> "However, I have not come forward either to oppose or to accuse in the matter of Mitylene; indeed, the question before us as sensible men is not their guilt, but our interests. Though I prove them ever so guilty, I shall not, therefore, advise their death, unless it be expedient; nor though they should have claims to indulgence, shall I recommend it, unless it be clearly for the good of the country.... We are not in a court of justice, but in a political assembly; and the question is not justice, but how to make the Mitylenians useful to Athens."

* * *

> "Confess, therefore, that this is the wisest course, and without conceding too much either to pity or to indulgence, by neither of which motives do I any more than Cleon wish you to be influenced, upon the plain merits of the case before you, be persuaded by me to try calmly those of the Mitylenians whom Paches sent off as guilty, and to leave the rest undisturbed."

[Book III, XLIV and XLVII]

> *O gods, spare me the sight*
> *of this thankless breed, these politicians*
> *who cringe for favors from a screaming mob*
> *and do not care what harm they do their friends,*
> *providing they can please a crowd!*

[Euripides: Hecuba, 255-259]

Diodotus won the day; another ship was sent to Mitylene to counteract the first decree, and arrived just in time to prevent the slaughter. For the Mitylenians, it was life spared. For Athens, if Thucydides' account is near the truth, it was the death of the spirit.

In a similar fashion, in the famed debate between the Athenians and the Melians, Thucydides has the Athenians insist that matters of justice must play no role in the argument. The island of Melos, off the coast of Peloponnese, had been allied with the Spartans. The Athenians decided to bring it forcibly into alliance with themselves. The Melians refused the offer, fought for their freedom, and lost. Before the battle was joined, Thucydides has the two antagonists debate the validity of their positions.

The Athenians insist that there should be no "specious pretences" about right and justice, that both parties should stick to "the real sentiments"—

> "...since you know as well as we do that right, as the world goes, is only a question between equals in power, while the strong do what they can and the weak suffer what they must."
>
> [Book V, LXXXIX]

But the gods are strong, and over them
there stands some absolute, some moral order
or principle of law more final still.
Upon this moral law the world depends;
through it the gods exist; by it we live,
defining good and evil.

[Euripides: *Hecuba,* 799-804]

One can argue with a tiger only on its terms. Reluctantly, the Melians conformed to the rules imposed by the Athenians: " 'For here again if you debar us from talking about justice and invite us to obey your interest, we also must explain ours, and try to persuade you, if the two happen to coincide.' " [Book V, XC.]

Faced with the obliteration of their city, the Melians pitifully tried to find some words—any words—that might move this monster of cruelty:

> "As we think, at any rate, it is expedient—we speak as we are obliged, since you enjoin us to let right alone and talk only of interest —that you should not destroy what is our common protection, the privilege of being allowed in danger to invoke what is fair and right, and even to profit by arguments not strictly valid if they can be got to pass current. And you are as much interested in this as any, as your fall would be a signal for the heaviest vengeance and an example for the world to meditate upon."
>
> [Book V, XC.]

Hecuba: And when you were at my mercy, my slave then.
Do you remember what you said?
Odysseus: Said?
Anything I could. Anything to live.

[Euripides: *Hecuba,* 247-248]

We know from the plays of Euripides what is the end of such appeals for compassion made to gods or to politicians. The scientific recorder of the facts informs us that "the Athenians...put to death all the grown men whom they took, and sold the women and children for slaves..." [Book V, CXVI.] Thucydides' descriptions of atrocious events could be so cold-hearted that, even in ancient times, it was customary for him to be censured for relating them without expressing any disapproval.[20]

Homer, despite his ambivalence, fundamentally believed in the cruelty which he exalted. It is true that he also repressed the moral voice within himself which proclaimed the actions of his heroes as something less than admirable. But on the whole, his faith in glory, honor, and courage in battle was firm. Thucydides, Pericles, and Alcibiades had lost that faith. They unconsciously knew, in a way in which Homer did not, that their commitment was not to glory and courage, but to evil. Yet they could not abandon that commitment. They loved cruelty, and pretended otherwise. The moral voice was the one thing they could not permit because it exposed the hypocrisy of their position. Intent on extirpating it, they accelerated the violence in their lives, hoping in that way to resolve their conflict and drown conscience in a river of blood. As Thucydides remarked, they used "sovereign reason to thrust aside what they did not fancy."

In the latter part of the fifth century, the inquiring intellectual mind of the Greeks attempted to deal with the problem that the gods of their culture were often depicted as conducting themselves in an immoral manner. As we have seen, Aeschylus believed that this necessitated a transformation of the gods. In the next century, Plato dealt with the problem by dictating that in his ideal state no stories could be told which showed the gods as acting unjustly. The aspect of this controversy about the gods which appealed most to the mind of Thucydides was the idea that the gods' immorality was a license for men to go out and do the same. The Athenians to their Melian victims, before the sacrifice:

"When you speak of the favour of the gods, we may as fairly hope for that as yourselves; neither our pretensions nor our conduct being in any way contrary to what men believe of the gods, or practice among themselves. Of the gods we believe, and of men we know, that by a necessary law of their nature they rule wherever they can. And it is not as if we were the first to make this law, or to act upon it when made: we found it existing before us, and shall leave it to exist for ever after us; all we do is to make use of it, knowing that you and everybody else, having the same power as we have, would do the same as we do. Thus, as far as the gods are concerned, we have no fear and no reason to fear that we shall be at a disadvantage..."

[Book V, CV]

I do not believe the gods commit

adultery, or bind each other in chains.
I never did believe it; I never shall;
nor that one god is tyrant of the rest.
If god is truly god, he is perfect,
lacking nothing. These are poets' wretched lies.

[Euripides: *Heracles,* 1341-1346][21]

The depths of Thucydides' immorality, under the disguise of amorality, is revealed in his descriptions of the class struggles that are shocking the Greek world at the same time as the great power struggle between Athens and the Peloponnesians. Thucydides' method is to equate these two struggles; he argues that the war between the commons and the aristocrats in the cities is exactly the same thing as the power struggle between Athens and Sparta. Just as Thucydides sees this latter conflict as a drama of power politics between two great states, with justice or the right on neither side, so he views the class conflicts within the cities. Commons and aristocrats both wanted power, as human nature dictates. Their interests were incompatible, and thus fighting and violence were inevitable. Thucydides never raises the question of whether the commons or their aristocratic rivals had more moral right on their side, as if the rule by the few or the rule by all were morally indistinguishable. By reducing *all* politics to a struggle for power, he forcibly represses the moral instincts:

The sufferings which revolution entailed upon the cities were many and terrible, such as have occurred and always will occur, as long as the nature of mankind remains the same; though in a severer or milder form, and varying in their symptoms, according to the variety of the particular cases.

[Book III, LXXXII]

When Thucydides addresses himself to the causes of these class struggles, we hear nothing of economic inequality, nothing of oppression and the tyranny of a few over the many. He is oblivious to the drive for freedom and liberty. It never occurs to him consciously that, if the struggle is for power, then justice dictates that power *ought* to belong to all the people in society, not to a tyrannical few. One thing he understands, and he understands it well, is the lust for power:

The cause of all these evils was the lust for power arising from greed and ambition; and from these passions proceeded the violence of parties once engaged in contention...

[Book III, LXXXII]

Having excluded all motives of justice and morality from his psychology, Thucydides is left with a brutish human nature, only too ready to commit brutal acts.

The creation of a viable democratic state, albeit slave-owning and imperialist, was one of the great moral achievements of Greek culture in the fifth century. It is reasonable to assume that there was a large group of decent, honorable people in such states, because no democracy can function for any length of time without them. In the pages of the historian Thucydides we get absolutely no hint that any such group of people ever existed. For this writer the democratic citizen is part of a violence-prone rabble, lusting for power, played upon by immoral demagogues, kept in control for a short while by the superior intelligence of Pericles. If such a description is accurate, if the decent citizen who understood democracy and its great moral purpose did not exist, we have a right to wonder how Athenian democracy lasted even for one month. Certainly we cannot explain its viability for over a hundred years on the evidence presented in this history.

We may turn to the words of Euripides for a complete picture of "human nature," for proof that such people did exist, even though for Thucydides they were invisible:

> *But at last*
> *someone stood up to take the other side.*
> *Nothing much to look at, but a real man;*
> *not the sort one sees loafing in the market*
> *or public places, ma'am, but a small farmer,*
> *part of that class on which our country depends;*
> *an honest, decent, and god-fearing man,*
> *and anxious, in the name of common sense,*
> *to say his bit.*

[Euripides: *Orestes,* 916-922][22]

In the play, the proposition of the honest, decent man was defeated. The vote in the assembly was for death. It was a vision of Athens.

CONSCIENCE AND PARANOIA

Despite Thucydides' overwhelming concern with power he fails to understand it, because his conception of power is essentially paranoid. The paranoid view of power knows only two alternatives: rule others tyrannically or submit to weakness and be tyrannized. A third possibility, the holding of power in a non-tyrannical way, it cannot conceive.

Once one assumes the world offers only tyranny or submission, there is no question what a "real man" will choose. Pericles to his constituents:

> "Besides, to recede is no longer possible, if indeed any of you in the alarm of the moment has become enamoured of the honesty of such an unambitious part. For what you hold is, to speak somewhat plainly, a tyranny; to take it perhaps was wrong, but to let it go is unsafe. And men of these retiring views, making converts of others, would quickly ruin a state...[I]n fine, such qualities are useless to an imperial city, though they may help a dependency to an unmolested servitude."
>
> [Book II, LXIII]

"Tyranny or servitude" is always the paranoid slogan. Those who advocate moderation or sanity in political affairs are always subject to the charge of being weak and unmanly.

This excuse for tyrannical behavior is repeated many times in the *History*. The Athenian ambassador to Sicily uses the new sophistic rationalism to explain the world to the incredulous Sicilians:

> "We assert that we are rulers in Hellas in order not to be subjects; liberators in Sicily that we may not be harmed by the Sicilians; that we are compelled to interfere in many things, because we have many things to guard against..."
>
> [Book VI, LXXXVII]

The mark of the paranoid mentality is that, in rhetoric, words are distorted to mean their opposites. Enslavers become "liberators"; a brutal, senseless war is undertaken "to save the world for Democracy"; a constant state of cold-war crisis becomes "Peace in our time." It is not merely a case of hypocrisy. The paranoid public personality, deeply committed to evil violence, cannot really ignore the demands of conscience, especially in public utterances delivered to the society as a whole. Unable to overlook conscience, it distorts the voice of it, and tries to make it appear that conscience itself is dictating the drive towards tyranny and violence.

The paranoid political personality lives in a constant state of crisis. If no crisis exists, it will invent one. We have seen, in the last thirty years of the United States' history, what great damage the paranoid mentality can do to a culture. We have observed Mr. James Forrestal, a U.S. Secretary of Defense, who, when sane, was making decisions that determined whether we would all be blown to pieces or not, go insane and declare that he could see the Russian tanks treading their way down Pennsylvania Avenue. We have watched a President of the United States, as he was

about to be reelected by one of the greatest margins in history, afraid
that he might be beaten, prepare a list of his "enemies" for retribution.
We have seen this country sacrifice 50,000 young men because, even
though China, the third-most powerful country in the world, had
become Communist twenty years before, the security of the United
States was being threatened. We would all be unable to sleep securely at
night if Ho Chi Minh became the ruler of Vietnam. The noise of the
dominoes falling would keep us awake.

Preferring crisis to peace, the paranoid mentality becomes reckless
when it cannot force a crisis, or resolve one that it has created. Ultimately,
it prefers suicide to a rational reconciliation of problems. The Athenian
expedition to Sicily was suicidally reckless. Alcibiades was the leader
of the faction advocating the move. Thucydides was an admirer of this
ward of Pericles, and puts into his mouth the paranoid creed, succinct
and unadorned:

> "Men do not rest content with parrying the attacks of a superior, but
> often strike the first blow to prevent the attack being made. And we
> cannot fix the exact point at which our empire shall stop; we have
> reached a position in which we must not be content with retaining
> but must scheme to extend it, for, if we cease to rule others, we are in
> danger of being ruled ourselves."
>
> [Book VI, XVIII]

The paranoid, constantly expectant of attack, sees enemies
everywhere, because, amongst other reasons, he is in fear of being
punished by conscience for his commitment to destruction. The repressed
conscience returns with a cry for vengeance. Thucydides is capable,
under certain circumstances, of using the normal standards of justice,
morality, and civilized behavior to condemn acts of brutality. These
judgments indicate that Thucydides understood how a normal human
conscience is supposed to react. That he would appeal to conscience in
some instances and totally ignore its existence in others is an indication
of the extent of the conflict he maintained in regard to moral considerations.

Twice in the *History* Thucydides unequivocally condemns acts of
brutality. Ultimately, these condemnations do not serve the general interest of morality. Like Homer's censure of Achilles "barbarism," they
serve another purpose: they excuse the common, ordinary, day-to-day
brutality of the heroes Thucydides admires.

The first of two instances concerns Corcyra. During the course of the
war, class warfare erupted in that city. The adherents of both sides
resorted to the most extreme measures in order to defeat their enemies. It

seemed that no aspect of human brutality, barring cannibalism, was excluded from the tactics used on both sides. In judging the actions of this social warfare, Thucydides even resorts to those age-old laws of right and wrong that Euripides desperately tried to maintain. "Thus religion was in honour with neither party; but the use of fair phrases to arrive at guilty ends was in high reputation" [Book IV, LXXXII], he tells us. And further:

> Indeed men often take upon themselves the prosecution of their revenge to set the example of doing away with those general laws to which all alike can look for salvation in adversity, instead of allowing them to subsist against the day of danger when their aid may be required.
>
> [Book III, LXXXIV]

Can this, indeed, be the same person who told of the massacres of Melos and Scione with no comment? Ironically, it was Thucydides himself who had the Melians warn the Athenians that if they overthrew all the rational laws of justice, their own fall someday would call forth the most terrible vengeance [Book V, XC]. The Athenians paid no heed to this reminder of "the general laws of which all alike can look for salvation in adversity," and went out and massacred the city. Why did Thucydides make no moral comment on that action, and yet, in the case of Corcyra, argue like Euripides at his best?

Corcyra, it must be remembered, was a circumstance of class struggle. Radical democrats, lusting for power, oblivious to the demands of traditional morality, contended against the established aristocracy in the most brutal manner, the historian tells us. This was not legitimate violence, Thucydides implies. Legitimate violence occurs when the two great powers, Athens and Sparta, commit genocide or massacre helots, in the service of "their interests" and "rational policy." When the "mob," the "democratic rabble," insists on doing the same kind of thing to serve its "interests," then it must be condemned and shown to be a destroyer of the culture. Thucydides' moral protestations in the circumstance of Corcyra were nothing more than a hypocritical use of a moral stance to serve a narrow, immoral political purpose.

Similar is Thucydides' telling of the story of Mycalessus. Some Thracian tribesmen had been enlisted by Athens. Having no further use for them, the Athenians sent them home. Traveling to Thrace by land, they used the opportunity to do some mischief to the enemies of Athens:

> The Thracians bursting into Mycalessus sacked the houses and temples, and butchered the inhabitants, sparing neither youth nor

age, but killing all they fell in with, one after the other, children and
women, and even beasts of burden, and whatever other living
creatures they saw; the Thracian race, like the bloodiest of the barbarians, being ever most so when it has nothing to fear. Everywhere
confusion reigned and death in all its shapes; and in particular they
attacked a boys' school, the largest that there was in the place, into
which the children had just gone, and massacred them all. In short,
the disaster falling upon the whole town was unsurpassed in
magnitude and unapproached by any in suddenness and in horror.

[Book VII, XXIX]

Such richness of detail, such delineation of the horror, we do not get
when the Athenians destroyed Melos. We are not told how or where the
Melians were killed, nor what was done with so many corpses. We are
not informed what were the reactions of the "fortunate" Melian women
and children who were not killed, but had to watch their husbands and
fathers being slaughtered. The Athenians never "butchered" anyone—
merely killed them. And the business-oriented saviors of Greece never
would have been so stupid as to kill valuable animals.

We have been to this immoral place before. We have witnessed
Homer's insistence that there is a profound difference between "barbaric
brutality" and the legitimate violence of his heroes. Thucydides' condemnation of the barbarians rings as empty as Homer's. For both, such
criticism was an excuse to go on killing other men in a "civilized" way.
Aeschylus' great lesson that all evil is connected to all other evil was lost
on Thucydides and Athens. Greek culture did not regress into barbarism—Homer and Thucydides made sure of that—but it never succeeded in freeing itself from the lust to annihilate. Thucydides and
Homer made that certain as well.

ILLUSIONS AND SUICIDE

The primary illusion of the "value-free" historian or sociologist is that
one can think productively about human culture even though one ignores
moral values. A second illusion of such analysts is that they have no illusions. Determined to be as "scientific" as possible, Thucydides prided
himself that his approach was devoid of the illusionary, that he dealt
with all matters in a hyper-rational manner. Such was not the case. The
moral instincts can only be repressed by denying reality; the denial of
reality results in a compensatory belief in what is not real. One of
Thucydides' most important illusions was his magical belief in the
power of the great man.

First there was Pericles. Pericles was wise, rational, and moderate in his approach, the historian tells us. He, and only he, had the power to control the destructive impulses in the democratic "rabble" at Athens. If he had only lived on, all the evils that befell this great state never would have happened:

> In short, what was nominally a democracy became in his hands government by the first citizen. With his successors it was different. More on a level with one another, and each grasping at supremacy, they ended by committing even the conduct of state affairs to the whims of the multitude.
>
> [Book II, LXV]

Thucydides' attitude towards Pericles is similar to those illusioned by Soviet Russia, who, when they began to be disillusioned by Stalin, still could not give up the fantasy and were determined to think that everything would have been all right "if only Lenin had lived." They failed to see that Stalinisn was implicit in Leninism. Similarly, Thucydides will not see that the accelerating violence of Athenian political life was implicit in Pericles' imperial policy, that the "mob" was only doing in its crude way what Pericles had done in a sophisticated manner.

The fact is that Pericles, even when alive, was never as much in control of the situation as Thucydides would have us believe. "Though Pericles was returned to office a few months before his death, the fact that he had been deposed as early as the second year of the war shows the disunion that already existed in Athens."[23] Having rejected a belief in moral values, Thucydides still had to believe in *something*. Amongst other things that he discovered for Western culture, he was also the first to give us the myth of the great man in history.

Secondly, there was Alcibiades. A person of enormous energy, capacity, and vanity, Alcibiades, a thoroughly amoral/immoral man, was a person about whom everyone had strong opinions. Thucydides was alone, among ancient and modern observers, in stating that Alcibiades, and only Alcibiades, could have kept, and would have kept, Athens from ruin, if he had not been banished by the state:

> For the position he held among the citizens led him to indulge his tastes beyond what his real means would bear, both in keeping horses and in the rest of his expenditures; and this later on had not a little to do with the ruin of the Athenian state. Alarmed at the greatness of his license in his own life and habits, and of the ambition which he showed in all things soever that he undertook, the mass of the people set him down as a pretender to the tyranny, and

became his enemies; and although publicly his conduct of the war was as good as could be desired, individually, his habits gave offence to every one, and caused them to commit affairs to other hands, and thus before long to ruin the city.

[Book VI, XV]

When Alcibiades fled from captivity in order not to be tried in Athens, he turned traitor and proceeded directly to *Sparta,* offering all his resources, knowledge, and intelligence to the Peloponnesians in order to revenge himself on those at Athens who had turned on him. Such a man Thucydides expected to be the savior of the city. If Alcibiades had only stayed in office instead of being hounded out by the "rabble," the historian tells us, everything would have been all right. From the creator of "scientific" history, a bedtime story.

And yet
we boast, are proud, we plume our confidence—
the rich man in his insolence of wealth,
the public man's conceit of office or success—
and we are nothing; our ambition, greatness, pride,
all vanity.

[Euripides: *Hecuba,* 623-627]

Alcibiades was a prime mover in the Athenian expedition to Sicily, the disastrous outcome of which was the single most important factor leading to the ultimate defeat of Athens in the war. Even though Athens continued to fight for more than ten years, her power had been broken in Sicily. The decision to invade Sicily was taken at a time when the Athenian military situation was somewhat stronger than it had been when the war started. Argos, a Peloponnesian land power, was now allied with Athens against Sparta. The deficiency of land forces was Athens' greatest weakness in the first ten years of the war; this alliance with Argos strengthened the Athenian military position in exactly the place where aid was needed. Despite the fact that the Athenians could now expect a great increase in their military effectiveness against the Spartans, the Athenian assembly voted to undertake a massive invasion of Sicily, the advantages of which were unclear and the risks enormous. Success in this expedition would not have made Athens invincible; failure might have jeopardized the whole war effort. There was something peculiarly reckless in risking all on one action by which there was so much to lose and not that much to gain—reckless to the point of suicide.

Opinion at Athens was divided on the advisability of going to Sicily. Nicias, an important general, a moderate man, for whom Thucydides has sympathy, was opposed to the expedition, and talked sense to a people unwilling to hear it:

> "A man ought, therefore, to consider these points, and not to think of running risks with a country placed so critically, or of grasping another empire before we have secured the one we have already; for in fact the Thracian Chalcidians have been all these years in revolt from us without being yet subdued, and others on the continents yield us but a doubtful obedience."
>
> [Book VI, X]

Nicias used all kinds of strategies to get the Athenians to desist. When they asked him what manner of forces he would need to succeed, he asked for an armament so large that he felt the assembly would decline to give it. He was wrong. They voted him the largest fleet ever assembled at Athens.

> *Hope has driven*
> *many cities against each other; she stirs*
> *an overreaching heart; she is not to be trusted.*
> *When the people vote on war, nobody reckons*
> *on his own death; it is too soon; he thinks*
> *some other man will meet that wretched fate.*
> *But if death faced him when he cast his vote,*
> *Hellas would never perish from battle-madness.*
> [Euripides: *Suppliant Women,* 478-485]

Thucydides prided himself on his moderation, which, he thought, separated him from the irresponsible democratic "mob." And yet, in the most crucial decision the "mob" took during the war, he is at one with it. Forswearing Nicias' sound advice, Thucydides' heart was with those bent upon self-destruction. The expedition, he tells us, did not fail because the original decision was reckless:

> This, as might be expected in a great and sovereign state, produced a host of blunders, and amongst them the Sicilian expedition; though this failed not so much through a miscalculation of the power of those against whom it was sent, as through a fault in the senders in not taking the best measures afterwards to assist those who had gone out, but choosing rather to occupy themselves with private cabals for the leadership of the commons, by which they not only paralyzed operations in the field, but also first introduced civil discord at home.
>
> [Book II, LXV]

This last is an incredible statement. His own evidence proves that such was not the case. The Athenians at home gave every support imaginable to the forces at Sicily. When Nicias found himself in trouble and asked for reinforcements, they were sent with dispatch and in large numbers. No discord at home kept the troops in the field in want.

Thucydides is intent on not seeing what is obvious: that Athenian failure to win the war and inability to make any kind of peace was producing a state of tension within the body politic. The city did what an individual might do under a similar state of severe tension, something grandly reckless to ease the conflict, no matter what the cost: "Triumph or death!" "Victory or suicide!" The moderate, rational Thucydides never condemned this most reckless action; he admired the "courage" that could make it happen:

> But what most oppressed them was that they had two wars at once, and had thus reached a pitch of frenzy which no one would have believed possible if he had heard of it before it had come to pass. For could any one have imagined that even when besieged by the Peloponnesians entrenched in Attica, they would still, instead of withdrawing from Sicily, stay on there besieging in like manner Syracuse, a town (taken as a town) in no way inferior to Athens, or would so thoroughly upset the Hellenic estimate of their strength and audacity, as to give the spectacle of a people which, at the beginning of the war, some thought might hold out one year, some two, none more than three, if the Peloponnesians invaded their country, now seventeen years after the first invasion, after having already suffered from all the evils of war, going to Sicily and undertaking a new war nothing inferior to that which they already had with the Peloponnesians?
>
> [Book VII, XXVIII]

> *And you have power,*
> *Odysseus, greatness and power. But clutch them gently,*
> *use them kindly, for power gives no purchase*
> *to the hand, it will not hold, soon perishes,*
> *and greatness goes.*
>
> [Euripides: *Hecuba,* 282-284]

It was, indeed, a tragic tale, but no great tragic poet lived to tell its story. Tragic poetry was also a victim of this war. What perished in the war of the Athenians against the Peloponnesians were not only the hundreds of thousands killed. Lost forever was an Athens that a great, moral man could believe in. Aeschylus' faith that his city would maintain the moral leadership of the world would never revive. Athens would continue to exist; Athens' great achievements would continue to be admired by many. But the Athens that had the possibility of permanently transforming the Homeric view of the world into a higher order of morality had been lost in a world of suicidal imperialism.

X
The Failure of Love

"Was it the horse that refused, or the rider? That is really the crucial question. Personally, I believe it was the horse—in other words, those irrational elements in human nature which govern without our knowledge so much of our behaviour and so much of what we think is our thinking."[1]

Granting the truth of Dodd's contention that Greek culture deliberately refused an advance that would have extended the boundaries of human independence, we are faced with an equally important question: Why did the horse refuse? Was it a "failure of nerve," as many have postulated, that inhibited the horse? Did Greek society suffer from a lack of courage and strength and a kind of reckless bravery that would make the horse jump? Does our reading of Homer, of Thucydides, of the conquests of Philip and Alexander convince us that what Greek culture lacked, and needed most, was more heroic courage? When we compare Greek culture with ancient Israel, our other ancestor, when we realize that it was the merging of those two cultures that finally enabled the horse to take that particular leap successfully, do we find that Israel brought to that union the "nerve" that was lacking in pagan culture? Was it a failure of nerve or a failure of love that caused the horse to recoil?

Dodds vividly describes the collapse of moral and intellectual power in Greek culture that ensued when the culture declined to take that fateful leap: "A prevision of this history would have surprised an observer in the third century B.C. But it would have surprised him far more painfully to learn that Greek civilization was entering, not on an Age of Reason, but on a period of slow intellectual decline which was to last, with some deceptive rallies and some brilliant individual rear-guard actions, down to the capture of Byzantium by the Turks; that in all the sixteen centuries of existence still awaiting it the Hellenic world would produce no poet as good as Theocritus, no scientist as good as Eratosthenes, no mathematician as good as Archimedes, and that the one great name in philosophy would represent a point of view believed to be extinct—Transcendental Platonism."[2]

It was Gilbert Murray who described that decline as a "failure of nerve"—a phrase, he explains, he took from J. B. Bury. "We were discussing the change that took place in Greek thought between, say, Plato and the Neo-Platonists, or even between Aristotle and Posidonius, and which is seen in its highest power in the Gnostics. I had been calling it a rise of asceticism, or mysticism, or religious passion, or the like, when my friend corrected me. 'It is not a rise; it is a fall or failure of something, a sort of failure of nerve.' "[3]

Dodds, in turn, relates this concept of failure of nerve to a fear of freedom: "But behind such immediate causes we may perhaps suspect something deeper and less conscious: for a century or more the individual had been face to face with his own intellectual freedom, and now he turned tail and bolted from the horrid prospect—better the rigid determinism of the astrological Fate than that terrifying burden of daily responsibility."[4]

What is so terrifying within the concept of freedom that a whole culture would move toward sixteen centuries of decline and stagnation rather than accept its challenge? When a culture develops the strength to take that challenge, to live with the anxiety of freedom, is it the killing-nerve of the warrior-hero that provides the essential ingredient necessary to avoid retreat? Or is it *Eros* that makes the crucial difference?

Dodds relates the new freedom, from which Greek culture eventually fled, to the unconscious drives of the Oedipus complex. When a child or a culture comes face to face with this seemingly grotesque trial of the psyche, such child or culture, or the horse of each, may either take the leap or hesitate before finally resolving on a panic flight. Is it "nerve" or love the child needs most at such a time?

When my son was five years old, he and I were feeding fish on a lake. "I could push you in," he said, "and you would sink to the bottom, and I would not save you, and then I would have mommy all to myself."

Clearly, it took courage for the child to verbalize such a fantasy to his "rival," but the crucial aspect of the situation was that he had no great fear of retribution. The Oedipus complex occurs in the fourth or fifth

year of the child's life. By that time, he or she already has a long history
with his or her parents. The child knows what to expect from them. If
Freud postulated that the Oedipus complex is "smashed to pieces by the
shock of threatened castration," he did so because the model he had of a
father was a domineering, unloving tyrant. If the father conforms to this
model, it is undoubtedly true that the fear of castration will play a crucial
part in the repression of the Oedipus complex.

I do not know whether mothers and fathers in ancient Israel were more
loving than parents in ancient Greece. That is a matter for the new field
of psychohistory, and it is questionable what evidence remains by which
we could try a conclusion. In the area of the history of culture, however,
we do possess strong, incontrovertible evidence: the god of Israel,
although jealous and vengeful at times, was also a god of love, who was
prepared to forgive the transgressions of his people, who was ready to
save the most sinful city for one good man.

In Greece, such a god, such a mythical father, never existed, despite
the efforts of Aeschylus and Plato to create one. It is one thing to live in
a culture where, finding one's parents inadequate, one can resort to a
god who is truly loving. It is quite another thing to live in a culture where
the only alternative to unloving parents is the vengeance of Hera and
Athene.

We read of the first feeble effort to create a god of love in the *Iliad*. In
the fourth book Zeus makes an attempt to be a god of affection and
compassion:

> "Let us consider then how these things shall be accomplished,
> whether again to stir up grim warfare and the terrible
> fighting, or cast down love and make them friends with each other.
> If somehow this way could be sweet and pleasing to all of us,
> the city of lord Priam might still be a place men dwell in,
> and Menelaos could take away with him Helen of Argos."
>
> [IV 14-19]

Hera will have none of this:

> "Majesty, son of Kronos, what sort of thing have you spoken?
> How can you wish to make wasted and fruitless all this endeavour,
> the sweat that I have sweated in toil, and my horses worn out
> gathering my people, and bringing evil to Priam and his children.
> Do it then; but not all the rest of us gods will approve you."
>
> [IV 25-29]

Zeus stands corrected by his wife. He will be as great a hero as she:

"And put away in your thoughts this other thing that I tell you:
whenever I in turn am eager to lay waste some city,
as I please, one in which are dwelling men who are dear to you,
you shall not stand in the way of my anger, but let me do it,
since I was willing to grant you this with my heart unwilling."

[IV 39-43]

What, then, can we expect from Pericles, Alcibiades, or Thucydides? To
what god could the cities of Melos or Scione appeal?

In terms of its final effect on the culture, even the great creative
criticism of the gods by the tragic playwrights was no more effective than
Homer's pitiful attempt. Despite Aeschylus' efforts to create a god of
love out of his own mind, Aristotle could write, "It would be eccentric
for anyone to claim that he loved Zeus."[5]

Euripides' bitter criticisms produced no transformation: "Euripides
has summoned up the reasoning in the well-known sentence: 'If gods do
anything base, they are no gods.' ...It was not that the way was being
prepared for a higher conception of the gods; the old gods were under-
mined without any new and better gods being put in their stead."[6]

The failure of the tragic playwrights to create one play of true reconciliation, their failure to imagine one convincing and sustained scene of
love between father and son, indicates that they also were trapped by
these unloving gods no matter how hard they fought to liberate
themselves. The great psychological and cultural problems subsumed
under the Oedipus complex were incapable of solution because the essential element in such a solution was lacking: the conception of a father, or
at least a god, who could love his son to the point of giving him the
freedom to experience and express what is a human necessity, without
fear of retribution. When Cassandra in Aeschylus' *Agamemnon* finally
tells the Chorus that Agamemnon will be killed by his wife, they plead
with her to be still: "Peace, peace, poor woman; put those bitter lips to
sleep." "Useless," Cassandra replies, "there is no god of healing in this
story."[7] [1247-1248.] It is a motto that could be written over every page
of Greek history.

In the fourth century A.D., when pagan culture was replaced by a
revolutionary world-view, what kind of god ruled? Was he a god of
nerve, providing that essence the failure of which had produced the
decline of the pagan world? Clearly not. He was a god of love and did
provide what had been sorely lacking in pagan culture; the barbarism of
the Roman arena was extirpated, the revolutionary doctrine that even
slaves possess a soul and are loved by God was proclaimed, the central
rite of the new religion was communion, a ritual of affection between
people and God and among the worshipers with each other. The new
religion was unlike the mystery cults of the pagan world, which had been

private, particular, and precious. It was the official religion of the state and had the power of the state behind it. The troubles of humankind were hardly over, but the vision of Aeschylus had been fulfilled: *Eros* had triumphed—a transformation in culture had brought the establishment of the ideal of love.

It is instructive to see what kind of epic poetry this revolution in culture produced. The *Iliad* and *Beowulf* are both epic poems, fundamentally concerned with the concept of the warrior-hero. The development of the hero from Achilles to Beowulf signifies a fundamental transformation of the world.

CHRISTIAN HEROIC POETRY: *BEOWULF*

In the view of most scholars, *Beowulf* was composed in the eighth century A.D. by one poet. It was written in Anglo-Saxon for a community that was thoroughly Christianized, although the poem itself contains many references to Barbaric armament, funerals, and social customs. A general knowledge of Germanic heroic poetry is assumed by the poet on the part of his audience.

England, in the eighth century, was one of the most intellectually advanced countries in Europe. At that time the great Bede flourished and Alcuin was invited by Charlemagne to bring intellectual learning to his court. The heroic past is very much alive in the poem, but the world-view expressed is a deeply, even devoutly, felt Christian one.

Hrothgar, a most successful king of the Danes, has built himself a great battle hall to celebrate his many victories. For a while all goes well with the Danish king. Suddenly, one night, the monster Grendel comes to the hall and kills several of the Danes sleeping there. He repeats his visits nightly, and the Danes, helpless before Grendel's power, abandon the hall.

Beowulf, a nephew of the king of the Geats, journeys to Denmark to try his power against Grendel, sleeps in the battle hall, and kills the monster. Grendel's mother, as fiendish and powerful as her son, returns the next night and avenges her dead child by killing several of the king's men. After tracking her back to her lair, Beowulf succeeds in destroying Grendel's mother.

Beowulf returns to Geatland in triumph. Years pass. The old king Higlac and his son both die, and Beowulf becomes king of the Geats. In Beowulf's old age, a dragon, having been disturbed in his den by the theft of the treasure he was guarding, starts to ravage the land. The old king goes to fight the dragon, succeeds in killing him, but receives his own death-blow from the monster. Beowulf is buried as his people sing his praises.

Like the *Iliad,* this poem celebrates physical strength and courage in battle. Each of the three important charcters in the poem—Beowulf, Hrothgar, and Higlac—are great warriors. Like all heroic poetry, this poem assumes that one cannot be a hero unless one is a formidable soldier. However, in this epic-heroic poem of 3,182 lines, the hero kills no other human being. In fact, although many references are made to killings in the past and portended killings in the future, in the course of the poem itself no human being kills another. It is a radically different view of the world than the one given in the *Iliad.*

The hero does kill three monsters. These monsters are deliberately described by the poet as symbols of evil—human evil. What Beowulf struggles against is hatred, the human commitment to violence. He has been a great warrior, but the poem does not concern itself with killings in battle. He becomes a great champion of the good against the forces of cruelty. "The author has fairly exalted the fights with the fabled monsters into a conflict between the powers of good and evil. The figure of Grendel, at any rate, while originally an ordinary Scandinavian troll, and passing in the poem as a sort of man-monster, is at the same time conceived of as an impersonation of evil and darkness, even an incarnation of the Christian devil. Many of his appellations are unquestionable epithets of Satan...[H]e belongs to the wicked progeny of Cain, the first murderer, his actions are represented in a manner suggesting the conduct of the evil one... and he dwells with his demon mother in a place which calls up visions of hell."[8]

The first description we get of Grendel makes it clear that the poet has no intention of creating mere fairy-tale monsters:

> So Hrothgar's men lived happy in his hall
> Till the monster stirred, that demon, that fiend,
> Grendel, who haunted the moors, the wild
> Marshes, and made his home in a hell
> Not hell but earth. He was spawned in that slime,
> Conceived by a pair of those monsters born
> Of Cain, murderous creatures banished
> Of Abel's death. The Almighty drove
> Those demons out, and their exile was bitter,
> Shut away from men; they split
> Into a thousand forms of evil—spirits
> And fiends, goblins, monsters, giants,
> A brood forever opposing the Lord's
> Will, and again and again defeated.
>
> [101-114][9]

After Grendel's first attack, it is clear that it is evil as well as death which has triumphed:

> ...the only survivors
> were those who fled him. Hate had triumphed
> So Grendel ruled, fought with the righteous,
> One against many, and won...
>
> [142-145]

Even when the poet recounts tales from older heroic poetry, he always puts them in a moral context, which we may assume they did not originally have. He is intent on making evil the real enemy of all heroes:

> And sometimes a proud old soldier
> Who had heard songs of the ancient heroes
> And could sing them all through, story after story,
> Would weave a net of words for Beowulf's
> Victory, tying the knot of his verses
> Smoothly, swiftly, into place with a poet's
> Quick skill, singing his new song aloud
> While he shaped it, and the old songs as well—Siegmund's
> Adventures, familiar battles fought
> By that glorious Son of Vels. And struggles,
> Too, against evil and treachery that no one
> Had ever heard of, that no one knew
> Except Fitla, who had fought at his uncle's side...
>
> [867-879]

The ideal that the principal function of the hero is to struggle against evil is a critical step in the development of culture and conscience. Nothing is more effective in the sublimation of aggression than the process of using aggressive energy to fight for morality against the forces of violence within the culture and within oneself. Such a process of sublimation goes far beyond mere substitution or displacement, as in the replacement of athletic competition for warfare. Beowulf is as large, as strong, as powerful, as capable of killing other warriors as any hero in his world, but his heroic prowess is used to civilize and moralize the world.

Klaeber writes that the morality of the hero is not merely one possible variation of an old heroic theme; it is central to the form of the poem: "The poet has raised him to the rank of a singularly spotless hero, a 'defending, protecting, redeeming being,' a truly ideal character. We might even feel inclined to recognize features of the Christian Savior in the destroyer of hellish fiends, the warrior brave and gentle, blameless in thought and deed, the king that dies for his people. Though delicately kept in the background, such a Christian interpretation of the main story on the part of the Anglo-Saxon author could not but give added strength and tone to the entire poem. It helps to explain one of the great puzzles of our epic. It would indeed be hard to understand why the poet contented himself with a plot of mere fabulous adventures so much inferior to the splendid heroic setting, unless the narrative derived a superior dignity from suggesting the most exalted hero-life known to Christians.''[10]

Culturally considered, the exciting thing about this poem is that the function of the good, loving hero is not merely to demonstrate the value of virtue over evil; Beowulf's function is nothing less than a transformation of the heroic world-view. Beowulf lives in the world of epic; he is better at being a warrior-hero than any of his contemporaries; no one can accuse him of choosing the loving virtues because he lacks manliness or courage. His true function is to provide the forms of transformation out of the old heroic trap. If Hektor had listened to his wife on the battlements and refused to go back into the fighting, what kind of life could he have lived? What would he have done with all his energy and power? In *Beowulf* a viable alternative is lived—the good hero uses his heroism to fight evil.

That such was the poet's deliberate intention is confirmed by the many examples in the poem where the loving virtues of the hero are contrasted with the moral inadequacy of the heroes of the older stories. The bard sings of the contrast between the life of Beowulf and that of Hermod, a legendary king of the Danes:

> ...he was once the mightiest
> Of men. But pride and defeat and betrayal
> Sent him into exile with the Jutes, and he ended
> His life on their swords. That life had been misery
> After misery, and he spread sorrow as long
> As he lived it, heaped troubles on his unhappy people's
> Heads, ignored all wise men's warnings,
> Ruled only with courage. A king
> Born, entrusted with ancient treasures
> And cities full of stronghearted soldiers,
> His vanity swelled him so vile and rank
> That he could hear no voices but his own. He deserved
> To suffer and die. But Beowulf was a prince
> Well-loved, followed in friendship, not fear;
> Hermod's heart had been hollowed by sin.

[901-915]

The last lines of this epic concern themselves with the funeral of the hero, just as the *Iliad* closes with the funeral rites for Hektor. All people are praised over their graves. The crucial question for a culture is what qualities of the hero are chosen for praise and what relationship that praise has to the reality of the hero's life:

> So should all men
> Raise up words for their lords, warm
> With love, when their shield and protector leaves
> His body behind, sends his soul
> On high. And so Beowulf's followers
> Rode, mourning their beloved leader,
> Crying that no better king had ever
> Lived, no prince so mild, no man
> So open to his people, so deserving of praise.

[3174-3182]

Homer's last words for Hektor were that he was a "breaker of horses." We know he was a breaker of men as well.

Intimately related to this general atmosphere of virtue and love is the fact that Beowulf's relationships to two older kings, father figures who wield legitimate power, were primarily affectionate. After reading of all the disasters of Oedipal aggression delineated by Homer, after regarding the disturbing failures of reconciliation conceived by the tragic poets, it is amazing to come into a world where the young hero regards old kings as a source and an object of love and not of ambivalent hatred. Beowulf kills evil monsters because he has gone beyond the limited, paralyzing aggression of the Oedipal situation. Beowulf returns home to Geatland and his king Higlac after his triumphs in Denmark:

> Beowulf had brought his king
> Horses and treasure—as a man must,
> Not weaving nets of malice for his comrades,
> Preparing their death in the dark, with secret
> Cunning tricks. Higlac trusted
> His nephew, leaned on his strength, in war,
> Each of them intent on the other's joy.

[2165-2171]

The *Beowulf* poet and his audience knew that the situation, often dealt with in older heroic poetry, of an old king dying and leaving the throne to a young or less-than-competent son was filled with the possibilities of treachery. There was always the danger that some ambitious warrior of ripe years would slay the legitimate heir to the throne and take over the kingdom. The poet tells us that in Beowulf's lifetime he himself had to respond to aggressive temptations in such a circumstance. The old king Higlac died when his son was not yet capable of assuming the full burden of the kingship. Higlac's widow even offered the kingdom to Beowulf, which would have given legitimacy but not moral sanction to rebellion on his part. However, Beowulf's unambivalent love for his king and uncle extended to the king's son as well:

> Higlac's widow
> Brought him the crown, offered him the kingdom,
> Not trusting Herdred, her son and Higlac's,
> To beat off foreign invaders. But Beowulf
> Refused to rule when his lord's son
> Was alive, and the leaderless Geats could choose
> A rightful king. He gave Herdred
> All his support, offering an open
> Heart where Higlac's young son could see
> Wisdom he still lacked himself: warmth
> And good will were what Beowulf brought his new king.
>
> [2369-2379]

In this Christian epic we are also witness to a full, loving, unambivalent embrace of the kind that Heracles intended to give his father before he was commanded to march. Beowulf is about to depart from Denmark, to return home:

> The old king kissed him,
> Held that best of all warriors by the shoulder
> And wept, unable to hold back his tears.
> Gray and wise, he knew how slim
> Were his chances of ever greeting Beowulf
> Again, but seeing his face he was forced
> To hope. His love was too warm to be hidden,
> His tears came running too quickly to be checked;
> His very blood burned with longing.
>
> [1870-1878]

Only after a pagan culture had been transformed by the ideals of Israel could such a scene have been written in heroic-epic poetry.

If *Beowulf* concerned itself only with a struggle against monsters and loving relationships between human beings, it might be important evidence for cultural development, but it would lack the tension

necessary for great art. If we were presented with no insight into cruelty
and evil, we would learn nothing of why love is so important—and so
difficult. The poem does abound with incidents of treachery and cruelty,
but these either have occurred in the past or are destined to take place in
the future. In the present, in the course of the poem, no such human
aggression occurs. The poet creates his form, in part, out of a profound
tension between an ideal of human behavior and the gross reality of
human existence. The tension is built temporally: to the present belongs
the ideal, to the past and the future belong the cruel reality. The heroes
of the past become examples of what one should not be. Hrothgar advises Beowulf in what manner he should lead men:

> "Be not
> As Hermod once was to my people, too proud
> To care what their hearts hid, bringing them
> Only destruction and slaughter. In his mad
> Rages, he killed them himself, comrades
> And followers who ate at his table. At the end
> He was alone, knew none of the joys of life
> With other men, a famous ruler
> Granted greater strength than anyone
> Alive in his day but dark and bloodthirsty,
> In spirit. He shared out no treasure, showed
> His soldiers no road to riches and fame.
> And then that affliction on his people's face
> Suffered horribly for his sins. Be taught
> By his lesson, learn what a king must be:
> I tell his tale, old as I am,
> Only for you."
>
> [1709-1725]

The one device, used over and over in the poem, which brings all the
major themes together, is the immediate juxtaposition of past or future
human violence with the present evil of the monsters. These juxtaposi-
tions clearly demonstrate that the author conceives the monsters as symbols of *human* evil and that Beowulf's great heroism is congruent with
his struggle against human cruelty and immorality.

The very first mention of Grendel occurs in line 86 of the poem. The
poet is describing the great battle hall built by Hrothgar:

> ...that most beautiful of dwellings, built
> As he'd wanted, and then he whose word was obeyed
> All over the earth named it Herot.
> His boast come true he commanded a banquet,

Opened out his treasure-filled hands.

[77-81]

In the future, however, long after Beowulf destroys the monsters who ravaged the great hall, Herot will be burned in a dispute over Hrothgar's throne. His sons will not peacefully succeed to his kingdom, and the violence done in those struggles will destroy the hall. The poet does not tell the story, but his contemporary listeners knew the tale. The poem continues:

That towering place, gabled and huge,
Stood waiting for time to pass, for war
To begin, for flames to leap as high
As the feud that would light them and for Herot to burn.

[82-85]

Immediately after we are told that the glory of Herot will be short-lived, destroyed by human violence, we are given our first introduction to Grendel:

A powerful monster, living down
In darkness, growled in pain, impatient
As day after day the music rang
Loud in that hall...

[86-89]

In a similar fashion, after Beowulf arrives in Denmark, when he sits down to table in the great hall, he is taunted by one of Hrothgar's men, Unferth, who questions Beowulf's powers and reputation. Beowulf first defends his own reputation and then turns to attack Unferth. We learn that Unferth has committed violent aggression in the past, immediately following the revelation of which a reference is made to what Grendel is doing to the Danes:

"...And there's more: you murdered your brothers,
Your close kin. Words and bright wit
Won't help your soul; you'll suffer hell's fires,
Unferth, forever tormented. Ecglaf's
Proud son, if your hands were as hard, your heart
As fierce as you think it, no fool would dare
To raid your hall, ruin Herot
And oppress its prince, as Grendel has done.
But he's learned that terror is his alone,

Discovered he can come for your people with no fear
Of reprisal; he's found no fighting, here,
But only food, only delight.''

[587-598]

After Beowulf has killed Grendel, and before Grendel's mother seeks
her revenge, a feast of celebration is held in the hall. Hrothgar's wife,
Welthow, pours wine for the warriors and addresses some portentous
words to Beowulf. We know that Hrothgar's and Welthow's son will be
killed by a usurper of the throne when the old king dies. Welthow asks
Beowulf's protection for her progeny:

"Spread your blessed protection
Across my son, and my king's son!
All men speak softly, here, speak mildly
And trust their neighbors, protect their lord,
Are loyal followers who would fight as joyfully
As they drink. May your heart help you as I ask!"

[1226-1231]

Once again, this dark intimation of future human violence is the immediate occasion for the introduction of a monster—this time Grendel's
mother, brooding on her revenge:

She returned to her seat. The soldiers ate
And drank like kings. The savage fate
Decreed for them hung dark and unknown, what would follow
After nightfall, when Hrothgar withdrew from the hall,
Sought his bed...

[1232-1236]

We observe the same device after Beowulf has returned home and his
king Higlac asks him to recount his adventures in Denmark. Beowulf
begins with his triumph over Grendel, but he interrupts himself with a
long digression about what is to happen in Hrothgar's family. The Danes
and the Hathobards having been quarreling, fighting, and killing each
other, Hrothgar will attempt to settle the feud. He will give his daughter,
Freaw, as a bride to a prince of the Hathobards, Ingeld. The gesture will
not work, Beowulf informs all, and the old hatreds will be stirred up
despite the Danish bride:

"But war will begin
As he runs, to the sound of broken oaths,
And its heat will dry up Ingeld's heart,

Leave him indifferent to his Danish bride.
Hrothgar may think the Hathobards love him,
Loving Freaw, but the friendship can't last,
The vows are worthless.
         "But of Grendel: you need to
Know more to know everything; I ought to
Go on. It was early in the evening..."

[2063-2071]

The method of juxtaposition is an external device, and this strength in the poem also contains its weakness. All the evil in past and future heroic tales and in present monsters lies outside of Beowulf, Hrothgar, and Higlac. None of these noble heroes struggles against evil within himself; we do not observe them when they are tempted to commit cruel acts and must use moral insight to forestall their own aggressive inclinations. Therefore, they cannot teach us how to deal with immorality within ourselves. There are no great scenes of reconciliation, because the good people have never been sundered from each other. Beowulf is a great, noble hero but he lacks the dimensioned humanity that would make him fully believable.

What the poet created was an ideal of human behavior and ideal heroes. His paradigm was the ideal god, full of love, forgiveness, and human compassion. Greek heroes were also godlike, but the gods they imitated were narrowly human. Beowulf possessed as much "nerve" as Achilles, Hektor, or Ajax, but he was also filled with a kind of love that was impossible for those heroes. His god was the god that Aeschylus longed for, that Hebrews created, and Christians institutionalized within a large, complex society. Only such a god had the power to transform the barbarism which had critically troubled pagan society.

THE TRANSFORMATION OF CULTURE

When analyzing the value-system of any culture it is necessary to differentiate between an ideal of human behavior and its implementation within society. The Hebrew-Christian ideal of human society has never been fully implemented. That does not mean that this ideal had no significance for the development of culture. We cannot dismiss the non-implemented ideals of a culture as mere "hypocrisy." It may be thousands of years between the birth of an ideal and the time when the ideal is fully institutionalized within society. However, it is clear that no society can implement an ideal that does not exist.

It took almost two thousand years from the time that Christianity, the official religion of the Empire, proclaimed that slaves were people, had souls, and were loved by God, to the time when slavery was abolished in the Western world. At any point during that period one could facilely describe the Christian attitude towards slavery as "hypocritical," and so it was. But one must also ask whether slavery could ever have been abolished if the ideal of human equality had not previously existed. The creation of an ideal that is *not* institutionalized within society creates an ambivalence. The tensions within this ambivalence may eventually resolve themselves in the implementation of the ideal. No ideal of human behavior is ever merely an ideal without power in the real world.

This discussion of the creation of a god of love has been about the birth of an ideal of human behavior, not its full implementation into society. One does not need to be a historian to know that the Hebrew-Christian god did not put an end to war and killing. However, the culture which cannot conceive of love as an ideal of human behavior, as Greek culture could not, is in a profoundly different state of development from that of a society which cannot yet implement, but which can conceive, this ideal. For such a society there is hope that someday the gap between the ideal and the reality may be bridged. For the society in which it is impossible to invent such an ideal, there is no hope. If ever a humane, democratic, socialist culture should be established, it will become a reality through the implementation of the Hebrew-Christian ideal of human society. Such a creation would need no ideals other than those we already possess; it would need only the radical implementation of ideal values that have been a part of our value-system for 2000 years.

This discrepancy between ideal human behavior and the gross realities of society did not always exist. In Primitive Civilization, there was no such tension; the power of custom guaranteed the congruence of what was and what should be. The same was true in the Barbarian Civilizations, such as those of Polynesia, ancient Mexico, and Buganda. In the West, it was only with the beginnings of Archaic Civilization, and the creation of law, that leaders of society began to proclaim ideals by which they did not live. The Egyptian pharaohs talked much of *ma-at* ("Justice"), and Gudea, the Akkadian prince of Lagash, at the end of the third millenium B.C., announced that he had restored justice to the people and put down tyrannical power.

It was not until the high Archaic Civilizations of Israel and Greece that we find the creation of ideals of human behavior that are far above what society was capable of implementing. What was crucial for the development of culture was that these ideals continued to exist as ideals, despite society's inability to fully institutionalize them. The discrepancy between ideal behavior and objective actions has created a moral tension within every society since those times. Consciously, and unconsciously, Western culture has known—sometimes with greater, sometimes with lesser, power—that the realities of political life fall far short of its own moral vision.

When the Christian revolution destroyed the pagan world in the fourth century A.D., two significant things happened to the West: firstly, the stated ideals of society took on a moral tone unknown before; secondly, slowly and almost imperceptibly, society began to transform itself in accordance with the new moral vision. No attempt is being made to write a cultural history of the "Dark Ages," but it is valuable to look at some developments in culture from 350 to 800 A.D. that help to demonstrate that Christian culture could deal with moral problems in a way that was impossible for the Greeks. The argument has been made here that the creation of the poem *Beowulf* is one strong piece of evidence that this was so.

The information we have indicates that infanticide and abandonment of infants, especially girls, was widespread in the pagan world.[11] At the beginning of the Christian era, this practice became a concern of the government of the Empire. "Imperial legislation from the fourth century onward suggests that the worst abuses of children were increasingly coming under the purview of governmental officials. The recurrence of legislation indicates how ingrained were the practices of infanticide and child sale..."[12]

Lactantius (d. ca. 340) urged that the strangling of infants was immoral, "for God breathes into their souls for life, not death....It is as wicked to expose as it is to kill."[13] A series of church councils preached against the practice, and set up means to assist children who had been abandoned and had managed to live. "Church Fathers...progress in compassion for children by asserting that children had souls, were important to God, could be taught, should not be killed, maimed, or abandoned...[T]he Church began to bring serious pressure on the State in the fourth century to legislate an end to the life-endangering practices."[14]

In this matter of infanticide and child abuse, we must look as much to the creation of the ideal as to the objective results. We know, from the later history of child abuse, that the practical results of these fourth century beginnings were paltry. No immediate revolution in the treatment of children occurred, but we must not underestimate the importance of the birth of an ideal of child care, and its preservation through millenia of actual mistreatment. A revolution in the care of children did take place, in *this* century, but it could not have happened if an ideal of child care had never existed in the value-system of our culture. That this ideal was given new power at the same time that Christian morality was institutionalized is no accident of history. A god who can love his people can easily love the children of his people.

Morally related to this enlightened view of child care was the proliferation of social criticism and concern in the early fifth century A.D. These radical views on social and economic inequality produced no practical results, but what is remarkable about them is that they read "as if they had been written yesterday." All the great criticisms of the cruelty of society that, in the nineteenth and twentieth centuries, helped to transform the moral bases of our political and economic life were available to a person of conscience in the fifth century A.D. About 400 A.D., Victricius, a follower of St. Martin, wrote:

> Men do not differ by nature, but only in time and place, in their occupations and ideas; for difference is foreign to divine unity... [D]ivinity spits upon degree, breaks beyond time and place... [G]reater is the glory of your authority if you protect those who toil, defend the oppressed against their enemies.[15]

At about the same time, the Sicilian Briton went even further in his condemnation of wealth, proclaiming it evil:

> One man owns many large mansions adorned with costly marbles, another has not so much as a small hut to keep out the cold and heat. One man has vast territories and unlimited possessions, another has but a little stretch of turf to sit upon and call his own....Are these riches from God?....If God had willed universal inequality, he... would not have permitted...equal shares...in the elements...Does the rich man enjoy the blessings of fresh air more than the poor man? Does he feel the sun's heat more keenly or less? When earth receives the gift of rain, do larger drops fall upon the rich man's field than upon the poor man's...? What God himself distributes...is shared equally; what we own in unjust inequality is everything whose distribution was entrusted to human control....Is there one sacrament, one law for the rich, another for the poor?...[I]nequality of wealth is not to be blamed upon the graciousness of God, but upon the iniquity of men.[16]

When nineteenth-century Socialists took up the cry, "All property is theft," the moral ideal expressed was no more profound than the outrage of this fifth century cleric.

In 793 A.D., Alcuin, an intellectual leader of Charlemagne's court, wrote to Ethelred, king of Northumbria:

> What also of the immoderate use of clothing beyond the needs of human nature, beyond the custom of our predecessors? The princes' superfluity is poverty for the people. Such customs once injured the people of God, and made it a reproach to the pagan races, as the prophet says: "Woe to you, who have sold the poor for a pair of

shoes," that is, the souls of men for ornaments for the feet. Some
labour under an enormity of clothes, others perish with cold; some
are inundated with delicacies and feastings like Dives clothed in pur-
ple, and Lazarus dies of hunger at the gate. Where is brotherly love?
Where the pity which we are admonished to have for the wretched?
The satiety of the rich is the hunger of the poor. That saying of our
Lord is to be feared: "For judgement without mercy to him that hath
not done mercy."[17]

Athenian Democracy was as close to the ideal of human equality as
pagan culture could come, but no one in fifth-century Athens went
around announcing that Zeus had created all men equal and that a society
which permitted political *and* economic inequality was sacrilegious.

In addition to child abuse and socio-economic protest, an important
matter of moral concern was the warrior view of reality, of which reform
was attempted, not only in art (as in *Beowulf*) but also on the stage of
social action itself. Attempts were made by the new Christian faith to
downgrade the occupation of the warrior. One of the canons of the
Council of Nice was that a Christian who had abandoned the profession
of a soldier, and then returned to it, "as dogs to their vomit," was to
become a penitent in the Church for some years.[18]

In Anglo-Saxon England a life-style evolved that indicated a deep ambivalence about real-world power, which, of necessity, included the
capacity to be a successful soldier. The small kingdoms of England were
almost constantly at war with one another in the seventh and eighth centuries. To be a successful king, even to maintain one's kingship, meant to
be proficient in battle. A truly Christian king might have remained a
Christian, but his kingship would have been quickly taken by others.

What many of these political leaders did was split their lives into two
parts. The first was devoted to pursuing real-world power, which included the art of killing, and the second was lived in an atmosphere of
piety. Caedwalla of Wessex was a successful and warlike king; in 688, at
thirty years of age, he gave up the kingly power and went to Rome to be
baptized. In 709 Coenred of Mercia and Offa of Essex followed the example of Caedwella. In 726 King Ine of Wessex did the same, after many
years of kingship, and "became a pilgrim (*peregrinari*) near the holy
places of Rome...to be received in consequence with readier recognition
by the saints in heaven."[19]

In Anglo-Saxon England the most vivid history of this kind concerns
the life of Saint Guthlac. In his youth, his imagination was inflamed by
the heroic world-view; he became an Achilles of the North:

Now when his youthful strength had increased, and a noble desire for command burned in his young breast, he remembered the valiant deeds of heroes of old, and as though awakening from sleep, he changed his disposition and gathering bands of followers took up arms...

Guthlac, however, was a future saint, and his ambivalence could be measured in mathematical terms:

...but when he had devastated the towns and residences of his foes, their villages and fortresses with fire and sword, and, gathering together companions from various races and from all directions, had amassed immense booty, then as if instructed by divine counsel, he would return to the owners a third part of the treasure collected.

Guthlac was not Achilles. The revolution in cultural life which had transformed the heroic world-view made it possible for ambivalence about violence to express itself in the rejection of the world. After years of being Achilles, Guthlac decided to give three-thirds to love:

So when about nine years had passed away during which he had achieved the glorious overthrow of his persecutors, foes and adversaries by frequent blows and devastations, at last their strength was exhausted after all the pillage, slaughter, and rapine which their arms had wrought, and being worn out, they kept the peace. And so when this same man of blessed memory, Guthlac, was being storm-tossed amid the uncertain events of passing years, amid the gloomy clouds of life's darkness, and amid the whirling waves of the world, he abandoned his limbs one night to their accustomed rest; his wandering thoughts were as usual anxiously contemplating mortal affairs in earnest meditation, when suddenly, marvelous to tell, a spiritual flame, as though it had pierced his breast, began to burn in the man's heart. For when, with wakeful mind, he contemplated the wretched deaths and the shameful ends of the ancient kings of his race in the course of the past ages, and also the fleeting riches of this world and the contemptible glory of this temporal life, then in imagination the form of his own death revealed itself to him; and, trembling with anxiety at the inevitable finish of this brief life, he perceived that its course daily moved to that end....Suddenly by prompting of the divine Majesty, he vowed that, if he lived until the next day, he himself would become a servant of Christ.[20]

Guthlac became as great a saint as he had been a warrior.

My book on cannibalism described how the Kwakiutl resolved their ambivalence about eating other people by splitting society into two parts: the cannibal society, which was permitted anthropophagous activity, and the balance of the tribe, for whom cannibalism was prohibited. After the advent of Christian culture, we can observe Western society performing the same kind of operation in regard to matters of aggression and morality. In the West the special segment of society has the task of nurturing, preserving, and developing the *moral ideals* of the culture, while the balance of society is free to pursue aggressive aims. The Christian priesthood becomes a special group within society, and society recognizes and protects its right to exist. Ambivalence is maintained by letting the Church speak for love and permitting everyone else to indulge in economic inequality, slave-owning, and killing.

Alcuin's letter, full of Socialist views on economic inequality, was written in 793. Twelve years earlier he had left England and gone to serve Charlemagne, the most powerful king in all Europe. At that court more riches had been seen than had been observed anywhere in Western Europe since the passing of the Roman emperors. Did Alcuin profess his egalitarian views to the King of the Franks? Did he say to Charlemagne's face, "The princes' superfluity is poverty for the people," or did he content himself with reserving these sentiments for a distant, powerless King of Northumbria? Evidence is lacking, but we may surmise the answers.

One must not denigrate the importance of this split in society between moral ideas and gross reality. If the Kwakiutl had had no cannibal society, the possibility is that all would have eaten. If the Church had not become the guardian of moral ideals, then society could have remained in the same trap that held Homer and Thucydides.

When a culture resolves its ambivalence about moral ideals by establishing an institution within society to be the guardian of those ideals, two things may happen. Firstly, the ideals may grow and develop, and gather strength by taking into account the society in which they exist. Secondly, as long as the culture accepts the legitimacy of such a moral institution, the way is prepared for the transformation of culture in the direction of the ideal. It is a continuing process, and we live in the midst of it.

WILL OUR HORSE TAKE THE LEAP?

Dodds closes his great book on Greek culture with a look at the culture in which we live: "But as a man cannot escape his own shadow, so no generation can pass judgement on the problems of history without reference, conscious or unconscious, to its own problems. And I will not pretend to hide from the reader that in writing these chapters...I have had our own situation constantly in mind. We too have witnessed the slow disintegration of an inherited conglomerate, starting among the educated class but now affecting the masses almost everywhere, yet still very far from complete. We too have experienced a great age of rationalism, marked by scientific advances beyond anything that earlier times had thought possible, and confronting mankind with the prospect of a society more open than any it has ever known. And in the last forty years we have also experienced something else—the unmistakable recoil from that prospect. It would appear that, in the words used recently by Andre Malraux, 'Western civilization has begun to doubt its own credentials.'

"What is the meaning of this recoil, this doubt? Is it the hesitation before the jump, or the beginning of a panic flight? I do not know. On such a matter a simple professor of Greek is in no position to offer an opinion. But he can do one thing. He can remind his readers that once before the jump, or the beginning of a panic flight? I do not know. On he can beg them to examine all the circumstances of that refusal."[21]

It has been one of the aims of this book to attempt to shed light on some of the problems that Dodds raises in these remarks. I have tried to demonstrate that the Greek irrational horse was suffused not so much with fear, although that must have been part of it, but with a commitment to sadistic violence, to cruelty, to a lust to annihilate—in short, to evil. It was this commitment to evil that forced the horse to recoil from that great moral leap; and the antidote to evil is not nerve, but love. Love does produce courage, and courage is needed to transform society radically, but one must not talk of courage or nerve separated from love, because without *Eros* courage ends up as the power to kill.

We must pursue even further Dodds' analogy with our present situation. We also, like fifth-century Athens, are on the verge of a revolutionary transformation of culture; we have reached a state of evolutionary cultural development where only a revolutionary change of moral values will work. This moral revolution may or may not happen in the immediate future; it may not occur at all. Our society, unconsciously at least, knows it has reached a critical stage. It knows it has come to the edge of a great leap. It may spend two or three hundred years ambivalently treading on the edge before it decides to jump or to take flight. If we are to understand the moral malaise that currently afflicts our culture, we cannot blame it on oil shortages or generation gaps or inflation or on the vague decline of traditional institutions and values. We must understand that we, as a culture, will never restore the liberating sense of being part of a good, moral society until we decide to take that leap.

Through either diffidence or confusion, Dodds' analysis of our present situation is unnecessarily tentative. The Western civilization that now doubts its own credentials is capitalist civilization, built upon economic inequality, imperialist wars, and that subtle form of human aggression called "competition," which insists that those who suffer in society somehow deserve that suffering. The great leap which culture has so far refused to take is towards a humane, democratic socialism which renounces aggressive warfare and insists that all people in society must be cared for. When the Reverend George Turner went to Samoa in the middle of the nineteenth century, he vainly tried to explain to the Samoans the English notion of "poverty." The Samoan had always taken care of the aged, the sick, the blind, and the lame, and would respond to Turner: " 'How is it?'...'No food! Has he no friends? No house to live in! Where did he grow? Are there no houses belonging to his friends? Have the people there no love for each other?' "[22]

The history of the United States in the last twenty-five years has shown remarkable similarities to the situation of Athens in the fifth century. We, too, came to world domination after being the foremost power in the defeat of the "barbarians." The United States also embarked on an imperialist policy and found itself reduced to genocide in order to preserve its power. We have had our Pericles in the person of John Kennedy, who would adorn his country with great cultural achievements and facile moral pronouncements and, at the same time, play the paranoid game of missile-gaps and counter-insurgency. We have had our Thucydides in the person of Henry Kissinger, the amoral practitioner of *realpolitik,* who, in a discussion of the 500,000 tons of bombs American planes dropped on Cambodia, said: "I may have a lack of imagination, but I fail to see the moral issue involved."[23] In Vietnam we have had both our Sicilian debacle and our Melian genocide.

However, we also have many in our culture who understand the moral passion in Aeschylus and Euripides. And we have something Athenian culture never had. We have an ideal of love, a moral vision, that has maintained its strength despite the Nazi holocaust and all the evils that real-world power has brought to humankind.

What we need, at this critical time, is not an infusion of more nerve. A country which could, senselessly, drop two atom bombs and kill nearly 200,000 people is not lacking in that quality. For our horse finally to decide to take that leap, what we shall need is the implementation of that ideal of human behavior which we have carried with us since the time when the prophet Amos implored us not to sell the poor for a pair of shoes. At this point in the history of the world, the cost of denying this great moral leap may be the world itself.

Footnotes

INTRODUCTION

1. Friedrich Nietzsche, "Homer's Contest," *The Portable Nietzsche,* ed. and trans. Walter Kaufman (New York: The Viking Press, 1954), p. 32.
2. George Thomson, *Aeschylus and Athens* (London: Lawrence and Wishart, 1946), p. 342.
3. Alvin W. Gouldner, *Enter Plato* (New York: Basic Books, 1965), p. 60.
4. Gilbert Murray, *The Rise of the Greek Epic* (Oxford: Oxford University Press, 1960), p. 3.
5. Ibid., p. 10.
6. Pindar, "The Power of Custom," trans. C. M. Bowra, *The Oxford Book of Greek Verse in Translation,* ed. T. F. Higham and C. M. Bowra (Oxford: Clarendon Press, 1938), p. 330.

CHAPTER I

1. All quotations from the *Iliad* are from Richmond Lattimore, trans. *The Iliad of Homer* (Chicago: University of Chicago Press, 1962). Roman numerals indicate the Book; Arabic numerals, the lines.
2. Eli Sagan, *Cannibalism: Human Aggression and Cultural Form* (New York: Harper and Row, 1974).
3. E. R. Dodds, *Euripides: Bacchae* (Oxford: Clarendon Press, 1960), p.v.
4. Simone Weil, *The Iliad or The Poem of Force* (Wallingford, Pennsylvania: Pendle Hill, n.d.), p. 11.
5. *Ibid.,* p. 25.
6. All quotations from Aeschylus' *Agamemnon* are from the translation by Richmond Lattimore in David Grene and Richmond Lattimore, editors. *The Complete Greek Tragedies* (Chicago: University of Chicago Press, 1959).
7. Friedrich Nietzsche, *The Birth of Tragedy,* trans. Francis Golfing (Garden·City, N.Y.: Doubleday Anchor Books, 1956), pp. 63-64.
8. Thomas Mann, "Introduction," *The Short Novels of Dostoevski* (New York: Dial Press, 1945), p. xii.
9. *Ibid.,* p. viii.
10. Quoted by Philip Wheelwright, *Heraclitus* (New York: Atheneum Press, 1971), p. 118.

CHAPTER II

1. W. P. Ker, *Epic and Romance* (New York: Dover Publications, 1957) p. 19.
2. Alvin Gouldner, *Enter Plato,* p. 26.
3. Sigmund Freud, "The Dissolution of the Oedipus Complex," trans. James Strachey, Volume XIX *The Standard Edition of the Complete Psychological Works of Sigmund Freud* (London: Hogarth Press, 1961), p. 173.
4. Ibid., p. 175.
5. Sigmund Freud, "Some Psychical Consequences of the Anatomical Distinction Between the Sexes," trans. James Strachey, Volume XIX *The Standard Edition of the Complete Psychological Works of Sigmund Freud* (London: Hogarth Press, 1961), p. 257.
6. Freud, "The Dissolution of the Oedipus Complex," p. 176.
7. Freud, "Some Psychical Consequences of the Anatomical Distinction Between the Sexes," p. 250.
8. Ibid., p. 256.
9. John Sandys, *The Odes of Pindar* (London: William Heinemann, Ltd., 1948), p. 15.
10. Richmond Lattimore, *The Odes of Pindar* (Chicago: The University of Chicago Press, 1959), p. 139.
11. E. R. Dodds, *The Greeks and the Irrational* (Boston: Beacon Press, 1957), pp. 46-47.
12. All quotations from Sophocles *Oedipus the King* are from the translation by David Grene in University of Chicago *The Complete Greek Tragedies.*
13. Plato, *The Republic,* Book II.

CHAPTER III

1. Erwin Rohde, *Psyche* (New York: Harper and Row, 1966), Volume I, p. 14.
2. Nietzsche, "Homer's Contest," p. 39.
3. Murray, *The Rise of the Greek Epic,* p. 10.
4. George Rawlinson, trans., *The History of Herodotus* (New York: Tudor Publishing Company, 1946), p. 507.
5. Ibid., p. 508.
6. A. M. Snodgrass, *The Dark Age of Greece* (Edinburgh: Edinburgh University Press, 1971), p. 392.
7. Lewis Richard Farnell, *Greek Hero Cults* (Oxford: Clarendon Press, 1970), p. 7.
8. Herodotus, p. 225.
9. Ibid., p. 212.
10. Ibid., p. 223.
11. Ibid., p. 223.
12. H. Munro Chadwick and N. Kershaw Chadwick, *The Growth of Literature* (Cambridge: Cambridge University Press, 1968), Volume I, pp. 92-93.
13. Richard Brayton Onians, *The Origins of European Thought about the Body, the Mind, the Soul, the World, Time and Fate* (Cambridge: Cambridge University Press, 1951), pp. 98-99.
14. All quotations from Aeschylus' *Libation Bearers* are from the translation of Richmond Lattimore in University of Chicago, *The Complete Greek Tragedies.*
15. M. I. Finley, *The World of Odysseus* (New York: Meridian Books, 1959), pp. 128-129.
16. Joseph Conrad, *The Heart of Darkness,* in *The Portable Conrad* (New York: The

Viking Press, 1947), p. 523.
17. Ibid., p. 511.
18. Ibid., pp. 511-512.
19. Ibid., p. 493.
20. Ibid., p. 526.
21. Ibid., p. 504.

CHAPTER IV

1. Rachel Bespaloff, *On the Iliad*, trans. Mary McCarthy (Princeton: Princeton University Press, 1970), p. 57.
2. Max Weber, *The Protestant Ethic and the Spirit of Capitalism*, trans. Talcott Parsons (New York: Charles Scribner's Sons, 1958), p. 105.
3. Richmond Lattimore, trans., *The Odyssey of Homer* (New York: Harper and Row, 1968).

CHAPTER V

1. J. M. Edwards, trans., *Elegy and Iambus* (London: William Heinemann Ltd., 1968), Volume II, p. 101.
2. Ibid.
3. Ibid., p. 127
4. Richmond Lattimore, trans., *Greek Lyrics* (Chicago: The University of Chicago Press, 1971), p.3.
5. Ibid., p. 2.
6. Ibid., p. 6.
7. J. M. Edwards, trans., *Lyra Graeca* (London: William Heinemann Ltd., 1958), Volume I, p. 87.
8. Ibid., p. 117.
9. Ibid., Volume II, p. 155.
10. Ibid., p. 99.
11. Edmonds, *Elegy,* Volume 1, p. 473.
12. Edmonds, *Elegy,* Volume I, p. 341.
13. Ibid., Volume II, p. 105.
14. Ibid., Volume II, p. 131.
15. Edmonds, *Lyra,* Volume II, p. 61.
16. Ibid.
17. Ibid, p. 371.
18. Ibid., p. 359.
19. Ibid., p. 357.
20. Ibid., p. 197.
21. Ibid., p. 53.
22. C. M. Bowra, *Greek Lyric Poetry From Alcman to Simonides* (Oxford: Clarendon Press, 1961), p. 255.
23. Ibid., p. 253.
24. Lattimore, *Lyrics,* p. 40.
25. Ibid., p. 25.
26. Edmonds, *Elegy,* Volume I, p. 47.

27. Edmonds, *Lyra,* Volume I, p. 337.
28. Lattimore, *Lyrics,* pp. 44-45.
29. Edmonds, *Elegy,* Volume I, p. 75.
30. Dodds, *Irrational,* Chapter II.
31. Bowra, *Lyric,* p. 240.
32. Jane Ellen Harrison, *Themis* (New Hyde Park, N.Y.: University Books, 1962), p. 470.
33. Erich Neuman, *The Origins and History of Consciousness* (Princeton, Princeton University Press, 1970), p. 121.
34. Lattimore, *Lyrics,* p. 4.
35. Bowra, *Lyric,* p. 138.
36. Lattimore, *Lyrics,* p. 5.
37. Ibid., p. 49
38. Edmonds, *Lyra,* Volume II, p. 127.
39. Ibid., p. 179.
40. Ibid., Volume I, p. 187.
41. Ibid., p. 263.
42. Edmonds, *Elegy,* Volume I, p. 305.
43. Ibid., Volume II, p. 101.
44. Edmonds, *Lyra,* Volume II, p. 97.
45. Ibid., p. 165.
46. Ibid., Volume I, pp. 285-287.
47. Ibid., p. 235.
48. Ibid., p. 279.
49. Ibid., pp. 439-441.
50. Ibid., p. 127.
51. Bruno Snell, *The Discovery of the Mind* (New York: Harper and Brothers, 1960), pp. 17-18.
52. Ibid., pp. 59-60.
53. Edmonds, *Lyra,* Volume I, p. 221.
54. C. M. Bowra in *Oxford ... Greek Verse,* p. 211.
55. Snell, *Discovery,* p. 19.
56. Edmonds, *Elegy,* Volume I, p. 313.
57. Ibid., p. 259.
58. Edmonds, *Lyra,* Volume I, p. 435.
59. Ibid., p. 87.
60. Edmonds, *Elegy,* Volume I, p. 349.
61. Ibid., Volume II, p. 151.
62. C. M. Bowra in *Oxford ... Greek Verse,* p. 201.
63. Edmonds, *Elegy,* Volume I, p. 247.
64. Edmonds, *Lyra,* Volume II, p. 173.

CHAPTER VI

1. Trans. S. H. Butcher in James H. Smith and Edd Winfield Parks, editors, *The Great Critics* (New York: W. W. Norton, 1939)
2. Trans. John Moore, Chicago, *Complete Greek Tragedies,* Volume II.
3. Trans. Ronald Willetts, Ibid., Volume IV.
4. All quotations from *Prometheus Bound* from translation by David Grene in Ibid., Volume I.
5. H. D. F. Kitto, *Greek Tragedy* (Garden City, New York: Doubleday and Company, n.d.), p. 67n.

6. All quotations from *Antigone* from translation by Elizabeth Wyckoff, in Chicago, *Complete Greek Tragedies,* Volume II.
7. All Quotations from *Oedipus The King* from translation by David Grene in Ibid.
8. Sigmund Freud, *A General Introduction to Psychoanalysis,* trans. Joan Rivier, in Michael T. O'Brien, ed., *Twentieth Century Interpretations of Oedipus Rex* (Englewood Cliffs: Prentice Hall, 1968), p. 105.
9. Translated by E. R. Dodds, "On Misunderstanding, *Oedipus Rex,"* in Michael J. O'Brien, ed., *Twentieth Century Interpretations of Oedipus Rex* (Englewood Cliffs: Prentice Hall, 1968), p. 28.
10. All quotations from the *Oresteia* are from the translation by Richmond Lattimore, Chicago, *Complete Greek Tragedies,* Volume I.

CHAPTER VII

1. William Arrowsmith, "Euripides' Theatre of Ideas," in Erich Segal, ed., *Euripides: A Collection of Critical* Essays (Englewood Cliffs: Prentice Hall, 1968), pp. 17-21.
2. Herodotus, *History,* pp. 41-47.
3. Ibid., pp 158-159.
4. F.M. Cornford, *Greek Religious Thought* (New York: AMS Press, 1969), p.71.
5. Trans. Richmond Lattimore in Chicago, *Complete Greek Tragedies,* Volume I.
6. Trans. David Grene in ibid., Volume II.
7. All quotations from *Hippolytus* from translation by David Grene in ibid, Volume III.
8. All quotations from *Orestes* from translation by William Arrowsmith in ibid., Volume IV.
9. All quotations from *Alcestis* from translation by Richmond Lattimore in ibid., Volume III.
10. All quotations from *Oedipus at Colonus* from translation by Robert Fitzgerald in ibid., Volume II.
11. Cedric Whitman, "Apocalyse: *Oedipus at Colonus,"* in Thomas Woodard, ed., *Sophocles: A Collection of Critical Essays* (Englewood Cliffs: Prentice Hall, 1966), p.153.
12. James Joyce, *A Portrait of the Artist as a Young Man* (New York: The Modern Library, 1928), p. 239.
13. Trans. Richmond Lattimore, Chicago, *Complete Greek Tragedies,* Volume III.
14. Trans. Michael Jameson, ibid., Volume II.
15. Trans. William Arrowsmith, ibid., Volume IV.
16. All quotations from *Heracles* from translation by William Arrowsmith, ibid., Volume III.
17. All quotations from *Ajax* from translation by John Moore, ibid., Volume II.
18. William Arrowsmith, "Introduction to *Heracles,"* ibid, volume III, p. 278.
19. Trans. Richmond Lattimore, ibid.
20. All quotations from *Heccuba* from translation by William Arrowsmith, ibid.

CHAPTER VIII

1. All quotations from *Medea* from the translation by Rex Warner in Chicago, *Complete Greek Tragedies,* Volume III.
2. Trans. William Arrowsmith, ibid., Volume IV.

3. Trans. Robert Fitzgerald, ibid., Volume II.
4. All quoatations from *The Trojan Women* from the translation by Richmond Lattimore, ibid., Volume III.
5. Clifford Geertz, "Religion as a Cultural System," in *The Interpretation of Cultures* (New York: Basic Books, 1973), pp. 107-108.
6. All quotations from *Herakles* from the translation by William Arrowsmith in Chicago, *Complete Greek Tragedies,* Volume III.
7. Trans. William Arrowsmith, ibid.
8. G. M. Kirkwood, "Two Questions of Dramatic Form in *Oedipus Tyrannus,*" in Michael S. O'Brien, ed., *Twentieth Century Interpretations if Oedipus Rex* (Englewood Cliffs: Prentice Hall, 1968), pp. 66-67.
9. Bernard Knox, "The *Ajax* of Sophocles" in Thomas Woodard, ed., *Sophocles* (Englewood Cliffs: Prentice Hall, 1966), p. 36.
10. E. R. Dodds, "On Misunderstanding the *Oedipus Rex,*" in O'Brien, ed., *Oedipus Rex,* p. 26.
11. Bernard Knox, *The Heroic Temper* (Berkeley: University of California Press, 1964), pp. 53-54.
12. F. M. Cornford, *Greek Religious Thought* (New York: AMS Press, 1969), p. 154.
13. C. J. Herington, "Aeschylus: The Last Phase," in Marsh H. McCall, Jr., ed., *Aeschylus: A Collection of Critical Essays* (Englewood Cliffs: Prentice Hall, 1972), p. 161.
14. William Arrowsmith, "Euripides' Theatre of Ideas," in Erich Segal, ed., *Euripides: A Collection of Critical Essays* (Englewood Cliffs: Prentice Hall, 1968), p. 22.
15. All quotations from Hippolytus from the translation by David Grene in Chicago, *Complete Greek Tragedies,* Volume III.
16. Bernard Knox, "The *Hippolytus* of Euripides," in Erich Segal, ed., *Euripides,* pp. 113-114.
17. Jan Kott, *The Eating of the Gods* (New York: Vintage Books, 1974), p. 14.
18. H. D. F. Kitto, *Greek Tragedy* (Garden City, New York: Doubleday and Company, n.d.), p. 93.
19. All quotations from *Eumenides* from the translation by Richmond Lattimore in Chicago, *Complete Greek Tragedies,* Volume I.

CHAPTER IX

1. David Grene, *Greek Political Theory* (Chicago: University of Chicago Press, 1965), p. 17.
2. Ibid.
3. Werner Jaeger, *Paideia* (New York: Oxford University Press, 1965), Volume I, pp. 410-411.
4. All quotations from Thucydides are from the Crawly translation published in various editions.
5. Trans. William Arrowsmith in Chicago, *Complete Greek Tragedies,* Volume IV.
6. All quotations from *Hecuba* are from the translation by William Arrowsmith in ibid., Volume III.
7. Trans. Rex Warner, ibid.
8. F. E. Adcock, "The Archidamian War," *Cambridge Ancient History,* Volume V (Cambridge: University Press, 1953), p. 199.
9. Alfred Zimmern, *Solon and Croesus* (London: Oxford University Press, 1928), pp. 92-93.

FOOTNOTES 223

10. Ibid., p. 93.
11. E. R. Dodds, *The Greeks and the Irrational* (Boston: Beacon Press, 1957), p. 191.
12. All quotations from *Heracles* from the translation by William Arrowsmith in Chicago, *Complete Greek Tragedies,* Volume III.
13. Trans. Richmond Lattimore, ibid.
14. All quotations from *The Suppliant Women* from the translation of Frank William Jones, ibid., Volume IV.
15. Francis M. Cornford, *Thucydides Mythistoricus* (Philadelphia: University of Pennsylvania Press, 1971), p. 4n.
16. Trans. Richmond Lattimore, Chicago, *Complete Greek Tragedies,* Volume III.
17. Grene, *Political Theory,* pp. 31-32, 50.
18. See ibid., p. 54.
19. Zimmern, *Solon,* pp. 95-96.
20. Cornford, *Thucydides,* p. 186.
21. All quotations from *Heracles* from the translation by William Arrowsmith in Chicago, *Complete Greek Tragedies,* Volume III.
22. Trans. William Arrowsmith, ibid., Volume IV.
23. John H. Finley, Jr., *Thucydides* (Ann Arbor: University of Michigan Press, 1963), p. 158.

CHAPTER X

1. E. R. Dodds, *The Greeks and the Irrational* (Boston: Beacon Press, 1957), p. 254.
2. Ibid., p. 35.
3. Gilbert Murray, *Five Stages of Greek Religion* (Garden City, New York: Doubleday and Company, 1955), p. xiii.
4. Dodds, *Irrational,* p. 246.
5. Ibid., p. 35.
6. Martin P. Nilsson, *A History of Greek Religion* (Oxford: Oxford University Press, 1925), p. 247.
7. Trans. Richmond Lattimore, Chicago, *Complete Greek Tragedies,* Volume I.
8. Fr. Klaeber, *Beowulf,* Third Edition, (Lexington, Mass.: D. C. Heath and Company, 1950), pp. l-li.
9. All quotations from *Beowulf* from the translation by Burton Raffel (New York: New American Library, 1963).
10. Klaeber, *Beowulf,* p. li.
11. Lloyd deMause, "On the Demography of Filicide," *The Journal of Psychohistory,* Vol. 4, No. 1, Summer 1976, pp. 16-30.
12. Richard B. Lyman, Jr., in Lloyd deMause, ed., *The History of Childhood* (New York: The Psychohistory Press, 1974), p. 90.
13. Ibid.
14. Ibid.
15. John Morris, *The Age of Arthur* (New York: Charles Scribner's Sons, 1973), p. 336.
16. Ibid., p. 340.
17. Dorothy Whitelock, ed., *English Historical Documents c. 500-1042* (London: Eyre and Spottiswoode, 1955), pp. 776-777.
18. Edward Westermarck, *The Origin and Development of Moral Ideas,* Volume I, (London: Macmillian and Co., 1906), p. 346.
19. Wilhelm Levison, *England and the Continent in the Eighth Century* (Oxford: Oxford University Press, 1946), p. 38.

20. Bertram Colgrave, *Felix's Life of Saint Guthlac* (Cambridge: Cambridge University Press, 1956), pp. 81, 83.
21. Dodds, *Irrational,* pp. 253-254.
22. George Turner, *Samoa* (London: Macmillan and Co., 1884), p. 159.
23. Quoted by Anthony Lewis, *The New York Times,* December 27, 1976, p. A23.

Index